D0840326

QUENTIN TARANTINO

INTERVIEWS

CONVERSATIONS WITH FILMMAKERS SERIES
PETER BRUNETTE, GENERAL EDITOR

QUENTIN
TARANTINO
INTERVIEWS

EDITED BY GERALD PEARY

UNIVERSITY PRESS OF MISSISSIPPI / JACKSON

c 1998

The paper in this book meets the guidelines for permanence and durability of the Committee on Production Guidelines for Book Longevity of the Council on Library Resources.

Insert photographs courtesy Museum of Modern Art, Film Stills Archives

Library of Congress Cataloging-in-Publication Data
Tarantino, Quentin.
 Quentin Tarantino : interviews / edited by Gerald Peary.
  p. cm. — (Conversations with filmmakers series)
 Filmography: p.
 Includes bibliographical references and index.
  ISBN 1-57806-050-8 (cloth : alk. paper).—ISBN 1-57806-051-6
(pbk. : alk. paper)
  1. Tarantino, Quentin — Interviews. 2. Motion picture producers and directors — United States — Interviews. I. Peary, Gerald. II. Peary, Gerald.
III. Title. IV. Series.
PN1998.3.T358A5 1998
791.43'0233'092 — dc21   98-17837
                                                               CIP

British Library Cataloging-in-Publication data available

CONTENTS

INTRODUCTION

EVERYONE WHO IS ABSORBED by cinema has a favorite video store employee to interact with during rentals, someone embarrassingly overqualified to be there, yet who does not let a six-dollar-an-hour salary curb a nonstop energetic discourse about film, film, all types of film, whether European auteurist masterpieces, Hollywood genre works, or Hong Kong kung-fu.

Quentin Tarantino, twenty-eight, was exactly that appealing person, when he arrived in January 1992 at the Sundance Film Festival. He was a California-reared, self-proclaimed "film geek" with five intense years behind the counter at Manhattan Beach's Video Archives, where he devoured countless movies, talked endlessly about them, and developed a game plan about making them himself. Now he'd struck gold with the premiere at Park City of his first feature, *Reservoir Dogs,* with credits as actor-writer-director.

In February 1992 Tarantino talked briefly to David J. Fox of the *Los Angeles Times,* admitting that his Sundance visit had been "the first time I was ever in snow." And when *Reservoir Dogs* went to Cannes in May 1992, he went too, an initial voyage to Europe. He conversed with Camille Nevers of France's film magazine, *Cahiers du Cinéma,* identifying himself as "first and foremost a film fanatic," and offering a list of admirations, from Nicholas Ray to Mario Bava to Sergio Leone.

Back in America in August–September 1992 Tarantino accompanied *Reservoir Dogs* to both the Montreal and Toronto Film Festivals in anticipation of the October opening in the U.S.A. Everyone who encountered

Tarantino that late summer recalls the most approachable and affable of filmmakers. Post-Cannes, he was buoyed in the spotlight, having an irrepressibly jolly time sounding off with journalists and critics not only about cinema in general—just as he'd done at Video Archives—but about *his* movie.

Those who sat down for a formal interview with "Quentin" (he was hardly "Mr. Tarantino") walked away satisfied and satiated. This young filmmaker answered all questions colorfully, knowledgeably, and without inhibition. His theme when explaining his work was that he had tried to free himself in terms of time, story structure, and characters by using literature as a model without constraints. Among his literary influences: J. D. Salinger's Glass family tales, the hardboiled books of Elmore Leonard, Charles Willeford, and Jim Thompson. He also enjoyed TV: *The Partridge Family* and *Baywatch*.

He was so fresh, so unconceited, a now twenty-nine-year-old mensch. And he capped his several weeks of one-on-one talks by being the charismatic center of a wildly entertaining press conference at the Toronto International Film Festival, where he was flanked by *Reservoir Dogs* actors Harvey Keitel, Michael Madsen, Steve Buscemi, and Tim Roth.

The text of the press conference, held on 16 September 1992, is printed here for the first time, as well as an unpublished interview with critic Peter Brunette, conducted at the Montreal World Film Festival. In the press-conference discussion, Tarantino revealed how he rehearsed the actors for *Reservoir Dogs*, how they staged for themselves the jewel robbery that never occurs on screen. And as he would do in many interviews, Tarantino balked at explaining the meaning of the film's title, saying, "It's more of a mood title than anything else. It's just the right title, don't ask me why."

With Brunette, Tarantino talked of structuring *Reservoir Dogs* as a dark gallows comedy: "I like the idea that the audience is laughing and that, BOOM, the next minute there is blood on the walls"; and of his unabashed romance with American pop and junk-food culture: "There's something very lovely in that, though I'm maybe saying it's very lovely because it's my culture. It's me!"

As Tarantino recalled for Brunette his first visit to Europe, something amazing occurred: he described his experience at a Paris McDonald's in words similar to those he would place into the mouth of John Travolta's well-traveled gangster, Vincent Vega, in *Pulp Fiction*. Tarantino said, "and they don't call it a Quarter Pounder because they have the metric system there: Le Royale with Cheese! They don't know what a fucking Quarter Pounder is!"

It is possible that Tarantino's "Quarter Pounder" observation has never been repeated in another interview. In virtually every Q&A, even with the most mundane journalist, Tarantino will press energetically into new territory. Though I only interviewed him for twenty minutes or so at the 1992 Montreal Film Festival, he confided to me a favorite bed-time dream that I've never found mentioned elsewhere, of attending a party at the home of director Howard Hawks, along with guests Robert Mitchum and John Wayne.

Tarantino is so friendly and ingenuous that I had no problem asking him for a great favor. He was coming soon to Boston, where I teach, to meet with local press before the *Reservoir Dogs* opening. I'd learned of his love for French New Wave filmmakers, Jean-Luc Godard and Jean-Pierre Melville.

"Is there any chance that you could drop by my Boston University course on the French New Wave and say a few words?" I asked him in Toronto. "Sure," he obliged. And so it was that a week later, he strolled into BU. It was September 1992, and I said (how could I forget?): "Class, this is Quentin Tarantino. You don't know yet who he is, because his film hasn't played in Boston. But you will: it's a *great* first feature." The students stared at him: he looked cool (a favorite Tarantino word), even if they had to take my word for his talent.

"Quentin has come to talk to us about French New Wave cinema. Quentin..." And away he went! I'd asked for a few minutes; he gave a generous hour-and-a-half, a gleeful soliloquy about the wonders of the Nouvelle Vague, not only about the films the directors had made (he knew it all forwards and backwards) but about their writings in the magazine, *Cahiers du Cinéma*. I remember him paraphrasing Godard in *Cahiers* enraptured by a war picture of Douglas Sirk: "What a great title: *A Time to Love and a Time to Die!* And any film with a title that great must be...a great film!"

What was most impressive was that Tarantino didn't speak at all about *Reservoir Dogs*. His heart and soul were in Paris in the 1960s; and we at Boston University were too mesmerized to remember to videotape this one-time happening. How momentous for this high-school dropout,

Tarantino informed me, to address his first-ever college class. (Robert Patton-Spruill is a young African-American filmmaker from Boston who made the feature *Squeeze,* released in 1997 by Miramax Films. "When people ask me what attending Boston University was like," he says, "I tell them that Quentin Tarantino came to my class the first week that I started there in graduate school.")

September 1992 was also, in the French magazine, *Positif,* the occasion of the first published "career" interview with Tarantino, a long discussion of his film-saturated childhood, his pre-*Reservoir Dogs* effort to make a feature film, *My Best Friend's Birthday,* and his attempts to direct two long-ago-written screenplays, *True Romance* and *Natural Born Killers.* Also, Tarantino mapped out his screenwriting methods and detailed how he worked with his cinematographer, Andrzej Sekula. (This far-reaching English-language Q&A profile, translated into French for *Positif* by the interviewers, Michel Ciment and Hubert Niogret, returns to English via the original tape transcripts for this book.)

In October 1992 *Reservoir Dogs* opened theatrically in the U.S. It was not a breakaway hit; that happened when it was issued on video some months later. But America's best critics wrote at length about it, praising Tarantino's precocious talents, his cheeky dialogue, his deftness with genre, but sometimes raising objections to the film's seeming embrace of the violence within it. A prime example of such an article is Ella Taylor's 22 October 1992 column in the *LA Weekly,* combining a generally enthusiastic review and a Tarantino interview, but concluding with a sharp rebuke for *Reservoir Dogs'* torture-by-straight-razor scene, labeling it an exercise in "spurious, sadistic manipulation, . . . pure gratuity, without mercy for the viewer."

Tarantino's answer, and in this he has been remarkably consistent interview after interview, is to dismiss such criticisms completely. Screen violence is not the same as real-life violence, which Tarantino insists he abhors. But he thoroughly enjoys watching well-turned violence in movies, and he also likes staging violent scenes. Violence in cinema is, for Tarantino, a matter of taste, just as some people like or dislike dance movies, or stupid comedies. As for shirking social responsibility, Tarantino claims that he has only *artistic* responsibility, to be true to his characters. If they are cold-blooded killers, so be it.

In 1993 *True Romance* was released, directed by Tony Scott, from the Tarantino screenplay. Approving Scott's adaptation, Tarantino joined a publicity junket in Los Angeles, and there continued the sustained defense of his murder-prone protagonists. "One of the things that I really like about the character of Clarence is that when he kills, it's without apology," he reported to the *Boston Phoenix*'s Peter Keough (10 September 1993, p. 3:6).

Tarantino's most extended explication of his screenplays—*Reservoir Dogs, True Romance,* and *Natural Born Killers*—was in a May 1993 dialogue with *Interview* executive editor, Graham Fuller. "To me, violence is a totally aesthetic subject," Tarantino said to Fuller, but this time he qualified his stubborn disregard for the ethical implications of his work. "I'm not trying to preach any kind of morals or get any kind of message across, but for all the wildness that happens in my movies, I think that they usually lead to a moral conclusion."

Meanwhile, Tarantino was writing, then shooting *Pulp Fiction,* which had its world premiere in May 1994 at the Cannes Film Festival, winning the Palme d'Or. By this occasion, Tarantino had become so incredibly popular that his interviews couldn't help but be restricted. The wide-open days of *Reservoir Dogs* were over, probably forever. Many journalists at Cannes were marched in for five to ten minutes, hardly time to learn substantial things about the movie. Luckily, there were exceptions.

Early on, he sat down with the *Sight and Sound*'s Manohla Dargis and plotted for her the process of the movie-making. As he had done for *Reservoir Dogs,* he cooperated with Michel Ciment and Hubert Niogret for a *Pulp Fiction* discussion in *Positif,* eventually published in November 1994. (For purposes of this book, the originally-in-English interview, translated into French, was put back into English by Boston University film professor, T. Jefferson Kline).

A West Coast journalist, Joshua Mooney, was on the set for a bit of the *Pulp Fiction* shooting—a real scoop—and his profile of Tarantino came out in the August 1994 *Movieline.* But the most in-depth conversation about what occurs on-screen in *Pulp Fiction* was with Gavin Smith. Additionally, Smith managed some canny questions about issues still unresolved about *Reservoir Dogs.*

Pulp Fiction opened in the U.S. in October 1994 to rousing reviews and excellent box office, and virtually every American newspaper had a Tarantino interview. For this book these have been narrowed to several in-depth conversations, including an obligatory at-home visit with the filmmaker (Hilary de Vries in the *Los Angeles Times*, David Wild in *Rolling Stone*).

At a lavish New York press junket, Tarantino offered his most provocative defense yet for his thesis that violence in his films is unharmful, purely "aesthetic." As quoted by Gary Susman in the *Boston Phoenix* (7 October 1994, p. 3:5), Tarantino opined, "I don't think anyone in Rwanda has seen any of my movies, and yet they've machete'd 500,000 people to death there."

It was a confident time for Tarantino, a time to stretch out. He and his co-writer Roger Avary, and his producer, Lawrence Bender, did a three-way conversation with Godfrey Cheshire in the September 1994 *Interview;* and Tarantino and director Robert Zemeckis had a mutual-admiration society dialogue that was published in the *Los Angeles Times* on 26 March 1995. (Tarantino, as it turned out, really liked Zemeckis's *Forrest Gump*.). Also, he had the chance to make a goofy guest appearance in the movie *Sleep with Me*, offering an absurdist monologue regarding the homosexual subtext of the movie *Top Gun*. It was to Peter Biskind in *Premiere* in November 1994 that Tarantino looked ahead also to his next project, the four-part *Four Rooms*, interconnected stories taking place in a grand hotel. He'd write and direct one part, and the other three would be done by his director friends, Roberto Rodriguez, Allison Anders, and Alexandre Rockwell. Some months later, again with Biskind, Tarantino and the three others submitted to a group interview shortly before *Four Rooms* was to premiere at the Toronto International Film Festival. Even as the quartet was putting on a brash, jocular front, it was clear the film was in trouble. And for the first time ever, Tarantino sounded bruised and burned. He had been unhappy about the reviews for his acting in Rodriguez's feature, *Desperado*. Every critic, he felt, was saying, "We're sick of this guy. We don't want to see his face anymore." Tarantino, overexposed in the media, was the new "fall guy."

Then disaster struck at the Toronto Fest in September 1995. (I was in the much-disappointed Closing Night crowd.) The Anders and Rockwell sections were despised by all, the Rodriguez story generally approved. Tarantino's story, though not exactly embraced, fell somewhere in the middle. *Four Rooms* played a couple of weeks theatrically in fall 1995, then disappeared from the screen.

Tarantino, as far as I can determine, did *no* interviews at all about *Four Rooms*, shaken by its instant failure. That's a pity, for his section of the film could be served well by his commentary about it, beginning with an elucidation of how it is an homage to the Hollywood comedies (*The Bellboy*, especially) of Jerry Lewis.

Several days prior to the *Four Rooms* screening at Toronto, I reintroduced myself to Tarantino, asking if he would care to give another lecture at Boston University. "Thanks," he said politely, "but I'm going to take a long vacation." However, three months later, Tarantino was back in the public eye. At the beginning of 1996, he was feeling revitalized, acting for his friend, Roberto Rodriguez, in the western horror film, *From Dusk Till Dawn*. The script was by Tarantino, too, so he agreed to magazine interviews promoting it.

He seems to have recaptured much of his former pop-culture spirit for the breezy, agreeably informal profile in *Axcess*. Speaking with Don Gibalevich, he rhapsodized about favorite recent Hong Kong action films. But even amidst fun teasing his *From Dusk Till Dawn* co-star Juliette Lewis in a twin interview with Mim Udovitch for *Details*, Tarantino suddenly veered to his new discontent being a media star. "It's funny," he confessed, "because the thing that I find really bizarre when I read interviews with myself is I start getting ridiculously self-conscious about just being me.... No one can deal with that kind of self-consciousness, and all of a sudden you're afraid to be who you are."

In a telling interview with critic Jim Hoberman, Tarantino unburdened himself of built-up discontents. Three biographies had come out which, he felt, were unnecessarily critical: "If they want their careers to be talking bad about me—well, have a nice career." He'd had a major breakup with his screenwriting partner, Roger Avary, "and not to get too melodramatic about it, but I've never been more betrayed by anybody I was close to." And his acting appearances, he felt, continued to be treated dismissively by the press. However, he would continue performing, even "if critics look at it like a celebrity turn."

Finally, he had tired of being stereotyped as a film freak and of the misconception "that I just completely live my life through movies—like that's the only thing I relate to. It's not true! I feel I've lived a life more than most of the people I bump into." How did he plan to clear his head? "I'm going on a sabbatical," Tarantino avowed. "Read books, reacquaint myself with friends, just have a good time."

Tarantino stayed true to a new resolve to step away from the spotlight by running a totally closed set for the shooting of *Jackie Brown*. Journalists and TV crews were kept away. During post-production, Tarantino made room for only one talk, an interview with Lynn Hirschberg for a special November 16, 1997, film issue of *The New York Times Magazine*. The piece called "The Man Who Changed Everything" featured a thoughtul, sedate, matured Tarantino, moved at last, as he certainly deserved, to a "palatial mansion in the Hollywood Hills."

He talked, of course, of the upcoming *Jackie Brown* and, revealingly, of how the Samuel Jackson character in the movie, Ordell, a violent and homicidal African-American con man, was actually very autobiographical. "If I hadn't wanted to make movies, I would have ended up as Ordell," he told Hirschberg. "I wouldn't have been a postman or worked in the phone company or been a salesman or a guy selling gold by the inch. I would have been involved with one scam after another. I would have gone to jail."

On another note, Tarantino complained with justification that the American press had always sought to talk to him, yet treated him badly for this very accessibility, calling him "a master of self-promotion." Tarantino noted, "...I didn't do anything different from what an actor does. I didn't do *one more interview* than an actor does."

But the stage was set for a quiet release of *Jackie Brown* by its once-chatterbox filmmaker. Tarantino appeared on a few TV talk shows, but newspapers and magazines had to make do with interviews with the actors, especially Pam Grier. Seemingly the only occasion that Tarantino discussed the movie with a gathering of press was at an LA junket several weeks before *Jackie Brown* opened on Christmas Day, 1997.

The Boston Phoenix's Peter Keough was there to record Tarantino's remarks. And it's with that occasion that this volume of interviews concludes, on the eve of *Jackie Brown*.

As with books in the Conversations with Filmmakers series, the interviews are reprinted unedited. Though the form followed by the series leads to a certain amount of repetition, Tarantino is one of those artistic people who says even the same things in oddly different ways. And these interviews are chosen out of many because, of course, they are the most insightful, informative, and unusual ones.

Thanks for their kind help on this book to David Bartholomew, Mark Bazer, Courtney Beliveau, Peter Biskind, Gerry Byrne, Michel Ciment, David Chute, Barbara Davis, Walter Donahue, Matt Drewein, Graham Fuller, Peter Keough, T. Jefferson Kline, Robin MacDonald, Michele Maheux, Howie Movshovitz, Lupe Salazar, Gary Susman, Sheila Trevitt, Josh Vallee, Bumble Ward.

Special thanks to my close friend, Peter Brunette, general editor of the University Press of Mississippi's Conversations with Filmmakers series, for allowing me this book of interviews with Quentin Tarantino, and to Seetha Srinivasan, editor-in-chief of the University Press of Mississippi, and to Kathy Greenberg, for their gracious editorial guidance.

Finally, thanks to my assistant editor, Jenn Sutkowski, for her many hours of diligent work. And a special dedication to Karen Schmeer, editor extraordinaire and my sweet companion.

— Gerald Peary, Cambridge, Massachusetts, 1 November 1997

CHRONOLOGY

1963 Born in Knoxville, Tennessee, on 27 March, son of Connie McHugh and Tony Tarantino

1965 Connie moves to Los Angeles, marries Curtis Zastoupil, and sends for Quentin.

1968 Enters kindergarten in the San Gabriel Valley, California

1971 Family moves to El Segundo, in the South Bay area of Los Angeles; attends the Hawthorne Christian School

1973 Parents divorce

1977 Writes his first screenplay, *Captain Peachfuzz and the Anchovy Bandit*

1979 Quits high school and works as an usher at an x-rated movie theatre in Torrance, California

1981 Starts taking acting lessons at the James Best Theater Company, where he meets Craig Hamann

   On 31 December, Connie marries Jan Bohusch.

1983 Works for Bohusch, selling trade-show booth space

   Moves out of his mother's house

1984 Craig Hamann comes up with a script for *My Best Friend's Birthday,* and he collaborates.

1984–89   Works at the Video Archives in Manhattan Beach, where he meets co-worker Roger Avary

1985   Starts studying acting at Allen Garfield's Actors' Shelter in Beverly Hills

1986   Principal shooting on the 16mm film of *My Best Friend's Birthday* (unfinished), with Quentin as director

1987   Writes the screenplay, *True Romance*

1989   Writes the first draft of the screenplay, *Natural Born Killers;* writes the screenplay, *Reservoir Dogs*

1989–91   Tarantino's romance with Grace Lovelace

1990   Writes the screenplay, *From Dusk Till Dawn;* works at CineTel, a production company, doing screenplay rewrites on *Past Midnight,* a 1992 cable TV movie

1991   June workshop of *Reservoir Dogs* script at the Sundance Institute, Utah; summer-fall five-week shoot of *Reservoir Dogs*

1992   January world premiere of *Reservoir Dogs,* Sundance Film Festival, Park City, Utah

Screenings of *Reservoir Dogs* at the Cannes, Montreal, and Toronto Film Festivals; October opening of *Reservoir Dogs* in the USA

1993   *True Romance* released, with Tarantino screenplay

1994   Winter filming of *Pulp Fiction*

In May, *Pulp Fiction,* written and directed by Tarantino, premieres at the Cannes Film Festival, where it wins the Palme d'Or.

In September, *Pulp Fiction* opens the New York Film Festival.

October opening of *Pulp Fiction* in the USA

Sleep With Me, with a comic acting role by Tarantino

Destiny Turns On the Radio, with an acting lead by Tarantino

Crimson Tide, with additional writing (uncredited) by Tarantino

It's Pat, with additional writing (uncredited) by Tarantino

Natural Born Killers, with a Tarantino story credit

1995   *Desperado,* with an acting role by Tarantino

Tarantino and Lawrence Bender form Rolling Thunder, to release others' films, new and revivals, through Miramax.

September premiere at the Toronto International Film Festival of *Four Rooms,* with one story written and directed by Tarantino.

September release of *Four Rooms* in the USA

From Dusk Till Dawn released, with acting and a screenplay by Tarantino

1996   *Girl 6* released, with an acting role by Tarantino

Appears at Academy Awards with girlfriend, Mira Sorvino

The Rock released, with additional writing (uncredited) by Tarantino

1997   Summer filming of *Jackie Brown,* written and directed by Tarantino

Christmas release of *Jackie Brown*

Crimson Tide (Hollywood Pictures, 1995)
Producer: Don Simpson, Jerry Bruckheimer
Director: Tony Scott
Screenplay: Michael Schiffer (**Quentin Tarantino,** uncredited), from a story by Schiffer and Richard Hendrick
Cast: Denzel Washington, Gene Hackman, George Dzundza, Matt Craven, James Gandolfini, Viggo Mortensen

Desperado (Columbia Pictures, 1995)
Producer: Bill Borden, Robert Rodriguez
Director: Robert Rodriguez
Screenplay: Robert Rodriguez
Cast: Antonia Banderas, Joaquim De Almeida, Salma Hayek, Steve Buscemi, Cheech Marin, **Quentin Tarantino**

Destiny Turns On the Radio (Rysher Entertainment, 1995)
Producer: Gloria Zimmerman
Director: Jack Baran
Screenplay: Robert Ramsay and Matthew Stone
Cast: **Quentin Tarantino,** James LeGros, Dylan McDermott, Nancy Travis, James Belushi, Tracey Walter, Allen Garfield

Four Rooms (Miramax Films, 1995)
Producer: Lawrence Bender
Director: Allison Anders, Alexandre Rockwell, Robert Rodriguez, **Quentin Tarantino**
Screenplay: Allison Anders, Alexandre Rockwell, Robert Rodriguez, **Quentin Tarantino**
Cast: Tim Roth, Antonio Banderas, Jennifer Beals, Paul Calderon, Sammi Davis, Valeria Golino, Madonna, David Proval, Ione Skye, Lili Taylor, Marisa Tomei, Tomlyn Tomita

From Dusk Till Dawn (Dimension Films, 1996)
Producer: Gianni Nunnari, Meir Teper
Director: Robert Rodriguez
Screenplay: **Quentin Tarantino,** from a story by Robert Kurtzman
Cast: Harvey Keitel, George Clooney, **Quentin Tarantino,** Juliette Lewis, Cheech Marin, Fred Williamson, Salma Hayek

The Rock (Hollywood Pictures, 1996)
Producer: Don Simpson, Jerry Bruckheimer
Director: Michael Bay
Screenplay: David Weisberg, Douglas S. Cook, Mark Rosner (**Quentin Tarantino**, uncredited), from a story by Weisberg and Cook
Cast: Sean Connery, Nicolas Cage, Ed Harris, Michael Biehn, William Forsythe

Girl Six (Fox Searchlight, 1996)
Producer: Spike Lee
Director: Spike Lee
Screenplay: Suzan-Lori Parks
Cast: Theresa Randle, Isaiah Washington, Spike Lee, **Quentin Tarantino**, Richard Belzer, Peter Berg, Halle Berry, Naomi Campbell, Ron Silver, John Torturro

Curdled (Miramax Films, 1997)
Producer: John Maass and Raul Puig (Executive Producer, **Quentin Tarantino**)
Director: Reb Braddock
Screenplay: John Maass, Reb Braddock
Cast: William Baldwin, Angela Jones, Bruce Ramsay, Mel Gorham, Lois Chiles, Daisy Fuentes, Barry Corbon

Jackie Brown (Miramax Films, 1997)
Producer: Lawrence Bender
Director: **Quentin Tarantino**
Screenplay: **Quentin Tarantino**, from the book *Rum Punch* by Elmore Leonard
Cast: Pam Grier, Samuel L. Jackson, Robert Forster, Bridget Fonda, Michael Keaton, Robert De Niro, Michael Bowen, Chris Tucker

QUENTIN TARANTINO

INTERVIEWS

Let's See. Whose Calls Won't I Return Today?

DAVID J. FOX/1992

IT'S JANUARY, 1991, AND Quentin Tarantino, 27, is in his fifth year of trying to become a movie actor or screenwriter. He's working at a video store in Manhattan Beach and getting rejection after rejection from Hollywood.

Flash forward to January, 1992. Tarantino returns to his mother's home in Glendale after a week at the Sundance Film Festival in Park City, Utah. The phone is ringing wildly. Agents are calling. Deals are being offered.

What changed Hollywood's view of Tarantino?

Simple. Tarantino's movie, *Reservoir Dogs*.

His script began attracting attention early last year when it was circulating among film industry agents. The movie, with prints still dripping wet, was completed just three days before the Sundance Festival began, and the five Park City screenings were among the hardest tickets to get, based on advance word from Hollywood, and word-of-mouth around the festival. The buzz seemed to be right, based on the reaction of those who saw it. Some festival-goers had problems with its violence and some called it one-dimensional, but most said Tarantino's touch as a writer and director was unmistakable. *Reservoir Dogs* was arguably the most talked-about movie of the festival.

Tarantino says he never "wrote things to sell. I wrote things to make. But I never had any success. It was a wasted life."

From the *Los Angeles Times* Calendar Section, 2 February 1992, pp. 21–22. © 1992 by the *Los Angeles Times*. Reprinted by permission.

That realization led him to the decision to finally write a movie he could produce. So he wrote *Reservoir Dogs* in four weeks and planned to shoot it on a $10,000 budget. But a friend and fellow would-be actor, Lawrence Bender, told him the script was "too good" to be made so cheaply, and persuaded Tarantino to hold off while he would take the script to some of his contacts.

"The script got circulated around Hollywood. Agents read it and gave it to all their actors. And that started people talking," Tarantino recalls.

The favorable reaction was quite a change from the days when Tarantino himself would try to sell his screenplays. "Script readers used to say my scripts were too vile, too vulgar, too violent. The scripts never got past the reader.

"Now, the scripts go right to the top guys.

"Before," he says, "the script readers reamed my screenplays. I still have the rejection letters.

"Now," after Sundance, he says, "I've gotten the Good Housekeeping Seal of Approval... people are even looking at my old scripts and saying, 'Oh, wow. This is so cool.'"

The script for *Reservoir Dogs* ended up with Monte Hellman and Richard N. Gladstein of Live America Inc. who, with Bender, decided to produce it. The film was shot in August with Tarantino directing on a budget that has been estimated between $1.5 million and $3 million.

"Quentin has written something that is challenging," Gladstein says. "It's a very, very, very, *very,* violent comedy."

How does Tarantino describe his own movie? "It's a heist film, about a bunch of guys who get together to pull a robbery and everything that can go wrong, goes wrong," said the writer-director. "It all leads to violence and blood, but it ends up being black, gallows humor." The 93-minute feature features Harvey Keitel, Tim Roth, Chris Penn, Steve Buscemi, Lawrence Tierney and Michael Madsen.

Gladstein said the movie didn't win any prizes at Sundance "because it, perhaps, wasn't the most politically correct movie. There's not a woman in it who has a spoken line of dialogue. It's a bit rough. Gritty. But the reaction by the people was fantastic."

He says the American release of the film will not come before the Cannes International Film Festival in May, where, Gladstein said that Live wants to enter the movie in the competition for first-time film directors.

Meanwhile, Hollywood is calling Tarantino about his future. But the director, who sleeps in his old room decorated with a Bobby Sherman lunch pail and posters of such movies as *Breathless,* and the French poster of *Dressed to Kill,* isn't answering.

"They're offering me X movies starring Mr. X, and I say, 'Send it over and I'll look at it.' But everyone knows what I'm going to do. You see, I'm spoiled now. On *Reservoir Dogs,* we never had a production meeting. It was kept pure. No producer ever monkeyed around with the script.

"So I have my own project and say, if you want to do it, then let's do it. If you don't like it, then I'll go somewhere else."

One project he has a deal to write and direct is *Pulp Fiction,* a film he will make for Danny DeVito's production company, Jersey Films.

And before that, he plans to travel. "I've been broke all my adult life... never been anywhere. This time in Park City? It was the first time I was ever in snow."

Encounter with Quentin Tarantino

CAMILLE NEVERS/1992

THEY SAY HIS FILM is violent. Indeed it is, a dense violence, in itself and for itself, and without a trace of self-consciousness. Violence is at the heart of *Reservoir Dogs*, not just its visceral pretext. It mirrors the film's music: pure movement which fuses in a centrifugal way, an appeal for outside help (to the voice on the radio or a police rescue team) to air out the suffocating, claustrophobic space of the film. Quentin Tarantino carries this film on his own shoulders, from the writing through to the editing: *Reservoir Dogs* is a work of raw theatricality (like Kazan's films) which is built around several hypotheses (like Mankiewicz's films); it hits first and thinks later (like Leone's films). However, you need more than good references to make a good film; and Tarantino proves that he's got something to say and something to film.

I liked the idea of beginning the film with a scene focusing on six characters for about ten minutes, which at first seems to have nothing to do with the rest of the film. There's nothing to indicate that they're all gangsters about to pull off a major heist. But I used it to situate the characters. This creates a sense of play with what's going to follow, and the idea that you have to make a mental effort to keep track of who's who (among Mr. Pink, Mr. White, Mr. Orange or Mr. Blonde).

From *Cahiers du Cinéma* 457, June 1992, p. 49. © *Cahiers du Cinéma*. Reprinted by permission. Translated from the French by T. Jefferson Kline.

A lot of people have told me that *Reservoir Dogs* is constructed like a puzzle. In fact, it's more like a novel in the way it's put together: no flashbacks, just chapters. But in America, movies have got to be linear: if you begin a scene at the beginning of a race, you have to end it at the end of the race. I prefer what Sergio Leone does in *Once Upon a Time in America,* which is true of all his films: "Answers first, questions later." The way it is in novels.

I am first and foremost a film fanatic. I've always wanted to make movies, to be part of that world. My most important experiences as a viewer are amazingly varied: they go from Nicholas Ray to Brian De Palma, from Terry Gilliam to Sergio Leone, from Mario Brava to Jean-Luc Godard and Jean-Pierre Melville, and even include Eric Rohmer.

I love it when someone just starting out in the movies reinvents an entire genre from the inside out, like Godard did with *Band of Outsiders* (one of the greatest films in the world) or *Breathless* or even *The Little Soldier,* which picked up stuff from American movies and went completely beyond them. I love playing with my viewer's expectations and, in the end, crossing him up. Take for example the "gas" scene in my film: what makes it work is that it unfolds in real time (the time it takes to play a song) and you can't cheat, it has to be played out to the end.

Every film should be better than its scenario, which is only a project, a kind of rehearsal for the film.

I don't really like the work of film writing. What's hardest is just sitting down to write. Afterwards, the fun comes from reading what I've written at the end of the day and wondering what's going to happen next. Shooting holds a different kind of pleasure for me: it's completely exhausting, crazy, hysterical. The connections people make with each other. Afterwards, the work of editing feels totally serene.

If *Reservoir Dogs* was written to take place entirely in one setting, it's because when I started out I thought I was going to have to make a film for $5000 in 16 mm and in black and white. Also, getting to a place and settling down allows you to devote your mind entirely to what the film will be like—you save time and energy that can be entirely focused on your work. Each time you change the setting you lose too much time moving everything, installing cables, lights, and rails, etc.

We spent two weeks rehearsing before the shoot, and in some ways the situation was just like the one in the film: I was "Joe," the guy who introduces these guys who don't know each other but who have to work together, who rehearse their crime down to the last detail before they set to work.

The reason I had only a cameo role in *Reservoir Dogs* is that the film had to have a kind of density that I needed to control, and I thought that my direction would be more aggressive if I kept my distance and concentrated entirely on directing. For me it's very simple, let me put it this way: Do I want to be a movie star? No, I just want to make films.

Interview at Cannes

MICHEL CIMENT AND

HUBERT NIOGRET/1992

MICHEL CIMENT/HUBERT NIOGRET: *So, you are twenty-eight?*
QUENTIN TARANTINO: Actually, I'm twenty-nine. I was twenty-eight when I made *Reservoir Dogs*.

MC/HN: *Was there earlier filmmaking?*
QT: The one thing I did as far as trying to make a movie was, when I was like twenty-two, I borrowed a 16mm movie camera. For three years I was doing this home-made feature, *My Best Friend's Birthday,* on weekends, or whenever I got some money. But I couldn't afford to process it. I was financing this movie from a minimum wage job at a video store. And after three years of just shooting it off and on, off and on, I finally got enough money to take it out of the laboratory. I started putting it together, and I was heartbroken. This was not what I thought it was going to be. It was useless. To finish it would have meant like another year-and-a-half of, "Okay, now we go into post-production." So I said, well, that's my film school. I learned how not to make a movie. So I started writing scripts in order to get money to do a real movie. *True Romance,* and then *Natural Born Killers.*

MC/HN: *What are they about?*
QT: *True Romance* is a love story, kind of, built around a drug deal. It's very much an Elmore Leonard novel kind of story. *Natural Born Killers* is

From *Positif* 379, September 1992, pp. 28–35. © *Positif.* Reprinted by permission of *Positif* and the authors.

the story of a husband-and-wife serial killer team who become culture heroes. They become teen idols for the teens of the world, especially in America, but then in Japan and France.

MC/HN: *Are they based on real people?*
QT: No, it's just an idea I got. There was a serial killer in America called "the Night Stalker," a guy named Richard Ramirez. And he had groupies who would go to his trial, like sixteen-year-old girls. They were asked, "What do you do in court all day?" And they said, "We try to catch Richard's eye." I thought, "That's interesting." So I came up with this black comedy about these serial killers who become media darlings.

My first script, the *True Romance* one, well I tried for three years to get the money to make it for a *Blood Simple* budget. I was very much inspired by the way the Cohen brothers and Sam Raimi for *The Evil Dead* raised money through limited partnerships and got doctors and gynecologists to give them some money. I tried that, but nobody gave me anything. Then I wrote *Natural Born Killers* to be done for $500,000, and I thought I could raise that. A year-and-a-half later, I hadn't raised anything. I just lost confidence that anybody would ever give me money to make a movie. "But I've got to shoot a film," I thought. So I sold off one of the scripts.

MC/HN: True Romance?
QT: Tony Scott's doing it right now. The money wasn't very much, but I was going to make *Reservoir Dogs* on that money. I wrote the script so I could do it on 16mm, black and white, like the one I did a long time ago, except now knowing what I was doing. I was going to shoot the warehouse stuff in, like, seven days, and then the rest on weekends, until I finished, on a budget like $30,000. I'd play it in festivals and stuff, but I just had to make a movie.

The script is exactly the same script that you see here, except Harvey Keitel wouldn't have been in it, it would have been me and my friends. I showed the script to my partner, Lawrence Bender, the producer of my film, and he said, "Quentin, this is really good. Why don't we really try to make this? This is going to be a real movie."

I said, "No, no no no. I've heard all that before. No one's going to give me money, and I'm not going to spend another goddamn year talking about making movies." I'd been burned so bad that he said, "Look, give me two months to try to get this going. You can wait three months to make the movie you have to make." So I said, "Okay," and in two months we got it going. We had a commitment to do it for $200,000. And that led to a commitment to do it for half a million. Eventually, we did it for $1.5 million.

MC/HN: *You were born in Tennessee?*
QT: Yeah, I was there the first two years of my life, then I moved to LA. I've lived in LA the whole rest of my life except for my fifth grade year, when I went back to Tennessee.

MC/HN: *And your parents?*
QT: My mom's from Tennessee. She's an executive in the medical insurance business, in HMOs. People who can't afford medical insurance can sign up, and they have hospitals for them.

MC/HN: *Your father?*
QT: My father, I never met my real father.

MC/HN: *As a child, were you a great film buff?*
QT: That's the only thing I ever was, a film buff. It's funny, I meet people who are twenty, twenty-five, whatever, and they don't know what they want to do with their lives. I've known since before I can remember. As a kid, I wanted to be an actor because, when you love movies, that's what you gravitate towards. That's the only thing I ever studied: acting, with some very good teachers.

I studied it for about six years. The first teacher was James Best, who starred in Sam Fuller's *Verboten!* He's the Confederate soldier in Fuller's *Shock Corridor* and Jerry Lewis's partner in *Three on a Couch*. Then I studied for years with Allen Garfield, a brilliant actor (he was in *The Conversation* and he's the movie producer in *The State of Things*) and just a wonderful, beautiful teacher. He gave me a lot of faith and just taught me an immeasurable amount about acting.

Jimmy Best had a school in Teluca Lake, California, and Allen had a theater group in Beverly Hills, so I'm an LA actor. When I studied with Best, I had the intention of being an actor. But little by little I realized that I didn't fit in with the rest of the actors in the school. I was too movie-mad, and my idols weren't other actors. My idols were directors like Brian De Palma. I decided I didn't want just to be in movies, I wanted to make movies.

Even though I'd switched hats to try to become a filmmaker, I started studying with Allen Garfield. I still wanted to act, and I was such a big fan of his work. It was so cool because I could direct scenes in his class. He'd say, "Quentin, you want to be a director? Every time you do a scene in my class, I expect it also to be directed." That's film school as far as I was concerned. He's my mentor.

MC/HN: *And what about being a film buff?*

QT: I just watched TV in my childhood all the time, and was taken to the movies all the time. As soon as I got old enough to go to the theater myself, that's what I did every weekend. If I'd seen every movie, I'd go see them again. Also during the weekend in Los Angeles, these old movies constantly played on TV all day long, and my parents would get mad at me. "Quentin, you're a little kid. Go outside. Play football, play something."

I was very much a "tunnel vision" kind of kid. I was really bad in school. I had no interest in it. I didn't like sports. I wasn't into model cars, or anything like that. I was into movies and comic books. And monster magazines.

MC/HN: *What was your film taste?*

QT: When I started to develop, for lack of a better word, my "aesthetic," I loved exploitation movies. I loved in the '70s when New World was cranking out their pure stuff, like Jonathan Demme's *Caged Heat*. And all the Roger Corman stuff, drive-in movies. At the same time, I loved crime films and horror films. Also at the same time I discovered, it sounds like a cliché, I discovered Godard. I love *Breathless,* but my favorite is *Bande à part.* That's what I named my company after.

Another gigantic influence definitely would be De Palma who, with Godard, are my first hero directors. Along with Sergio Leone. When I decided to become a director, it just came on TV, Leone's *Once Upon a Time in the West.* It was like a book on how to direct, a film so well designed. I watched to see how characters entered the frame and exited the frame.

Those were my cinema teachers. And the other one was Pauline Kael. I got her book, *When the Lights Go Down,* when I was sixteen. I read it and thought, "Someday maybe I'll be able to understand a movie like she does." I've read everything she's ever written for *The New Yorker* and got all her books, and I've learned as much from her as I have from filmmakers. She taught me a sense of how to be dramatically engaging, how to make a connection with the audience. She was my professor. In the film school of my own making, she was my Kingsfield, like in *The Paper Chase.*

MC/HN: *Did you ever meet her?*
QT: Never.

MC/HN: *And since she's retired, you'll never be reviewed by her.*
QT: Believe me, believe me, I know. That was like the final irony. I'm in *Reservoir Dogs* pre-production, and that's when she retires. What's going on here? But maybe it's for the best. Maybe I really don't want to know what she thinks of the movie.

MC/HN: *How did you start to write a script?*
QT: I just come up with what I feel is a neat idea for something, and I'll put in mind. And I'll let it incubate for years. When I want to write, I figure out what genre and what style I want to work in. And I just kind of flip through the old backlog to see which idea's time has come. For *Reservoir Dogs,* about eight years ago I had the idea of a heist film told through the point of view of the rendezvous, where everyone will meet after the robbery. One by one, they show up. You never see the heist, though something horrible has happened.

MC/HN: *Did the title,* Reservoir Dogs, *come before or after the script?*
QT: I came up with the title before I had a movie. "This is a great title," I thought. "I'd go see a movie called this." So it was finding the right movie to go with it. When I came up with this story, it was like, "Boom! That's it!"

MC/HN: *Is it a slang expression?*
QT: No. It definitely means something to me, but I don't like to say because I am knocked out by people coming up to me telling me what

they think it means. The minute I say what it means to me, all of that will stop. I don't want it to stop. I can tell you that, when I went into meetings with people about making the movie, I was very nervous that the title might be changed. If I told them an obscure meaning, they'd say, "Well, we can do without that," or I could call it instead, *Dog Eat Dog,* or *Guys with Guns,* or *The Big Shootout.*

I didn't want any of that, so I said, "It's an expression used in French New Wave gangster films. It's an expression meaning 'rat.' It's in *Breathless,* it's in *Bande a part.*" A total lie, but they believed it. They hadn't seen those movies.

"It's a common expression," I said. Hopefully it will be, after the movie. And one of the reasons I liked it was that it sounds like something in an Alain Delon movie of Jean-Pierre Melville, who very much influenced me. I could see Alain Delon in a black suit saying, "I'm Mr. Blonde."

MC/HN: *Could you describe your writing process?*
QT: It's always a big deal for me when I'm going to write a new script, to go into the stationery store and buy the notebook. I've really romanticized it. I buy the three red ink pens I'm going to use, and the notebook. "This is the notebook I'm going to write *Reservoir Dogs* with," I say. It's a big ritual. But I can't spell, and I can't punctuate. My stuff is unreadable. So when I've finished, I try to give it to friends of mine to type it for me. But when I was finishing *Reservoir Dogs* and needed a typed hard copy very fast, my friends who used to do it for me for free were all busy on scripts.

So I got my girlfriend's computer, it's the most rudimentary computer in the world, you had to print after every page you wrote, and I typed it myself. And the thing that kind of blows away my theory that I had to have a pen in hand to create was that the characters started arguing by themselves about the colors of their names. They just kept talking to each other, so I wrote it down and it was like, "Wow!"

People come up to me and say, "You write great dialogue," and I feel like a fraud taking credit for it. It's the characters who write the dialogue. I just get them talking and I jot down what they say. To me, dialogue is very, very easy. As long as I care about the people and I know them, they just go off. And that's why my dialogue is about things that don't have anything to do with anything. They'll go off and talk for ten minutes about Pam Grier. Or ten minutes about Madonna, or Coca-Cola, or maca-roni and cheese. Like the conversations I have in real life.

M C / H N : *The opening scene was really great in that way, the conversations about Madonna and "Like a Virgin" and tipping or not tipping.*
Q T : That scene doesn't have anything to do with the movie storywise, but it's a character piece that hopefully you're always dipping back to during the course of the film to help get a bead on some of those guys. I'm offering you little as far as defining those characters except their personalities, and I wanted you to get a glimpse of personality outside of this horrible situation in their face in the warehouse.

In the script I make it all sparse except the dialogue. For instance, I can tell you the exact narration on the first page was, "Six guys wearing black suits, black thin ties are sitting around a table eating breakfast in a restaurant. Their names are Mr. Brown, Mr. blah, blah, blah" and then, boom, the dialogue starts. I didn't want to describe the characters, like, "This guy has blonde hair, this guy's fat, this guy's old." Nothing. I wanted the characters' personalities to be expressed through the dialogue.

The film you see is exactly the script. That's the structure which always existed. We didn't do anything in the editing room, like jumping around. I think one of the reasons the film works on a tension level is because of the use of real time. The real time of the movie is an hour, the time they're in the warehouse. It takes longer to see because it goes back and forth in the story. But they're stuck in the warehouse, and every minute for them is a minute for you.

M C / H N : *Do you let others read your scripts while you work on them?*
Q T : I don't give anything to people until I'm done with it. The first draft to you will be the sixth draft to me. That's the only way I'll be able to take the criticism is when I'm secure with it. But as far as testing it out, while I don't let anybody read the whole script, I may write a scene and be all excited about it and, it'll be twelve o'clock at night, I'll call up friends and say, "Listen to this!" I'll just want to read it. It's a stage of the game. It's not even that I want to hear their reaction. I'm sure their reaction will be good. It's saying it out loud and knowing someone is listening to it. It's almost like I can hear it through their ears. I do that all the time, call up friends.

MC/HN: *In the heist genre,* Reservoir Dogs *is obviously close to John Boorman's* Point Blank *because the heist is seen through fragmented editing.*

QT: Yeah, *Point Blank* and other Parker novels by Richard Stark were very influential to this film. I was kind of misquoted in the press book that this was like a complete homage to Kubrick's *The Killing.* I asked for it, because of a statement I made, "This movie is my *The Killing.*" What I meant by that was if I was going to make a war movie where a bunch of guys get together and blow up a Nazi gun, that would be my *Where Eagles Dare.* If I was going to do a western, it would be my *One-Eyed Jacks.* I just talk in movie terms. *The Killing* is my favorite heist film, and I was definitely influenced by it.

MC/HN: *But the two films are very different. There's no scene in common, and they're structured differently.*

QT: The big difference is that *The Killing* is done in the format of a newsreel or documentary: "At 5:15 on the last day of his life, so-and-so wakes up and…" I do mine in the style of a novel. I've always considered *Reservoir Dogs* as the pulp novel I'll never write. I tried very hard for a novelistic structure. I don't consider what I did as flashbacks but as character chapters. That's why they have chapter headings like "Mr. White," "Mr. Brown," "Mr. Blonde," so when you go back to the warehouse, you'll think, "Okay, I see where he's coming from."

MC/HN: *The warehouse is almost a stage.*

QT: Definitely. That made a hard time getting the movie made. We'd give the script to people and they'd say, "Well, this is a play." I'd say, "No, it's not. I have no interest in doing this on stage." The camera is very important to me. If it wasn't, I'd be directing on stage. But the script was done that way for two reasons. One, remember, I was planning on doing it in 16mm, so I had to try to stay in one place as much as possible. Second, I just like using theatrical elements as long as I can pull off the cinematic quality.

I'm really knocked out about how people catch the theatricality of how Mr. Blonde is introduced into the movie. When the guys are at each other and the camera pulls back, it's like, "Oh! He's been there all along."

Also, you need to feel the claustrophobia of these guys. You need to be locked in there with them. A film that actually did that was John

Carpenter's remake of *The Thing*. In some ways, it's exactly the same story as my movie. A bunch of guys are trapped in one place that they can't leave.

In *The Thing*, the tension and distrust and betrayal and paranoia those guys had going toward each other on that little outpost: it went right through the audience. I felt it, like a character in the movie, and it was freaking me out. That was what I was trying to achieve with *Reservoir Dogs*. I was hoping that lightning would strike twice and I could make an audience feel paranoid, creeped out, not knowing who to trust.

MC/HN: *But isn't your film more like Jacobean tragedy, in that blood is essential and spills over? Like the man on the floor, where you see blood oozing out?*
QT: That's the only thing in the film I would concede is graphic. The reason it freaks out people is that it's not theatrical, it's realistic. When somebody gets shot in the stomach that way, they bleed to death. It's the most painful place a person can get shot because, once the stomach is pierced, all the acidic juices are released into your body. It's a horrible, horrible pain, until you get too numb to feel it. Yes, the blood in that scene is realistic. We had a medic on the set controlling the pool, saying, "Okay, one more pint and he's dead."

MC/HN: *What did you shoot first, the warehouse or the other scenes?*
QT: It worked out wonderfully the way we did it. The first week was the opening and all the office scenes. The second week was all the action stuff, the chase with Mr. Pink and the stuff in the alley. And then it was two straight weeks of warehouse. And the last week was the Mr. Orange chapter, which is almost like another movie. I wanted it to be like a TV show, a *Starsky and Hutch* episode. We had said goodbye to Harvey Keitel, then everyone else in the movie except Tim Roth went away. And so it felt like we were making another movie with Tim Roth. We weren't that smart, but it just worked out in a good way.

MC/HN: *And your cameraman, Andrzej Sekula?*
QT: You have to understand, I was very intimidated about the idea of choosing both my cinematographer and my editor because I knew whoever I chose would know a hell of a lot more about their job than I knew about their job, but I knew about my movie. And I didn't want some old

salty dogs, you know, "Aww, kid, that's not how you do it." So I was prepared to fight constantly with them, but life's short, I didn't want to.
What happened with Andrzej, it was a great leap of faith on my part and
even more on the part of my producers, the company financing the
movie. He'd never done a feature before, and we had cinematographers
who wanted to do the movie whose work was definitely respectable.
Actually I don't mean just respectable: I mean I was a great fan of their
work.

MC/HN: *And Sekula?*
QT: He's a Pole who lives in London. He'd done some BBC films. He did
one called *Honey and Venom* for the BBC that's just beautiful. And he'd
done a lot of European commercials. I saw his reel. And the reason we
hired him, besides his passion, his love for the movie, was that he comes
across as a mad genius. Compared to everyone else's, his reel is the difference between the good and the arguably great. And he was a wild man! We
shot *Reservoir Dogs* in 50 ASA, which is the slowest film stock that Kodak
makes. Low-budget pictures are shot with the fastest film stock because
you don't need that much light. Instead, we were pumping in light from
everywhere; every shot in the movie was miserable to get. I mean, that
warehouse was an oven. It roasted you, but it was worth it because it gave
you those deep, deep colors.

I don't know a whole lot about lighting. I know what I want, but every
time I talked to Andrzej about how I wanted the film to look, I just talked
in terms of colors. I wanted the reds to be eye-popping reds, the blues to
be blue, the black to be black, no gray. I just talked in terms of the clarity
of the colors and that's what the film stock gave us.

I didn't use storyboards because I can't draw, and I don't like the idea of
someone else drawing them because they wouldn't get the framing right.
But I can write, so I did extensive shot lists, where I just describe everything. The camera will do this, at this point it will do that, all the different
set-ups. We'd discuss every scene, and then Andrzej would do some of his
own, and come back and I'd say, "Yeah, I like that"; "No, I don't like that";
"Yeah, I like yours here better than mine, I think that's more interesting."

His stuff was more aggressive than mine, and I was, like, we can't make
every shot a dolly shot. We'll never get finished. Actually, someone made a
suggestion to me, "Quentin, you're so wild. Your cinematographer shouldn't

be the adult, telling you, no, no, you can't. You should find someone more wild than you so that you'll be put in the position of the adult." Who gives you a great piece of advice like that? That was exactly our situation.

I had all these movies I wanted to watch with Andrzej. "I want you to look at this and look at that." And he'd say, "I will watch any movies you want but we must watch them with the sound off." So we watched eight movies I wanted him to see completely silent. I'd never done that before, and that's the difference between night and day. Then you really see the photography, the color, the style the film is being shot in. It's an eye-opener.

M C / H N :   *One of your producers is film director, Monte Hellman. Did he bring something special to the making of* Reservoir Dogs?

Q T :   I have nothing but respect for him, because he's a wonderful film-maker. I think *Ride the Whirlwind* is probably the most naturalistic Western ever made. It's beautiful, and *Ride the Whirlwind* and *The Shooting* are prob-ably the most authentic Westerns when it comes to the dialogue of the Old West. The slang they use in *Ride the Whirlwind* should be put in a time capsule. You know you're hearing the truth. But for *Reservoir Dogs,* he gave me freedom and respect. He was constantly shielding me, or knocking himself out to give me support. But he never talked to me about how to make a movie because he doesn't believe in that. As a film director, he doesn't like when people do that stuff to him.

There was one time when we were doing rushes when he said he thought I didn't accomplish the power of the scene. But he never sug-gested how I shoot anything. At the end of the first day, I was like, "So, Monte, what do you think about the way we're going to shoot the movie?" And he was like, "I wasn't even paying attention to that, Quentin. However you want to do it is how you want to do it. I'm just making sure you can accomplish in the course of the day what we expect of you."

M C / H N :   *Was Hellman considered to direct the film?*

Q T :   Well, it was weird. He wasn't considered; it was a miscommunication. I'd never met Monte, but I was a big fan of his work, and a mutual friend said he was going to get the script to him. I thought, great, I would love to hear what Monte Hellman had to say about the movie, though I wasn't willing to give it up. But Monte thought he was being offered to direct it. So he read it like that! And he said, "I want to meet Quentin Tarantino."

We got together at this place on Hollywood Boulevard, CC Brown's, a little ice-cream parlor, and we're having a hot fudge sundae, and he says, "I can get the money for it. I'm going to direct it myself." And I'm like, "There'd be no greater honor than to have Monte Hellman direct a script of mine, but this one's for me!" So we're eating, and he goes, "Well, how do you intend shooting it?" And I'm like, "Well, this is all theory," and I'm pontificating. But when I finish, he goes, "Well, that sounds really good. How about if I come aboard as executive producer?" I thought, "Oh, my God! Monte Hellman! It's a deal!" He's a lovely man, truly lovely.

M C / H N : *Where did you get the idea of calling your characters Mr. Blue, Mr. Brown, Mr. White, etc.?*

Q T : I just liked the idea that nobody knows anyone else. That way, if one guy is caught, he can't tell anybody anything. When I needed to decide what to use for pseudonyms, or aliases, I just came up with the idea for colors, partly because it just sounded like a French New Wave gangster film. I could see Jean-Pierre Melville doing something like that. It had the right tone, I thought, of tough-guy existentialism. Once I started saying it, "Mr. White, Mr. Blonde, Mr. Blue," I thought, "That sounds cool. I like that!" If I hadn't used colors, I probably would have named them after comic book characters or something. You know: "You're Spider Man, you're Thor, you're The Thing."

M C / H N : *The poster of "Kamikaze Cowboy"? Is that an American comic strip?*

Q T : Well, along with movies I'm a comic-book geek. I wanted to have a poster of the "Silver Surfer" in Mr. Orange's room. He's not only one of the great comic-book characters, he was on a wall in the American remake of *Breathless*, with Richard Gere, which I love. The character was first drawn by Jack Kirby, and that's the official "Silver Surfer," so I asked these friends of mine, Danny and Manny Villa Lobos, to draw me a Jack Kirby version of the "Silver Surfer." They did, and I put it on a wall, but they had also created their own comic-book poster character called "Kamikaze Cowboy." I put that on the wall in Tim's Mr. Orange apartment. Some journalists have been saying, "How do I get a copy of 'Kamikaze Cowboy'?" which should make my guys happy.

M C / H N : *Tell us about the radio playing in the movie.*

Q T : The radio station is sort of this invisible character that goes throughout. Me and Roger Avary wrote all the commercials that went into the
movie, traffic reports, editorials, everything. We got a bunch of actors and
recorded them, and that's what's playing. You can't hear them that well,
but it was great fun creating your own world that way.

M C / H N : *And the music?*

Q T : Those songs were hits in the '70s. I liked the idea of using pop bub-
blegum music, rock'n'roll for 14-year-olds. That's what I grew up with as a
teen in the '70s. And I thought it's a great ironic counterpoint to the
roughness and rudeness and disturbing nature of the film to have this
"What's wrong with this picture?" music playing along with it. In some
ways, it takes the sting off, in some ways it makes it more disturbing.

M C / H N : *There's an incredible scene where the gangster is running and the cops
are running after him. Were you more comfortable shooting action scenes like
that, or talking scenes?*

Q T : As long as you have good actors and get along with them, dialogue
scenes are far easier. Actors like Harvey Keitel and Tim Roth are easy to
work with, and you know they're going to be wonderful. You point the
camera at them, and you know they're going to get something. People ask,
"Were you intimidated working with actors like that?" How can you be
intimidated by them? I'd be intimidated working with really bad actors
because the movie's going to be crap. You can get a good actor who's a
jerk, but you can get a bad actor who is equally a jerk. Good actors make it
easy because you know it's going to be good.

Shooting that action stuff is tough. It's really tough, especially when
you only have a one-million-dollar budget. In fact, I said while I was doing
it that I will never shoot an action scene like that again on a low budget
because, for a chase like that, you need to close down the street. But we
didn't have the money to do that, we didn't have control of our environment. We needed five cops to stop traffic; we had two.

I was literally telling Steve Buscemi, "Okay, what's going to happen is
you're going to take the gun, you're going to empty it on the cops, you're
going to jump in the car, and, if the light is green, you're going to drive
away." He was like, "If the light is GREEN??? You mean you're not stop-

ping traffic?" "Well, kind of, we're stopping it from this side and this side. And the cops said, if you're going with the light, you can go."

Steve had just got through doing *Billy Bathgate*, which was like a 50-million-dollar movie. He was assuming we'd close down the town, too. It was really funny: in one of the car scenes he did, he's picking up full speed and driving away, and the road we used had a stop sign at the end, but we couldn't afford to put a cop down there. Well, Steve ran it, and I'm in the back seat of the car, and we hear on walkie-talkie, "That was totally illegal. You ran a stop sign, the cops are pissed. Get back here."

Hopefully, on the next movie we'll have more money.

MC/HN: *How many weeks shooting?*
QT: Five weeks. It was 30 days.

MC/HN: *You only did a few takes?*
QT: Most of the time, I didn't shoot from a million different angles and then try to put it together in the editing room. But some scenes like the opening had to be shot a bunch: get a ton of footage and then put it together in the best way. That scene is so dependent on the rhythm of the actors that you can't predetermine it. But listen to the actors' voices and that will dictate how to cut it together.

The one thing I did know was that, during the scene, I wanted to juggle the film styles. The first part of it, during the whole Madonna business, there's moving camera, and you don't quite get a bearing on anybody, who's talking, who are these people, you're slightly confused. The second part of it, when they're talking about the radio station, it's a bit more normal, two shots and masters, also a bit of movement. Then the whole tipping business is all closeups.

Most everything else, I only shot one way. Because I didn't want to have all these options. I just figured, look, this is going to work, and if it's not going to work, I'll make it work in the editing room.

MC/HN: *The casting was people you wanted?*
QT: Yeah. The only person who was pre-cast in the movie was Harvey Keitel. As I told you, we never dreamed we'd be able to get Harvey. Understand, he's my favorite actor in the world. I don't mean because I worked with him and he's a nice guy, and I've seen what he's capable of. I

mean I was fifteen years old and I saw him in *Taxi Driver* and *The Duellist* and, you know...

M C / H N : *In James Toback's* Fingers?
Q T : Fantastic! Since I've seen Harvey's performance in Toback's *Exposed,* as the terrorist. Oh, he's wonderful in that. He give such a wonderful speech about terrorism that he completely convinces you. He brings you over to his side. He's like, "What do I want? What do you think I want? What I want is a nice hotel room, to sleep in fine sheets. Fine food, Clint Eastwood westerns, that's what I want."

I approached Harvey, and he committed to the film. Everyone else we brought in to read. It was a great way to work on an ensemble piece, when you have someone who's perfect, and then you build around him. We knocked ourselves out getting just the right collection of guys. We were lucky because actors in LA and New York responded incredibly enthusiastically to the script.

We could have cast the film sixteen different ways and had sixteen different movies. It was very important that we had the right dynamic. We didn't want to do a lot of pre-casting: "Kevin Bacon and Kiefer Sutherland, we'll put them together, and boy, won't it be fun!" No, we wanted the right balance. Everyone had to be different, different rhythms, different looks, different personalities, different acting styles. But everyone had to be a unit. Also, we had actors who would come in and read wonderfully, but they didn't look like career criminals. I couldn't believe that Lawrence Tierney's Joe would hire those guys. And especially if you put them up against Eddie Bunker. He's the genuine article. He's the real thing.

M C / H N : *And your acting in the movie?*
Q T : When I was going to do it in 16mm, I was going to play a bigger part. I still could have, Harvey was all for it, but I decided I wanted to be outside the ensemble. I thought if I wasn't acting in the movie, I could pull it off. I felt the film could be just that much more aggressive, cinematically, because I was really 100% concentrating every day on the camera. So I took a smaller part, Mr. Brown. But I'd like to be able to jump back and forth. I've always admired the way Roman Polanski acts in some of his movies for two seconds, and others he's got a giant big part like *The Tenant* or *The Fearless Vampire Killers.*

MC/HN: *As the budget was very small, did you make special preshooting preparation with your actors?*

QT: We had two straight weeks of rehearsal, which was an immeasurable help. I demanded it, saying, "Look, not only is this the right thing to do, but it's going to save us money because we're not going to be sitting around asking these important questions while the clock is running." That's how it worked. We hammered things out. Of course, you're never giving a performance in rehearsal. It's like the difference between living with somebody and being married to somebody. The day you're shooting, that's when it really comes together. But you've answered questions on rehearsal days. Also, rehearsal is very much discovery. The script is a map and the rehearsal is a journey, but you don't know where you're going. And an actor like Harvey needs to go all around the world to get to where he starts. But when we started shooting, BOOM! We knew what we were doing, no messing around!

MC/HN: *How did you workshop your film at the Sundance Institute?*

QT: That happened literally just before the shoot. My script had gotten accepted into the Director's Workshop, which was normally for two weeks. But I didn't even know if I could go because we were in pre-production, and the film was completely cast. But I was able to be there for eleven days, and my producer partner, Lawrence Bender, held the fort and did all the pre-production work while I was messing around at Sundance.

I imagine that it's in pre-production when you can start losing your grip on the artistic side of the movie because you're dealing with money and time and schedules. You're dealing with everything except the script. So just when the machine was started going and going fast, I was able to escape, far far from Hollywood, in the middle of the mountains at the beautiful Sundance resort. The only thing I was doing was diving into the script for eleven straight days. It was remarkable. I mean, I'll never have that again. Just when everything is supposed to be hysterical, I had serenity and calmness.

MC/HN: *That's where you met Alison Maclean, the filmmaker of* Crush?

QT: Yeah, she was up there at the time, though she had to leave. Her film started earlier than mine. We were the only ones that were using the experience to jump into our own movies. Everyone else had projects that they were trying to get made, and ours were already going. Sundance was also a great experience because you had a little crew. A cinematographer, a production designer, and I was able to do two scenes. We had a day of rehearsal, then we had a day of shooting, and I was able to experiment with the scenes. That was a wonderful experience, but I would have done it anyway. To break the ice on filming, before shooting I would have got out a 16mm camera and some friends and just shot over a weekend. Good, bad, or indifferent, just to get used to the idea again.

MC/HN: *What's your next project?*
QT: I'm writing it now. It's called *Pulp Fiction.*

MC/HN: *A picture about the Pope?*
QT: Exactly! No, not "pope." "Pulp." It's a crime film anthology. Three crime stories like the old *Black Mask* magazine. The stories are completely separate, and they're the same stories you've heard a zillion times. You know, the staples of the genre, but hopefully taken where you've never seen them taken before. It's like the same group of characters in each of the different movies. A guy who's the star of the first story can be killed in two seconds in the third story. It's one of those scripts I won't know if I'm successful until I write the last page. I've written the first story, and so far so good, so we'll see.

MC/HN: *You're writing it here in Europe?*
QT: Not here while I'm in Cannes. I'm staying in Amsterdam, and that's where I'm writing it. It's a coproduction with Danny DeVito's company, Jersey Films. Danny won't be in it, but he'll be one of the executive producers of the film.

MC/HN: *Why Amsterdam?*
QT: I'd never been to Europe before, so I wanted, as soon as I was finished with *Reservoir Dogs,* to visit for the first time. Things are getting kind of crazy for me right now in Los Angeles, so Amsterdam is great because I don't have a phone and I don't have a fax, and I'm just writing. Nobody knows me, so it's been wonderful for me to just sit in my studio apartment and look at the canals and write. It's been a dream. I got there in March,

and I'll be going back in mid-July. And I'm going to visit London again and visit Paris before I go back.

MC/HN: *Do you have a shooting date?*

QT: No. I'll probably be finished with the script at the end of the summer, and we're thinking about shooting in winter. But it might get pushed back a little bit because I want to go to some countries and publicize *Reservoir Dogs* when I get there. I'll be coming back to France when it opens, and I'll be going to Britain and Japan. I've never been anywhere, so I'm looking to my movie as my passport to the world.

A Talk with Quentin Tarantino

GERALD PEARY/1992

GERALD PEARY: *Your publicity biography lists you in the cast of Jean-Luc Godard's* King Lear.
QUENTIN TARANTINO: It's a lie. I put it on my résumé as an actor, and said I was in that, because nobody would ever see the film.

GP: *Were you intimidated by the* Reservoir Dogs *cast?*
QT: Good actors don't intimidate me. After two weeks of rehearsal, they were ready to pop. They had some egos there, but they left them at the door.

GP: *Could you talk about casting Hollywood "B" veteran Lawrence Tierney in* Reservoir Dogs *as the gang's mastermind, Joe Cabot. He's someone who has been in a lot of trouble in his personal life.*
QT: I met him at a party at the Actors' Studio. He's an older guy, and had only so much to give in terms of stamina. He's a good guy, but he can slow you up 30 percent. He's alternately a teddy bear and a grizzly bear. He had a gun-firing incident. Do you remember his 1947 film, *The Devil Thumbs a Ride?* That could almost be entitled *The Lawrence Tierney Story.*

GP: *What's the connection of director Monte Hellman, the cult film director of* The Shooting *and* Two-Lane Blacktop, *to* Reservoir Dogs?
QT: He's worked on all these different projects that didn't happen. Three years ago, he made a film called *Iguana,* that never got released. A mutual

From the Montreal World Film Festival, August 1992.

friend gave Monte the script of *Reservoir Dogs,* and he wanted to direct it. We went to CC Brown, an ice-cream parlor, and I said to him, "As much an honor as that would be, this one is mine." "Well, OK." We continued eating ice cream. He said, "I'll be executive producer." He'd show up on the set every once in a while, and he gave the film to Tony Safford, who submitted it to Sundance.

I probably would write something for Monte to direct, possibly a remake of his western *Ride the Whirlwind* set in the 1930s.

G P : *You've mentioned John Carpenter's claustrophobic redoing of* The Thing *as an influence on* Reservoir Dogs.
Q T : One of the great remakes ever made: see *The Thing* again! Kurt Russell is just excellent. I've never met him: hopefully, he'll read this! And I should say that John Woo is also inspirational.

G P : *Describe yourself at age 29.*
Q T : I'm first and foremost a film geek, and making movies is a film geek's dream. All I ever spend money on is movie posters, videotapes, and books. Now I can buy a ton of film books, and they're all tax deductible.

When I was 18 or 19, I was going to write a book on genre filmmakers — John Flynn, Joe Dante, John Milius, Richard Franklin — and engage them in a conversation with movies. My four favorite directors in the world are De Palma, Leone, Godard, and Howard Hawks. I once had a dream that I was invited to a party at Hawks's house. Robert Mitchum was on a balcony and said, "You're here to see the old man." Hawks was on a patio with John Wayne. He said, "Hey, Quentin, come down, kid." I woke up. I was sad, it was so real.

G P : *Has Sam Fuller seen* Reservoir Dogs?
Q T : We hung out together, and he rips up your movie: "You make a movie for idiots! Too much gibble-gabble! Too much talk! Harvey Keitel? He's not an actor! He's a planet!"

G P : *And Michael Madsen as an actor?*
Q T : Michael conjures up so much to people: a handsome Neville Brand, Robert Mitchum in *Thunder Road.* Michael reminds me of Michael Parks, who, in the TV show, *Then Came Bronson,* is the greatest living actor!

G P : *And when Madsen's dancing about, before the famous razor blade scene?*

Q T : I love the time he takes playing the tape. He was great. It's my favorite scene in the movie. A female director said to me, 'What's scary about it is how much you enjoyed it." Early on, Harvey Weinstein of Miramax asked, "What do you think about taking the torture scene out?" Cut it out? I wouldn't. "Look," I said, "it's part of the movie, for people who appreciate the whole package." If violence is part of your palette, you have to be free to go where your heart takes you.

Sure, I think the scene is pretty horrible. I didn't make it for yahoos to hoot and holler. It's supposed to be terrible. But I didn't show it to convey a message. I don't think Stanley Kubrick was condemning violence in *A Clockwork Orange*. He wanted to film that stuff. It was cinematically exciting. He loved mocking "Singin' in the Rain."

Clint Eastwood fortunately decided to finish *The Unforgiven* in the right way, by taking everyone out. Did you see *Patriot Games*? It's a revenge movie, but they don't let Harrison Ford get to kill the bad guy at the end. The guy falls on a shovel, which is an asinine, chicken-shit way to kill the villain. They should go to movie jail for this! The only way to end it is for Harrison Ford to beat this guy to death.

G P : *What about the comparisons of you and Scorsese?*

Q T : Like him, I like mixing fast-cutting scenes and more deliberate ones, and I'm very particular with the frame. But he's almost a stone around young filmmakers' necks. So many new films are aping Scorsese. I don't want to be a poor man's Scorsese.

Interview with Quentin Tarantino

PETER BRUNETTE/1992

PETER BRUNETTE: *Could you explain your rationale for the odd chronology in* Reservoir Dogs?

QUENTIN TARANTINO: I wanted to break up the narration, not to be a wise guy, a show guy, but to make the film dramatically better that way. If I pulled it off, I got a resonance, so I liked the idea of giving the answers first, getting the questions later. Novels do that all the time, but when they make novels into films, the stuff that is most cinematic, that's what usually goes. A novelist would think nothing about starting in the middle. And if characters in a novel go back and tell past things, it's not a flashback, it's just telling a story. I think movies should benefit from the novel's freedoms.

PB: *So what was your strategy in structuring* Reservoir Dogs?

QT: I had the idea of how I wanted to reveal all the pieces of the story. *Reservoir Dogs* looks very structured, and it is, but it's A is structured, B is structured, but inside of A and B there's writing, with the characters deciding what will happen. If a character does something real that doesn't fit with the plan, well, that's what he does. I don't play God and mess with it. I then have a new reality: okay, this is what Mr. Pink does. That's how I work: letting the characters improvise, and I'm like a court reporter writing it down. I get a chance to be both an actor and a director. As an actor I get to play all the characters, get them work filmically, be rid of the extraneous stuff.

Published by permission of Peter Brunette.

P B : *There's a lot of theatricality in* Reservoir Dogs. *Was it written as a play?*
Q T : No, but it could be done as a play. It all takes place in one room, after the heist, beginning at the point where every other heist movie ends. I do have stage rights. If I were to make it a play, it would probably be a quick adaptation, and then I'd give it to someone else: "You do it. I'll come see it."

A "play" isn't a dirty word, it's just that I wanted to make a movie. But I don't like most plays made into movies. They're just recording the play, and what they offer is only actors playing parts that you didn't see them play in the theater. I want to offer much more.

When I was at the Sundance Institute in the Directors' Workshop, Terry Gilliam was one of the resource directors and we talked of this. It had always been his opinion, though he'd never tested it, that, if you did a movie in one set, you came close to pure cinema. You weren't spending hours and days moving from one place to another, breaking down, schlepping in cars, putting up things again. You were *there to create,* to film and film and film.

P B : *When I try to define your aesthetic sensibility, I think maybe David Letterman with Gus Van Sant, ultra-realism taken so far it becomes campy, funny, tongue-in-cheek.*
Q T : I wouldn't say tongue-in-cheek. But I do look at everything as a comedy, and *Reservoir Dogs* is structured to get laughs. I like the idea that the audience is laughing and that, BOOM, the next moment there is blood on the walls. Then there are more laughs. For example, after the torture scene, there's the scene where Joe hands out the colors, and the audience laughs again. And I like the idea that there are lots of smiles on faces while Michael Madsen is doing his razor dance.

To me, ultra-realism is *absurd,* real life is *absurd,* like the conversation you hear at Denny's in the next booth. My characters define themselves and talk to others through pop culture, because they all understand it. If one guy started talking about Longfellow, they wouldn't know who that is. But if he talked about Madonna or McDonalds, everybody knows. Or Elvis Presley. Everybody has an opinion. My mom can talk about all kinds of pop culture. She never goes to the movies, but she knows who Madonna is, who Richard Gere is.

PB: *Do you see anything wrong with being so enmeshed in popular culture?*
QT: I don't think it's the worst thing in the world. That's what makes America what it is, what gives it its charm, part of its personality. It's a junk-food culture. There's something very lovely in that, though I'm maybe saying it's very lovely because it's my culture. It's me!

I'd never been to other countries before this year, but I've now been to other countries, and I love going into McDonalds. The difference? In the Paris McDonalds, they serve beer. And they don't call it a Quarter Pounder, because they have the metric system there: Le Royale with cheese! They don't know what a fucking Quarter Pounder is!

PB: *What were you trying to do in conceptualizing your gangsters?*
QT: First, they're real people talking. That gives them a heartbeat. They have normal, childish, human responses. And they don't say "jokes," because you can imagine people actually saying shit like that. But they have the movie swagger, the movie sense of fun. So what I'm looking for is that wonderful blend of a highly stylized artistic aesthetic and a completely realistic aesthetic. An example is they're all wearing black suits.

PB: *Which they match with the same stupid thin ties. It's like the Blues Brothers.*
QT: There's a cool, stylized feel, and it scratches my movie itch. On the other hand, it's realistic, because robbers on the job often wear a uniform, whether baseball caps, jumpsuits, or trenchcoats, to take away from remembering faces. "At the robbery, what did they look like?" "I don't know, a bunch of black suits."

PB: *There's a difference, however, between "realism" and "reality." What you show in one scene is reality, that huge pool of blood.*
QT: Tim Roth is lying there, saying, "Please hold me." That scene makes people uncomfortable. They say, "Why don't you move on? You've made your point." But it ain't about making points! This guy is shot in the stomach and he's begging to be taken to the hospital! You can't deal with that in one or two sentences, and then move on!

PB: *Everybody asks you about the violence in your movie.*
QT: And I say, I love violence in movies, and if you don't, it's like you don't like tapdancing, or slapstick, but that doesn't mean it shouldn't be

shown. My mom doesn't like Abbott and Costello or Laurel and Hardy, but that doesn't mean they shouldn't have been making movies.

P B : *Does she like violence?*

Q T : The torture scene was her favorite in my movie.

P B : *I'm from Washington DC, where there are 500 murders a year. What do you say when people say that movies like* Reservoir Dogs *do nothing to discourage violence?*

Q T : If you're not part of the solution, you're part of the problem? My answer is that I can't worry about that. As an artist, violence is part of my talent. If I start thinking about society, or what one person is doing to someone else, I have on handcuffs. Novelists don't have to deal with that, painters don't have to deal with that, musicians don't have to deal with that.

There are two kinds of violence. First, there's cartoon violence like *Lethal Weapon.* There's nothing wrong with that. I'm not ragging on that. But my kind of violence is tougher, rougher, more disturbing. It gets under your skin. Go to a video store, to the horror section or the action-adventure section, nine out of ten of the films you get there are going to be more graphically violent that my movie, but I'm *trying* to be disturbing. What's going on is happening to real human beings. There are ramifications to it.

P B : *Well,* Reservoir Dogs *might make people think more about violence because it's so disgusting, so revolting. And what about your gangsters getting off on their own professionalism?*

Q T : They bullshit themselves into thinking it's a regular job, like a carpenter or a craftsperson. But being a crook is not a regular job. You are going against society. You can't do this kind of job and not have it be messy. Putting guns into people's hands and having them achieve things with the threat of murder? At some point that stops being a profession.

P B : *However "realistic" the film becomes, having the characters talk about Mr. Orange and Mr. White makes it all weird.*

Q T : I know, I know, I know! It's like Jean-Pierre Melville's French gangster films. He was basically taking the old Michael Curtiz and Raoul Walsh

Warner Brothers gangster pictures with Cagney and Bogart and almost doing them verbatim story-wise. But by putting them in Marseilles and giving them a French feeling, French pace, French sensibility, they were not only very realistic but, to me, insanely absurd. A French sensibility to an American pulp genre: I loved that! What I'm trying to do is put the American vernacular back into what Melville was doing.

With my characters, I love playing with their vocabulary. Some say weird poetic things, especially Mr. Pink. One of my favorite lines from him, buried in the middle of the movie: "I doubt that Joe is going to have a lot of sympathy for our plight." That's the way he talks, that's Mr. Pink's rhythm!

PB: *What's your answer for people who criticize* Reservoir Dogs *for its absence of women characters?*

QT: It's actually a sore point for me. Everything else I wrote has great parts for women, some of my proudest characters. There are no women in *Reservoir Dogs* because they wouldn't work in the reality of this story. They're in the warehouse. What, they're going to bring girlfriends to the rendezvous? Or I could have shown Mr. White with a wife, but that wasn't the story I was telling.

PB: *Did you go to film school?*

QT: I never went to college or film school. I studied acting, but I didn't have much of a career. I was on an episode of *The Golden Girls,* and some LA TV. But when I was 21 or 22, I decided to become a film director, and try and make a 16mm film called *My Best Friend's Birthday.* Rather than spend $60,000 for film school, spend $6,000 for a movie. That's the best film school in the whole world, learning how to go out every day and keep it alive, when you are not able to pay anybody. Even if the film fails.

None of the film books about directing made any sense. "What you need to do with rehearsal is..." I didn't buy into any of that. And I tried to read technical books about lenses and stuff, but they only confused me, gave me headaches. I did read books on how to form limited partnerships, how to get people to give you money.

Reservoir Dogs Press Conference

TORONTO INTERNATIONAL FILM FESTIVAL/1992

HENRI BÉHAR, *LE MONDE* (MC): We'll start the press conference concerning *Reservoir Dogs*, and I'll introduce quickly the people who are here at the table. On the far left, Mr. Blonde, Michael Madsen. Next to him, Mr. Orange, Tim Roth, Next to me, Mr. Pink, Steve Buscemi. Next to him, and also the co-producer, Mr. White, Harvey Keitel. And dead center, Mr. Rainbow, I guess.

QUENTIN TARANTINO: Mr. Brown! Mr. Brown!

TIM ROTH: Mr. Merde!

BÉHAR: The director, Quentin Tarantino. (Applause) The first question from the press?

QUESTION: *I wonder if at any point you considered putting the jewel robbery on screen?*

TARANTINO: Maybe at the earliest stage, I thought of, well, not really showing it, but a little flash, maybe just to get you a sense of the mayhem. But as shot, the first half of the movie generates a lot of suspense because you keep waiting to see what it is that everyone is talking about, and that's neat. By the second half, when you realize you're probably not going to see the robbery, it doesn't matter anymore because the movie has become about something else besides what happened at the robbery.

Toronto International Film Festival, 16 September 1992. With Quentin Tarantino, Harvey Keitel, Tim Roth, Michael Madsen, Steve Buscemi. Printed by permission of the Toronto International Film Festival Group.

QUESTION: Am I right to understand that the actors went through a robbery sequence themselves to prepare for their roles?

TIM ROTH: We knocked over a fruit stand. We wanted to start small and work our way up.

TARANTINO: Tim Roth put a quarter in a newspaper machine and took out a bunch of them as opposed to one, to get that "living on the edge" feel, you know? Actually, since we weren't going to show it, we wanted to know, as actors, what actually happened for ourselves. At a certain point, we actually staged the robbery in the rehearsal room. We all had our jobs, we knew what we were supposed to do, so we just came in there and did it. It was fun and it was goofy and we had a blast doing it, but when it was finished, for all intents and purposes we kind of knew what happened. We also saw how things got out of hand. Well, that was a big mistake, right there, having Mr. Blonde do crowd control. (laughter)

STEVE BUSCEMI: He controlled them!

MICHAEL MADSEN: I definitely controlled the crowd. They needed a little control, don't you think?

QUESTION: *Quentin, was there more to your character, Mr. Brown, or to Edward Bunker at any point?*

TARANTINO: No, we were always meant to be peripheral characters, but in that opening scene these guys don't know they're peripheral characters. As far as they're concerned, they're the stars of the movie, you know? So all the guys are talking and they're all doing things, and one of the things that's freaking these guys out is they're talking about how Mr. Brown was killed but you don't know who Mr. Brown is until later in the movie. They say, "Where's Mr. Blue?" Did he get away? Does he have the diamonds? Or do the cops have him? Are they sweating him down at the station house or is he going to show up? I wanted the audience to think it was possible that we could be walking through the door at any moment.

QUESTION: *Mr. Keitel, since you were instrumental in getting* Reservoir Dogs *made, can you tell us how you got involved, and why it was so important to you?*

HARVEY KEITEL: A woman colleague at the Actors Studio called and said she had this script she thought I'd be interested in. When I read it, I was just very stirred. Quentin had a new way of seeing those ancient themes of cameraderie, trust, betrayal, redemption. I called Lawrence Bender and told him I wanted to help the movie get made. Then we all spoke, Quentin, Lawrence, myself, and we set about trying to raise funds.

QUESTION: *But you had cast approval.*
KEITEL: I didn't have cast approval. I keep hearing this today. Why?

QUESTION: *It's in the press kit.*
TARANTINO: Yeah, it's in the press kit.
KEITEL: Well it's a mistake.

QUESTION: *Is there extra juice working with a first-time director?*
KEITEL: It's not just indigenous to a first-time director, but Quentin you can see has energy and enthusiasm, intensity, intelligence, and vulnerability. He has a great willingness to want to learn, and he's very open to the process of the actors to arrive at the characters he wrote. To handle eight actors like these would be hard for anybody, and for a first-time director, it was an enormous task.

I could only compare this particular group to *The Last Temptation of Christ,* to those actors playing the apostles. All these guys were supportive of each other, and if someone fell down, they helped him up. I'm privileged to have worked with them.

QUESTION: *For Quentin. Did you improvise that Madonna scene at the beginning, with the dirty interpretation of "Like a Virgin," or was it scripted?*
TARANTINO: That scene was written a long time ago, actually, from when I was an actor. That was one of my pieces, you know, when you're an actor you have different things under your sleeve you can just whip out and do at a minute's notice. That was one I wrote for myself. So of course I did it.

Has Madonna seen the movie? No, she hasn't. She knows of it. She's very *aware* of it. Her lawyers are very *aware* of it. My lawyers are very *aware* that her lawyers are very *aware* of it. There's talk that she may come to the New York premiere, and she knows there's a thing about "Like a Virgin" and its inner meaning, and it's a situation where she'll go and tell me if it's the truth or not. I have no doubt in my mind that she's going to come up to me and say, "Quentin, you're 100 percent right, that's exactly what the song is about. And I was laughing my ass off when all these 14-year-old girls were singing it."

QUESTION: *Could Michael Madsen describe his involvement with* Reservoir Dogs?

MADSEN: I read the script. I thought it was the kind of material that doesn't come around every day, and I wanted to meet Quentin and do it. But rehearsal is something I must say I never believed in until I worked with Harvey. He really convinced me of the value of rehearsal, and whatever we found out we found out during that time. When we got down to shooting, everything was where it should be.

QUESTION: *Do you think of your character as a psycho?*

MADSEN: No, I actually don't. When I was nine or ten years old, I saw *White Heat* with James Cagney, and there was a scene where he puts a guy in a car trunk and he asks the guy if he needs some air, and he shoots a couple of holes through the deck lid, but at the same time he's eating a piece of chicken. It gave a little normalcy to what he was doing and it was a bizarre contradiction. It kind of stuck in my mind my whole life, and I thought about it when I was doing Mr. Blonde. I think "psychopath" is a little too easy word to describe him. He was just a guy who was in the circumstances he was in and he did what he had to do. (Laughter.)

BUSCEMI: Just another misunderstood soul.

QUESTION: *What does the title,* Reservoir Dogs *mean?*

TARANTINO: Well, it's funny, I don't answer that question. And the reason I don't answer is that, basically, it's more of a mood title than anything else. It's just the right title, it just sums up the movie, don't ask me why. But the main reason that I don't go on record is because I really believe in what the audience brings. With movies as an art form, I think 20 percent of that art form is supplied by what the audience brings to the movie. People come up to me and tell me what they think it means and I am constantly astounded by their creativity and ingenuity. As far as I'm concerned, what they come up with is right, they're 100 percent right.

BUSCEMI: Tell them the Lawrence Tierney definition.

TARANTINO: When we were doing the movie, this journalist from West Germany came down to interview Joe, Lawrence Tierney, and that was it.

We could all take a shit, he didn't care. He came down to interview Lawrence Tierney, all right? And so they're in the trailer, and Steve Buscemi's there, and the journalist asks (imitation, German accent), "So what iz ze meaning of ze 'Reservoir Dogs'?" And Lawrence Tierney says (imitation, booming voice), "Well, as you know, '*Reservoir Dogs*' is a very famous expression in America for dogs who hang around a reservoir." (Laughter)

QUESTION: *A question for the actors. Was it hard to find your performance in a story with so many registers, going from incredible realism, blood, tough-edged, to the next scene, totally silly?*

ROTH: There was really no division. It was all of a piece, Quentin talks of writing in comedic terms, and I think that's essentially true. We found it very funny, but it was a very shocking thing, too.

MADSEN: I thought it was a bit like *Last Tango in Paris*: we want to make love but I don't really want to know your name, you know? To me, that's what it was.

BUSCEMI: I just tried to play it straight the whole way through. When I read the script, I certainly laughed, so I was aware that certain lines were funny. I didn't see it as jokes, you know? But I knew if you just play it as written, there are going to be laughs. I mean, these guys are so different from each other: just put them in a room. There's comedy there.

QUESTION: *Could you talk about a script you are doing for John Woo? That's an amazing combination.*

TARANTINO: Thank you for putting me in the same category with him. I mean, he's such a hero. He's making the best action films, bar none, since Sergio Leone. He's reinventing the genre there in Hong Kong, and it was an honor to meet him. I really liked him a lot, and, for him, I came up with a good story. Writing a lunk-headed action movie would be really hard work and it wouldn't be worth my time, and I'd be doing a disservice to John Woo. But I came up with an interesting story that I could be excited about and, to tell you the truth, I could be really excited about collaboration. I think I have a few things I could give him, and he could have a motherload to give me. Also, I would take the responsibility of bringing John Woo into the American market unfiltered. Not a half-way John Woo, or a John Woo for American audiences, but the John Woo for the people who love John Woo and who John Woo wants to be.

QUESTION: *Why are there no women in* Reservoir Dogs?

TARANTINO: It's because in the structure of the film, in the time in which I'm telling the story, women just don't present themselves. It's like, how are women going to end up on the submarine in *Das Boot*? I mean, they're not going to! Well, in this situation Joe would not hire a female to be part of the gang and that's the bottom line: Joe wouldn't do that. But the script I'm doing now has probably the best character I've ever written: this female character who I'm proud of.

QUESTION: *It is a problem that some people don't get the humor in* Reservoir Dogs?

TARANTINO: I've seen it with audiences that didn't know they were supposed to laugh, so that's like a pain, a problem. They'd eventually catch on by the last half hour of the movie, but they still didn't really know if they were supposed to laugh. So they wouldn't let the laugh out, even with lines that they felt were funny. It's really weird. I've watched the film with such an audience and thought, "They hate it. They hate it." And then afterwards, they'd say, "Oh, man, that was wonderful."

But the humor is now being talked about, alright?

Anyway, this movie isn't supposed to be for everybody. I made this movie for myself, and everyone is invited, But I'd be a fool to think everyone is going to get it. Nine out of ten people in America aren't going to see this movie. But *Reservoir Dogs* cost so little to make that I think it's going to do very well. And before the movie even opens, the people who came up with the money to film it have made their money back three times over selling it around the world. So as far as I'm concerned, *Reservoir Dogs* is a smash because the people who took a chance on me have been paid back in spades.

BÉHAR: Ladies and gentlemen, thank you very much,

(Applause.)

Quentin Tarantino's *Reservoir Dogs* and the Thrill of Excess

ELLA TAYLOR/1992

A FRIEND CALLS FROM the Sundance Film Festival to say that an unspeakably violent movie has taken the festival by storm. I carry on plucking my eyebrows. "So what else is new?" I answer listlessly. "This is the year of slash and burn. Is it any good?" She grins audibly and tells me that in the post-screening discussion *Reservoir Dogs* director Quentin Tarantino, a pipsqueak in his 20s from L.A., brazened out questions about a gratuitous torture scene by declaring that he loved violence. I start tweezing furiously and launch into my rant about how sick I am of black-clad film hacks with geometric haircuts who imagine that one splatter pic garnished with a few slo-mo sequences is going to make them the next Sergio Leone and who think any serious argument about the politics of screen violence is uncool. "That's my girl," crows my friend and hangs up, leaving me to stare moodily at two wildly non-aligned eyebrows.

But the fact is that, torture and all, *Reservoir Dogs*, opening in Los Angeles next week, is one of the most poised, craftily constructed and disturbing movies to come out this year. It's a fond genre movie that's forever chortling up its sleeve at the puerile idiocy of the genre: a heist caper without a heist, an action movie that's hopelessly in love with talk, a poem to the sexiness of storytelling, and a slice of precocious wisdom about life. All this from a first-time filmmaker whose training consists of six years behind the counter of a Manhattan Beach video store, a stint at the Sundance Institute Director's Workshop, and a lot of acting classes.

From *LA Weekly*, 16 October 1992, pp. 18–25. Reprinted by permission of the author.

Quentin Tarantino is a self-described movie expert who never set foot in film school and who never wanted to do anything but direct movies. "I'm trying to wipe out every movie I ever wanted to make in the first one," he says happily.

For Tarantino, derivation is the sincerest form of flattery. His most obvious homage is to the B-movie, specifically to Stanley Kubrick's 1956 caper, *The Killing*. In *Reservoir Dogs*, six smalltime Los Angeles hoods are hired by mastermind Joe Cabot (Lawrence Tierney) and his son Nice Guy Eddie (Chris Penn) for a major diamond robbery. They bond, they josh, they swagger, they kill; the one thing they don't do is confide. They've been chosen because they know nothing about each other; Joe assigns them color-coded names—Mr. White, Mr. Blue, Mr. Orange. When the heist, which we never see, is interrupted by a waiting phalanx of police, the thieves retreat to a meeting place in a disused warehouse. There, with one dead, one missing, and one seriously wounded, what's left of the group plunges into a morass of paranoid recrimination when it becomes clear that one of their number has set them up and another (Michael Madsen) has shot several bank employees for pressing the alarm.

It sounds odd to say this about a film that has a 10-minute torture scene shot in real time, but *Reservoir Dogs* is a romp: a brave, cocky, enormously self-satisfied adventure in film as manipulation. Tarantino loves to toy with the forms of his beloved action genre: with his favorite themes of professionalism, loyalty and betrayal; but most of all with us, flipping us from laughs to sympathy to horror and back again—he's the maestro of mood swing. Talk about the cinema of excess: from its opening sequence in which Tarantino, in a small part as Mr. Brown, entertains his fellow thugs in a café with a psycho-literary interpretation of Madonna's "Like a Virgin" ("Dick dick dick dick dick dick dick...it hurts...The pain is reminding a fuck machine what it once was like to be a virgin"). *Reservoir Dogs* throws down a challenge a minute to the politically correct. Its unheroes are a bunch of career criminals who kill cops without batting an eyelid but show a chivalrous concern for innocent bystanders (so long as they don't get in the way) and spend as much time debating the ethics of tipping waitresses as they do the semiotics of Madonna. Tarantino's dialogue drips with go-for-it racism, sexism and enough undeleted expletives to gladden the heart of David Mamet. And though he insists that he's just letting his characters be who they are, it's clear he relishes the effect they're going to have on audiences and critics shackled by a decade of what he calls a "square dance" mentality in filmmaking.

Quentin Tarantino shows up for lunch at Denny's on Sunset and Gower (his choice) driving the world's smallest rental car. Rumpled in a white T-shirt that says "Tin-Tin in America," badly in need of a shave and *any* kind of haircut, he apologizes cheerfully for being late and applies himself to a meal rich in bad cholesterol. We resume an amiably fractious argument about screen violence that began weeks earlier over the phone from Paris, where Tarantino was attending his film's world premiere. (*Reservoir Dogs* has made its money back three times over in world sales before even opening in the U.S.)

Tarantino would just as soon not have an abstract conversation about movie violence; he would rather talk about his movie's structure. *Reservoir Dogs* is laid out like an exquisitely paced piece of pulp fiction, divided into chapters and moving back and forth in time to explain the characters and the action. "I've always thought that the closer we can hitch movies to books, the better off movies will be," says Tarantino. "There's a complexity to a novel that you don't get in original screenplays. A novel thinks nothing of starting in the middle of its story. And if a novel goes back in time it's not a flashback, it's so you learn something. The flashback is a personal perspective. What I'm doing as the narrator is rearranging the order in the way I want you to get the information."

Tarantino's a showoff, and he has much to show off, smoothly trading off among black comedy, realism and horror as *Reservoir Dogs* swims around in time. After 10 minutes of ballsy man-talk around the café table, the credits go up, and the hoods in their black suits and shades saunter onto the streets in slow motion, backed by the Super Sounds of the '70s score that will provide a hilariously inane counterpoint to the action throughout the film. Cut to a blood-soaked Mr. Orange (Tim Roth) squealing like a stuck pig in the back of a get-away car while a panicked Mr. White (Harvey Keitel), trying to calm him, drives him to the warehouse that will become the center from which the film's multiple stories fan out.

With the exception of the ridiculously saintly cop he played in *Thelma & Louise,* Harvey Keitel has never put a foot wrong. He can carry a movie or disappear into an ensemble; in *Reservoir Dogs* he does both as a team-playing professional for whom loyalty and knowing the rules are paramount. He can also shoot three cops at close range and go for a taco.

It's largely because of Keitel, who was given the script for *Reservoir Dogs* by a friend of Tarantino's partner, that the film got made at all. Tarantino had resigned himself to being a "film geek" living on the fringes of the industry and was prepared to shoot the film guerrilla style. But Keitel was so impressed with the script that he not only agreed to star, but helped raise the money to put the film into production and probably attracted the rest of an all-male ensemble any director, let alone a new one, would kill for.

At the Toronto film festival, where *Reservoir Dogs* wins the specially created critics' prize for extraordinary achievement by a first-time filmmaker, Tarantino and some of the cast stalk the screenings, dinners and parties in shades and regulation black, backslapping and insulting one another for the benefit of anyone listening. The press conference for *Reservoir Dogs* could pass for a locker-room booster session. A reporter asks Tarantino why there are no women in the film. I choke back a snort; the movie practically wears a placard saying *Girls Keep Out*. (There *are* two women, onscreen long enough for one to shoot somebody before she's shot herself, while another is pulled through the driver's window of her own car and left sprawling in the road.) "It would be like women turning up on the submarine in *Das Boot*," Tarantino answers sweetly, "There's no place for women in this movie." Thank God, I mutter under my breath.

Like his film, Tarantino zigzags between boyishness and streetwise savvy. He peppers his speech with "cool" and "man" and other speech disorders of the excitable high-schooler. Yet he thinks aloud with the sharp independence of an autodidact (he never went to college) who has read and seen and thought widely without having had to toe the line for a grade-point average.

A boy who was frightened by *Bambi* but saw *Carnal Knowledge* when he was 4 and understood genre distinctions before he turned 10, Tarantino always chose a movie for his birthday over Disneyland or Magic Mountain. ("And it wasn't like I didn't go all the time.") His mother and the uncle they lived with took him to everything. "The ratings system meant nothing to them. They figured I was smart enough to tell the difference between a movie and real life, and they were right. There was only one movie that my mom wished she hadn't taken me to, and that was *Joe*, with Peter Boyle. I fell asleep. She was really happy because she didn't want her kid to see the cops kill those hippies.

"When I was a little kid, I thought the height of moviemaking was Abbott-and-Costello monster movies. I was just amazed at the genius of the concept of a horror film and a comedy together—two great tastes that taste great together." *Reservoir Dogs* is the work of a man who has lived his life inside movies. Tarantino thinks the death of the mother in *Bambi* would be much more horrifying to kids than the torture scene in *Reservoir Dogs*, which would go straight over their heads. Would he show *Reservoir Dogs* to his (hypothetical) 8-year-old? I ask. He shrugs: "If she [nice choice] reacts harshly and it gives her nightmares, so what? Part of being a kid is having nightmares."

Here's how Tarantino explains the mentality of the hoods in *Reservoir Dogs:* "These guys aren't like the guys in *Goodfellas*. They're not wise guys or gangsters. They're like Dustin Hoffman in *Straight Time*: they do jobs. And a big thing in that line of work is professionalism, which is a way to bullshit themselves into thinking that this is an actual job and profession, not just hooliganism." I ask how he knows this. "It's just the truth. You read a little of this and you see a little of that. And you know the truth when you see it. The truth makes sense."

You probably have to be 29 years old to have that sort of confidence in The Truth. But *Reservoir Dogs* is true to its own imagination, especially when Tarantino stops trying to control our responses, when he lets the genre breathe and allows his characters to expand into life: Steve Buscemi as the opportunist survivor Mr. Pink, sounding off about why he doesn't tip; Keitel combing his hair in the mirror and lecturing Buscemi on the difference between a professional and a psychopath; Keitel compromising his loyalty to his father figure, Tierney, when he becomes a father to Roth; Madsen and Penn competing for Tierney's approval and going at each other with homoerotic jock-speak. Toward the end of *Reservoir Dogs*, there's a dazzling chain of scenes that pile one virtuoso piece of storytelling on another for the sheer pleasure of playing one narrative voice off the next. "You're fucking Baretta," an undercover cop tells himself in the mirror. "They believe every word, cuz you're super cool."

Tarantino doesn't so much write his characters as hover over them, protecting their freedom of expression. "I don't play God with my work or clean it up. I don't know what these guys are going to do. I set up the situation and they start talking to each other and they write it. If you had asked me one thing that is powerful about this film, it's that there is no committee saying yes, no, he can't do that because that would make him unsympathetic. I think that while the characters come across insanely brutal, they also come across insanely human."

Yes and no. As an exuberant flirtation with genre, *Reservoir Dogs* is a fabulous accomplishment; but when it pushes to extremes, it becomes an exercise in spurious, sadistic manipulation. At his most self-consciously "cinematic," Tarantino is all callow mastery, and nowhere more so than in his favorite scene in which Madsen, dancing around to the tune of "Stuck in the Middle With You," gets creative with a razor and a fairly crucial part of a cop's anatomy. "I sucker-punched you," says Tarantino, all but jumping up and down with glee. "You're supposed to laugh until I stop you laughing." The torture scene is pure gratuity, without mercy for the viewer. "The cinema isn't intruding in that scene. You are stuck there, and the cinema isn't going to help you out. Every minute for that cop is a minute for you." He's wrong; the cinema *is* intruding. That scene is pure set piece; it may even be pure art. That's what scares me.

We're really arguing not about violence but about the politics of style. It's partly a question of different sensibilities — Tarantino likes emotional storm trooping, I prefer a slow-building opera — but there are still distinctions to be made between legitimate and gratuitous violence. Tarantino couldn't care less; he's an aesthete. "Violence is a very cinematic thing," says Tarantino, "like dance sequences are cinematic." Though he appears to have seen every movie ever made (his taste runs from Douglas Sirk to Eric Rohmer), for Tarantino the guys who really do it right are the auteurs of excess — Dario Argento, Abel Ferrara, Brian De Palma, Paul Schrader, all of whom, he says, "go beyond gratuity. They are so broad, so stylistic and so loving towards it that it becomes a justification unto itself."

His current hero is Hong Kong noirist John Woo ("He's re-inventing the action movie"), whom Tarantino considers the most talented action director since Sergio Leone and with whom he's collaborating on a treatment. I remark that even Leone's *Once Upon a Time in America,* an exercise in the theater of cruelty if ever there was one, used its brutality to say something about the way the world works, but Tarantino believes that filmmakers who work in his genre often use social relevance as a cover. "John Woo's violence has a very insightful view as to how the Hong Kong mind works with 1997 approaching and blah, blah, blah. But I don't think that's why he's doing it. He's doing it because he gets a kick out of it." While Stanley Kubrick used the social commentary in *A Clockwork Orange* to get away with one of the most violent movies Tarantino has ever seen, the social analysis was just an umbrella. "He enjoyed the violence a little too much. I'm all for that."

Tarantino isn't above covering his own ass. "I didn't do that [torture] scene just to say, 'Boy, I'm going to have a boner when this thing comes out,'" he insists. "If you're with the movie, you feel for these people at the end. Does violence put ideas in people's minds? It probably does. You can't make a blanket statement that it does or it doesn't." Nine hundred pages of the Surgeon General's Report on media violence, and countless other studies, agree with him; we haven't a clue how or if people are affected by what they see on the screen. And shot for shot, there is actually less physical violence in *Reservoir Dogs* than in any average action movie. Some of the gunplay is very funny (the hoods are a bunch of little boys playing with water pistols that happen to be loaded) and, aside from Madsen's frolic, you could argue that the brutality in *Reservoir Dogs* is "responsible" because, like Clint Eastwood's *Unforgiven*, it shows violence as it would really be—bloodsoaked, panicky, inglorious and slow. But that's not the point. "I'm not going to be handcuffed by what some crazy fuck might do who sees my movie," concludes Tarantino. "The minute you put handcuffs on artists because of stuff like that, it's not an art form anymore."

Tarantino, however, can afford to be the spokesman for art without politics. He's a straight, white male working in a genre that can do no wrong at the box office, and he'll never run afoul of the ratings board, which gets less prissy about violence than sex. (How very '90s that Tarantino's backers were untroubled by the torture scene but raised their eyebrows at the racism and sexism.) Critics also don't like talking about movie violence anymore, partly because the debate has gotten so mangled between the pieties of the left and the right, and partly because the celebration of style is an easy way out of taking any position at all.

I wasn't having fun in the torture scene; from foreplay to climax I watched it through my fingers, and if this wasn't my job I'd have rushed out of the theater, much as I did when Bambi's mother died. The torture scene infuriates me because it has no point other than to show off its technique, and to jump-start our adrenaline, which takes some doing these days; we've grown so numb to images of brutality that they have to be jacked up to fever pitch to stir us at all. It's not just *Reservoir Dogs*. Some of our most talented young filmmakers seem to be specializing in designer brutality: Gregg Araki with *The Living End*, Tom Kalin with *Swoon*, Robert Rodriguez with *El Mariachi* (as yet unreleased, but Columbia has snapped it up for a remake)—all highly stylized films that bring to the hot material of random violence a cool, giggly insouciance. (When women work in this mode—Kathryn Bigelow with *Blue Steel*, Katt Shea with *Poison Ivy*—they do it badly.) In the current season only Nick Gomez's *Laws of Gravity* and Anthony Drazan's *Zebrahead* have the guts and the heart, as did *Unforgiven*, to tell a story quietly and with a genuine feel for tragedy.

Reservoir Dogs is far and away the slickest and cleverest of the bunch. Tarantino brims over with ideas for future movies, including love stories and musicals. He has no doubt that he can continue to make the movies he wants within the studio system. "I'm not coming from the attitude that I want to run as far away from the studios as I can, or the attitude that I want to run up to the studios as much as I can, because there's danger in both. You don't watch out and next minute you're Richard Donner. At the same time, if all you can do is these little art films for 10 years for a million or two dollars, you're going to climb up your own ass. When was the last time Nicolas Roeg did a good movie? I'm not ragging on other people, but after I saw *Twin Peaks—Fire Walk With Me* at Cannes, David Lynch has disappeared so far up his own ass that I have no desire to see another David Lynch movie until I hear something different. And you know, I loved him. I *loved* him. I think Gus Van Sant, after *My Own Private Idaho*, has become a parody of himself. A lot of these guys, they become known for their quirky personality, and when they can do whatever they want, they showcase their quirky personality."

Tarantino has made several dazzling movies at once in his first feature—gangster flick, comedy, character study and horror show—and Miramax, an independent distributor, has let him get away with it. Will his future backers (the studios), who are already crawling all over him, give him the room to make more than a standard action picture? His next film, which will be co-produced with Danny DeVito's Jersey Films for $6 million, has a first-look deal with Tristar. It's an anthology called *Pulp Fiction*, three crime stories for the price of one. After that he joins forces with John Woo—for a musical love story, no doubt.

Answers First, Questions Later

GRAHAM FULLER/1993

QUENTIN TARANTINO WAS BORN in Knoxville, Tennessee, in 1963, the year when Monte Hellman's *Back Door to Hell* and *Flight to Fury*, Don Siegel's *The Killers*, and Sergio Leone's *A Fistful of Dollars* were also in gestation — as Tarantino himself could probably tell you. The writer/director of *Reservoir Dogs* (1992) and writer of *True Romance* (1993) and *Natural Born Killers* (1994), Tarantino is the most extreme instance of a movie-struck kid who has parlayed his obsession with cheap thrillers and Westerns into a career at a time when both forms are being reinvented and revitalized by Hollywood.

Tarantino was raised by his mother in Southern California and received his movie education at the Carson Twin Cinema, Scottsdale, and later as an employee of Video Archives, Manhattan Beach, where he worked while training as an actor. His scripts pullulate with references to his movie diet during those days. The story of two kids, Clarence (Christian Slater) and Alabama (Patricia Arquette), on the run with a cache of cocaine they've offloaded from the Mob, *True Romance*, directed by Tony Scott, is set up by Tarantino as a self-conscious analogue to Terrence Malick's *Badlands*, replete with the same Erik Satie theme and a gauche voice-over by the female lead.

The point is that Tarantino is not so much a post-modern *auteur* as a *post*-post-modern one, for he is feverishly interested in pop-cultural

From *Projections* 3, *Filmmakers on Film-making* (London, 1994), pp. 174–95. Reprinted by permission of Faber and Faber and the author.

artifacts and ideas (television, rock music, comics, and junk food, as well as movies) that themselves spring from earlier incarnations or have already been mediated or predigested. Because *Badlands* was made with *They Drive By Night, You Only Live Once, Gun Crazy,* and James Dean in mind, *True Romance* has a double frame of reference. In *Reservoir Dogs*—Tarantino's update on Stanley Kubrick's *The Killing* and/or Larry Cohen's *Q*—the pre-heist debate about the possible meanings of Madonna's "Like a Virgin," as implausible as it is funny, is an anti-intellectual demystification of Madonna's much chewed-over status as a post-feminist icon in books like *Madonnarama: Essays on Sex and Popular Culture.* It's not Madonna that concerns Tarantino in this scene—but what Madonna has come to represent.

All of which might seem like mere dressage for Tarantino's tough, cynical, and exuberantly amoral genre-bending scripts. Except that his appreciation of pop ephemera is as central to his movies—you could say it is the world they move in—as their rabidly talky flow, their intricately structured plots, their casual explosions of violence, and their reverse psychology. (Brought together in anonymity, for example, *Reservoir Dogs'* hoods form immediate allegiances, while the coolest among them turns out to be a psychopathic killer and the angriest the most professional.) That delight in contradiction is really Tarantino's calling card, for he writes pulp movies for audiences who want more than mere visceral thrills, who may not have read much Tolstoy, and even less Michael Crichton or John Grisham, but who might figure out how bloody a 'Douglas Sirk steak' can be, or the qualitative difference between *Bewitched* and *I Dream of Jeannie*—to cite Tarantino's *Pulp Fiction.* This was the script he had just finished writing, for himself to direct, when we talked, in May 1993.

GRAHAM FULLER: *When you started writing scripts, was it as a means to becoming a director or because you had specific stories you wanted to tell as a screenwriter?*

QUENTIN TARANTINO: I've never considered myself a writer writing stuff to sell, but as a director who writes stuff for himself to direct. The first script I ever did was *True Romance.* I wrote it to do it the way the Coen Brothers did *Blood Simple,* and I almost directed it. Me and a friend, Roger Avary, were going to raise about $1.2 million from a limited partnership and then go off and make the movie. We worked on it for three years, trying to get it off the ground like that, and it never worked. I then wrote *Natural Born Killers,* again hoping to direct it myself, this time for half-a-million dollars—I was shooting lower and lower. After a year and a half I was no further along than at the beginning. It was then out of frustration that I wrote *Reservoir Dogs.* I was going to go really guerrilla style with it, like the way Nick Gomez did *Laws of Gravity.* I'd lost faith in anyone giving me money—and then that's *when* I got the money.

G F : *What was your response to relinquishing* True Romance *and* Natural Born Killers *as scripts you would direct yourself?*
Q T : After *Reservoir Dogs* I was offered both of them to direct. The producers who had *Natural Born Killers*—before Oliver Stone acquired it—tried like hell to talk me into directing it. Tony Scott and Bill Unger had *True Romance.* I had convinced Tony to direct it, but Bill was saying, "Look, Quentin, would you be interested in doing this as a follow-up to *Reservoir Dogs?*" And my answer was no. I didn't want to do either one of them because they were both written to be my first film and by then I'd made my first film. I didn't want to go backwards and do old stuff. I think of them as like old girlfriends: I loved them but I didn't want to marry them any more. The thing that I am the happiest about is that the first film of mine produced was one that I directed.

G F : *How had you originally gone about positioning yourself in the industry?*
Q T : During the time I wrote these things, I wasn't anywhere near the industry. Eventually, what got me inside was moving to Hollywood and making some friends who were film-makers. One of them was Scott Speigel, who had just written the Clint Eastwood movie, *The Rookie* [1990], and people were calling him to write things he didn't have time to do, so he would suggest me. The next thing I knew, I was sending out *True Romance* and *Natural Born Killers* as audition scripts and, little by little, I started doing a little rewrite at this company, doing a little dialogue polishing at that one.

G F : *You say you're not a writer, but the narratives of each of your scripts is very carefully crafted and rich in imagery. You establish your characters very fast.*
Q T : I'm not trying to be falsely modest. I am a pretty good writer—but I always think of myself as a director.

GF: *In the* Natural Born Killers *script you wrote in a lot of the camera directions, so it was clearly a blueprint for a film you'd direct yourself. I remember Ken Russell saying he gets irritated when he sees scripts telling him where to put the camera.*

QT: Writing for somebody else and writing a movie for yourself to do are completely different. I'm not ragging on screenwriters, but if I was a full-on writer, I'd write novels.

GF: *You've talked about directors that have influenced you—including Samuel Fuller, Douglas Sirk, and Jean-Pierre Melville—but were you also influenced by specific screenwriters or novelists?*

QT: I think Robert Towne is one screenwriter who deserves every little bit of the reputation he has. I'm also a fan of Charles B. Griffith, who used to write for Roger Corman. But most of my writing heroes are novelists. When I wrote *True Romance*, I was really into Elmore Leonard. In fact, I was trying to write an Elmore Leonard novel as a movie, though I'm not saying it's as good.

GF: *What about earlier writers? Is your script for* Pulp Fiction *modelled on Cain, Chandler, and Hammett?*

QT: I don't know how much I am actually influenced by those guys, but I have read them all and I like them. The idea behind *Pulp Fiction* was to do a *Black Mask* movie—like that old detective story magazine. But I just finished the script and it's really not like that at all; it kind of went somewhere else. Two other writers I'm crazy about are Ben Hecht and Charles MacArthur, both as playwrights and as screenwriters. In fact, on the first page of *Pulp Fiction*, I describe two characters talking in "rapid-fire motion, like in *His Girl Friday.*"

GF: *How do your screenplays evolve?*

QT: One of the main things I like to do with my scripts is monkey with structure a little bit. I always know the structure I am going to employ in advance, and all the whys and the wherefores of the story when I start writing, but there's always some unanswered questions, ideas I want to explore. I don't know how effective they're going to be, but I want to try them out. When I start writing I let the characters take over. If you read my scripts, you'll see that the dialogue scenes just go on and on and on. I

never went to a screenwriting or creative writing class, but I did study acting for about six years and I actually approach writing the way an actor
approaches acting.

G F : *Do you write in a linear way?*
Q T : I have to write from beginning to end because the characters are kind
of telling the story.

G F : True Romance*'s narrative is linear, but with your script for* Natural Born
Killers, *you wove in a lot of flashbacks and a long sequence involving a tabloid-
TV-film-in-progress. Then you made another leap forward with* Reservoir Dogs,
which has a kind of dovetailed structure.
Q T : *True Romance* had a more complicated structure to start with, but
when the producers bought the script they cut-and-pasted it into a linear
form. The original structure was also an answers-first, questions-later structure, like *Reservoir Dogs.* Thinking back on it, that version probably wasn't
the most effective script that I've done, but I still think it would have
worked. Tony [Scott] actually started putting it together that way in the
editing room, but he said it didn't work for him.

I guess what I'm always trying to do is use the structures that I see in
novels and apply them to cinema. A novelist thinks nothing of starting in
the middle of a story. I thought that if you could figure out a cinematic
way to do that, it would be very exciting. Generally, when they translate
novels to movies, that's the first stuff that goes out. I don't do this to be a
wise guy or to show how clever I am. If a story would be more dramatically
engaging if you told it from the beginning, or the end, then I'd tell it that
way. But the *glory* is in pulling it off my way.

G F : *When you sat down to write* Reservoir Dogs, *did you have a structure or a
stratagem in your head?*
Q T : Definitely. I wanted the whole movie to be about an event we don't
see, and I wanted it all to take place at the rendezvous at the warehouse—
what would normally be given ten minutes in a heist film. I wanted the
whole movie to be set there and to play with a real-time clock as opposed
to a movie clock ticking. I also wanted to introduce these guys in a series
of chapters. Like, when you're reading a book, you're reading about Moe,
Larry and Curly doing something in chapters one, two, and three, and

then chapter four is about Moe five years before. Then, when that chapter is over, you're back in the main thrust of the action again, but now you know a little bit more about this guy than you did before.

GF: *Did* Reservoir Dogs *go through rewrites?*
QT: Not really. I wrote it real quick, and six months after I wrote it, we were shooting it. After I did the first draft, the big change I made was to include the scene where Mr. Orange is in the bathroom telling his story—that whole undercover-cop training sequence. I had written it earlier and then, when I was putting the script together, I'd think, "No one cares about this; they want to get back to the warehouse." So I left it out and put it in my drawer. But when we were trying to get the movie made, I dug it out and read it and I went, "Quentin, are you insane? This is really good. You've got to put this in." That was the only major change to the second draft.

I also kept changing who said what in the opening scene. That was the thing that went through the most metamorphosis. At one time, Mr. Blonde made this speech, and another time Mr. White said it, and so-and-so said this and so-and-so said that. I just kept switching speeches all the time. It's really funny, because when I look at it now, it doesn't look like it went through all that. But maybe it was good that it did—because all the right people ended up saying all the right things.

GF: *Did you have to fix things during shooting at all?*
QT: The only thing I did was a little polish after auditions, because auditioning shows you what lines don't work. So I got rid of them. Also, actors will come in and either improvise deliberately or they'll accidentally say something and it's funny.

GF: *I don't know if you've ever seen Michael Powell and Emeric Pressburger's* The Life and Death of Colonel Blimp . . .
QT: I never have—I've always wanted to.

GF: *The key event in the first half of the film is a duel between Roger Livesey and Anton Walbrook. There's a great deal of rigmarole leading up to it concerning the rules and codes of duelling. Then, just at the moment the duel is about to start, Powell cranes away from it and you never actually see it. It functions in the film in the same way the heist functions in* Reservoir Dogs. *My question is: do you consider omission part of the art of screenwriting? Is what you leave out as crucial as what you put in?*

Q T: I completely think so. To me, it even applies to the way you frame a shot. What you don't see in the frame is as important as what you do see. Some people like to show everything. They don't want the audience to have a second guess about anything; it's *all* there. I'm not like that. I've seen so many movies that I like playing around with them. Pretty much nine out of ten movies you see let you know in the first ten minutes what kind of movie it's going to be, and I think the audience subconsciously reads this early ten-minute message and starts leaning to the left when the movie is getting ready to make a left turn; they're predicting what the movie is going to do. And what I like to do is use that information against them.

G F: *You do that in your* Natural Born Killers *script, which opens with a lazy coffee-shop scene that suddenly turns into a massacre.*

Q T: Also the scene in *True Romance*, when Alabama has a terrifying fight with the hit man. One of the reasons that I think that scene is so exciting is because dramatically, in the context of where it falls in the movie, Alabama could get killed. We like Alabama, but it's getting towards the end of the movie and it would make a lot of sense for her to die. It would give Clarence something to do for the last fifteen minutes.

G F: *To avenge her, you mean.*

Q T: Yes. I once saw this Stephen King movie called *Silver Bullet* [1985, directed by Daniel Attias] with Gary Busey, who's really entertaining in it. It's got this little kid [Corey Haim] in a wheelchair and this young girl [Megan Follows] who's narrating the story. At the end, there's a big fight with a werewolf—and I was so scared for Gary Busey! I knew they weren't going to kill the little kid in the wheelchair or the girl because she's the narrator, but Gary Busey *could* die. Dramatically, they could have killed him—and so it was really scary. My sympathy was with him, because he was perishable. The point is, I didn't know what was going to happen.

G F: *In your own scripts, you tend to be unrelenting. The Mob execution of Clarence's father in* True Romance *comes as a major blow. Even the deaths of*

the cops played by Tom Sizemore and Chris Penn are surprising, because in the
short time they're on screen we get to like those guys.

QT: Throughout *True Romance*, Clarence and Alabama keep running into
all these people, and when they do, the movie becomes the story of the
people they meet. When they're with Clarence's father, I treat him as
though the whole movie is going to be about him. When Vicenzo Coccotti, the gangster that Christopher Walken plays, comes in, the whole
movie could be about him. The same thing with Drexl, the Gary Oldman
character. But particularly the father—you just figure he's going to play a
central role. One of the things I don't like about comedy-action films is
comic villains. They're never a threat; they're usually just buffoonish. The
villains in *True Romance* rub Dennis Hopper out. That's a shock. All right—
so now these guys are really, really scary, and every time they come in you
think the worst thing in the world could happen.

GF: *At the end, Alabama cradles Clarence in her arms and you think he's dead,*
but he's not. Did you actually think of letting him die?

QT: In my original script, Clarence gets killed. If I were to write a script
and sell it now, I would make the provision that they couldn't change anything. I can do that now, but at the time I was selling *True Romance* to get
the money to make *Reservoir Dogs* it never occurred to me it would get
changed. When I read the new ending, in which Clarence survives, I felt
that it worked—I just didn't think it was as good an ending as mine. My
ending has a symmetry with the whole piece. At first, I was really dis-
traught about it; in fact, I was talking about taking my name off the film. I
had a lot of faith in Tony Scott—I'm a big fan of his work, especially
Revenge—but where I was coming from, you just couldn't change my ending, you know?

Anyway, we got together and talked about it, and Tony said that he
wanted to change the ending in particular, not for commercial reasons,
but because he really liked these kids and he wanted to see them get away.
He said, "Quentin, I'm going to defer to you. I'm going to shoot both endings, then I'm going to look at them, and then I'll decide which one I
want to go with." As much as I didn't want my ending changed, I figured I
couldn't really ask for more than that. When it came to it, he really liked
the happy ending and went with it.

G F : *Oliver Stone has substantially reworked your script of* Natural Born Killers.

Q T : Yes.

G F : *Whereas your* True Romance *script was pretty much left alone.*

Q T : Yes. Except for the ending, Tony did my script. Aside from that, I am really proud of the film. *True Romance* is probably my most personal script because the character of Clarence was me at the time when I wrote it. He works at a comic-book shop—I was working in a video store. When my friends from that time see *True Romance,* they get melancholy; it brings back a certain time for us. It was weird when I first saw the movie because it was like looking at a big-budget version of my home movies, or memories. What happened with that film was exactly what I wanted to happen, in that I saw my world through Tony Scott's eyes. As I say, I'm a big fan of Tony as a director and I knew I would probably never be in a situation where I would be writing anything for him to do again, so *True Romance* was my one chance. Oddly enough, our aesthetics are similar. Tony keeps trying to do darker things and then keeps bumping up against the studios and having his rough edges rounded off. I remember when he was editing *The Last Boy Scout,* I showed him *Reservoir Dogs* and he was depressed. Because here I was doing this little no-budget movie with all its sharp edges intact, and here he was doing this big-budget movie, watching the studio round him off.

But if our natural instincts are similar, his shooting style is completely different to mine. I love the way he shoots; it's just not my way. He uses a lot of smoke and I don't want any smoke in my movies. I have a lot of long takes, whereas for Tony a long take is twenty seconds. But I like the idea of seeing my world look like that, through someone else's eyes.

G F : *What, though, is your stance on a situation where you sell a script and effectively lose control of it?*

Q T : I think it's a really thankless situation. That's one reason why I wouldn't be a screenwriter—it just seems like it would lead to ulcers. You can make more money than a novelist will probably ever make, unless you're Stephen King, but ultimately your work has to stand on its own. Everyone thinks that people just rewrite screenwriters' work and that's the way it has to be, but it isn't. You could do a script and put in the contract that they can't change a word of it unless you say so. It can be argued that nobody would then buy the script, but that's not necessarily true. If you wrote a very good script and a studio thought they could make money from it, they'd buy it. It would be a pretty revolutionary thing if some unknown writer tried to do that. In making the deal for *Pulp Fiction* as a writer-director, I realized that a studio has no right to bring in another writer to do any rewriting at all. My lawyer put such a proviso in there and he thought he was going to have to fight for it, but he didn't have to.

G F : *Do you feel that* Natural Born Killers *will still, in some way, be a Quentin Tarantino film?*

Q T : Not even remotely. I had bad feelings about *Natural Born Killers* for a long, long time, but I've come to terms with them now. I got together with Oliver Stone recently. I haven't read his version of the script but in the course of talking to him, I realized something that helped defuse my feelings about it. Where you can see some affinity between Tony Scott and me, there's really none between Oliver and me in terms of what I am trying to do with my movies and what he's trying to do with his, except that he's a really cinematic director, too. I don't show you events. I like things to be ambiguous. Constantly people will ask me, "Why did Mr. Orange tell Mr. White that he was a cop at the end of *Reservoir Dogs?*" And my answer to that is, "If you have to ask that question, you didn't get the movie." I doubt Oliver would ever let a question like that be asked in one of his movies. He wants you to know exactly where he's coming from and his movies are making *points* and going for big emotions. He doesn't want ambiguity. He twists emotions entirely and he's hammering his nails in. He wants to make an impact. He wants to punch you in the face with this stuff and when you leave the theater, he wants you to leave with a big idea. I'm more interested in telling the story. It's not better or worse in the grand scheme; it's just two completely different styles. When we were talking, he goes, "You know, Quentin, you're like Brian De Palma or John Woo. You like making movies. You make movies and your characters are movie characters—I am making *films.*" And it's true. I am not into making *films*. To me, Oliver Stone's films are very similar to the kind of films that Stanley Kramer used to make in the fifties and sixties, the big difference being that Stanley Kramer was kind of a clumsy film-maker and Oliver Stone is cinematically brilliant.

GF: *Are you going to take screenwriting credit for* Natural Born Killers?
QT: As of now, yes, and I wish the movie well. It's not going to be my movie, it's going to be Oliver Stone's, and God bless him. I hope he does a good job with it. If I wasn't emotionally attached to it, I'm sure I would find it very interesting. If you like my stuff, you might not like this movie. But if you like his stuff, you're probably going to love it. It might be the best thing he's ever done, but not because of anything to do with me. Apparently, he's planning stuff that's going to put *JFK* to shame as far as experiments. I actually can't wait to see it, to tell you the truth.

GF: *It will be curious to see which aspects of your original screenplay will emerge.*
QT: I have no idea when I will raise my ugly head in the course of that movie! I am not expecting to do it much, but when I do, it will make it all the more interesting. If *True Romance* was my world through Tony Scott's eyes, this is my idea in Oliver Stone's world and through Oliver Stone's eyes.

GF: *Do you feel that your screenplays provide a kind of legitimate forum for violence?*
QT: I don't quite look at it like that. I don't take the violence very seriously. I find violence very funny, and especially in the stories that I've been telling recently. Violence is part of this world and I am drawn to the outrageousness of real-life violence. It isn't about people lowering people from helicopters on to speeding trains, or about terrorists hijacking something or other. Real-life violence is, you're in a restaurant and a man and his wife are having an argument and all of a sudden the guy gets so mad at her, he picks up a fork and stabs her in the face. That's really crazy and comic-bookish — but it also *happens*; that's how real violence comes kicking and screaming into your perspective in real life. I am interested in the act, in the explosion, and in the entire aftermath of that. What do we do after this? Do we beat up the guy who stabbed the woman? Do we separate them? Do we call the cops? Do we ask for our money back because our meal has been ruined? I am interested in answering all those questions.

GF: *What about the visual aesthetics of violence, which seem to be writ large in your films? You mentioned John Woo. In his films, the violence in them is pleasurable to watch if you accept it as stylized comic-strip violence.*

QT: Well, like I say, I get a kick out of violence in movies. The worst thing about movies is, no matter how far you can go, when it comes to violence you are wearing a pair of handcuffs that novelists, say, don't wear. A writer like Carl Hiassen can do whatever he wants. The more outrageous, the better for his books. In movies, you don't really have that freedom.

GF: *When I asked you if your films provide a legitimate forum for violence, what I meant was that—within reason, obviously—it can be acceptable to see on screen that which is unpalatable in real life.*

QT: Oh, I completely agree with that. To me, violence is a totally aesthetic subject. Saying you don't like violence in movies is like saying you don't like dance sequences in movies. I do like dance sequences in movies, but if I didn't, it doesn't mean I should stop dance sequences from being made. When you're doing violence in movies, there's going to be a lot of people who aren't going to like it, because it's a mountain they can't climb. And they're not *jerks*. They're just not into that. And they don't *have* to be into it. There's other things that they can see. If you *can* climb that mountain, then I'm going to give you something to climb.

GF: *Conventional notions of morality are made complicated in your films. You give your characters a license to kill.*

QT: I'm not trying to preach any kind of morals or get any kind of message across, but for all the wildness that happens in my movies, I think that they usually lead to a moral conclusion. For example, I find what passes between Mr. White and Mr. Orange at the end of *Reservoir Dogs* very moving and profound in its morality and its human interaction.

GF: *In the same way that Tony Scott wanted Clarence and Alabama to survive* True Romance, *do you suppose audiences might want Mickey and Mallory, the serial-killing couple in* Natural Born Killers, *to escape? I feel that the point you are making is that the world they are seemingly intent on blowing away is so sleazy that it almost warrants it. Perversely, it's almost as if they are a moral force.*

QT: In writing *Natural Born Killers*, though, I didn't necessarily want the audience to sympathize with Mickey and Mallory. I want the audience to

enjoy them, because every time they show up on the screen they create mayhem that is exciting to watch. You watch that opening scene, and you think,
"Yeah, that was really neat, that was really fun." You see them posturing
and being cool and surly, and they're romantic and they're exciting. Then
you see them killing people that you know *don't* deserve to die and, hopefully, the audience will turn back on it and say, "Wait a minute, this isn't
fun any more. Why aren't I having fun? And, more important, why was I
having fun at the beginning?" But Mickey and Mallory will still be charismatic. By the end, when Mickey is doing the big TV interview, the audience
won't know what it feels about these guys or what it wants to happen to
them—which, actually, is my problem with serial killers. I don't believe in
the death penalty. I don't believe the government should have the right to
kill people. However, I find serial killers so *foul* that, in my heart, I wish
they could just be executed. The trouble with that is that it's making me
go against what I believe in. I don't even know if that worked itself into the
writing. At the time I wrote it, I was kind of fascinated with serial killers;
and I got sick of Mickey and Mallory really quickly. In fact, to this day,
people who've read the script come up to me and start talking to me like
I'm some serial-killer nut and I go, "Oh, you're talking to the wrong guy."

G F : *The Belgian documentary spoof* Man Bites Dog *[1992, directed by Remy
Belvaux, Andre Bonzel, and Benoit Poelvoorde] starts out as a very funny satire
about a serial killer, but as it becomes more graphic, it makes you question what
you are watching and how you are responding to it.*
Q T : Exactly, but the serial-killer guy never stops being funny. *Man Bites
Dog* does exactly what I was trying to do in the original *Natural Born Killers*.

G F : *Why do you think pop culture, comics, and movies themselves proliferate
in your scripts?*
Q T : I guess it just comes from me, from what I find fascinating. If I have
an interesting take on it, it's not that I'm necessarily lacing it with irony or
showing it to you so you can laugh at it. I'm trying to show the enjoyment
of it.

G F : *Junk food, too.*
Q T : Cap'n Crunch cereal or whatever! It's funny, because I'm actually getting on a more nutritious diet myself. I started writing down this list of

bad fast-food restaurants [where] I'd go to eat a bunch of stuff that I really didn't want to eat. I'm looking at it right now in my apartment and it says, "Stay away until you absolutely have to go there. Then enjoy it. But don't get used to it." Then there's a list that says, "Hanging out with Scott, Roger, and this group of guys!"

G F : *Scott and Roger being the prototypes for the TV crew guys with those names in* Natural Born Killers?
Q T : Yeah. And then underneath it says, "I want to still do that, so I must not do it frequently, and cut down in other areas, so I can still have fun with those guys." And then another bad place: "The kitchen at the office" — Cokes and cookies and stuff like that; stay away from there. Empty calories.

G F : *Do you see yourself writing scripts in a more classical style, perhaps less charged with pop-cultural references, and perhaps less frenetic? A period film?*
Q T : I don't necessarily want to make anything less frenetic. Not right now. I'll give you an example. L. M. Kit Carson let me read his script for *The Moviegoer,* and indicated that it would be cool by him if I wanted to direct it. I read it and I liked it a lot, but I told him, "I'm not mature enough to make this movie right now." Not that the work I'm doing is immature, but I'm still on my own road. Eventually, I'll get off it and want to go in a different direction, or do somebody else's work. As far as a period piece is concerned, I want to do a Western.

G F : *Were you influenced by Sam Peckinpah at all?*
Q T : Not as much as people think I am.

G F : *Sergio Leone?*
Q T : Oh, very much so. But if I had to pick my three favorite Westerns, they would be *Rio Bravo,* number one; *The Good, the Bad and the Ugly,* number two; and *One-Eyed Jacks,* number three.

G F : *There are references to* Rio Bravo *in* True Romance.
Q T : And *Natural Born Killers.* When Mickey kills Wayne, he goes, "Let's make some music, Colorado."

GF: *What has changed about your writing since you began?*

QT: I think it's more sophisticated. I am not chasing it as much. I know the effects I'm after, and I eventually get them. I trust myself more that it will all work out—just keep the characters talking to each other and they'll find the way. After you've done it a few times, you fly blind for a little while, not knowing how you're going to wrap a script up, and then at the last minute something really cool happens. Constantly, what happens in my scripts is that the characters will do something that just blows me away. With regard to the torture scene in *Reservoir Dogs,* I try to explain to people that I didn't sit down and say, "OK, I'm gonna write this really bitchin' torture scene." When Mr. Blonde reached into his boot and pulled out a straight razor, I didn't know he had a straight razor in his boot. I was surprised. That happens all the time when I'm writing. I equate it to acting. If you're improvising, all of a sudden you say or do something that puts this charge into a scene. That's what it's like writing. The other thing I've learned through acting is that whatever's affecting you that day needs to find a way to be filtered into the work that you're doing. Because if it doesn't, you're denying it.

Basically, I don't come up with any new ideas. I have a stockpile of ideas in my head that goes back five or six years, and when it comes time to write another script or to think about what I want to do next as a writer, I flip through them and find the right one. They're incubating. I'll come up with one of them and say, "OK, it's not this one's time yet. Let it just sit here and get a little better. Let's do this one instead." I want to do them all eventually; I know I never will.

GF: *Do your stories come fully formed?*

QT: I always start with scenes I know I am going to put in and scenes from scripts I never finish. Every script I have written has at least twenty pages that are taken from other things I've done. I had the idea for *Pulp Fiction* a long time ago, and then I came up with the idea of how to do it in the editing room when we were cutting *Reservoir Dogs.* I thought about it and thought about it, way past the point I normally do. Normally when I can't think about anything else but the script, then I write it. I couldn't do it while I was in the lab, but I finally moved to Amsterdam for a couple of months and started writing *Pulp Fiction* there. After thinking about it for six or seven months straight, suddenly what I was writing was completely different. Even though the movie takes place in Los Angeles, I was taking in all this weird being-in-Europe-for-the-first-time stuff and that was finding its way into the script. So some genre story that I'd had for five years started becoming very personal as I wrote it. That's the only way I know how to make the work any good—make it personal.

GF: *How many drafts will you do before you hand it in?*
QT: When I hand in the first draft of a script, it's probably my third draft of it. That's why I'm pretty comfortable with it and can say, "If you don't like it, then you don't want to do it, because this is what I'm going to do."

GF: *Do you revise as you proceed, or do you go back and redo the whole thing?*
QT: I revise scenes as I go along, minimally. Usually, I'm just trying to keep going on it.

GF: *Do you write overnight?*
QT: I write into the night.

GF: *On a word processor?*
QT: No, I don't know how to type properly. When I know I'm going to do a script, I'll go to the stationery store and buy a notebook with eighty or a hundred pages in it, where you rip the pages out of the ring file, and I'll say, "OK, this is the notebook I'm going to write *Pulp Fiction* or whatever in." I also buy three red felt pens and three black felt pens. I make this big ritual out of it. It's just psychology. I always say that you can't write poetry on a computer, but I can take this notebook places, I can write in restaurants, I can write in friends' houses, I can write standing up, I can write lying down in my bed—I can write everywhere. It never looks like a script; it always looks like Richard Ramirez's diary, the diary of a madman. When I get to my last stage, which is the typing stage, it starts looking like a script for the first time. Then I start making dialogue cuts and fix up things that didn't work before.

GF: *Do you enjoy the process?*
QT: I usually think it's going to be horrible, but I always have a great time.

GF: *Does it pour out?*

QT: If it doesn't, then I just don't do it that day. If I can't get the characters talking, then I ain't gonna do it. If it's *me* making the characters talk to each other, then that's phoney baloney. It becomes exciting when a character says something and I'm like, 'Wow, he said this? I didn't know that he had a wife or I didn't know he felt like that!'

GF: *So it's a process of discovering what's locked away inside there?*

QT: Very much so. That's why I could *never* do a script treatment where you take the story from beginning to end. I'm not that kind of a writer. There are questions I don't want to answer until I get to writing.

Quentin Tarantino on *Pulp Fiction*

MANOHLA DARGIS/1994

WHEN I STARTED *PULP Fiction* I was trying to figure out a way to get a feature going and I came up with the idea of writing a crime short story, shooting it as a short film, then doing another and another and putting them together like a crime-film anthology. It seemed like a good idea because it would be something I could manage: finish it, take it to festivals, get notoriety, feel like a film-maker. It could be a thing in itself, and I could keep building on it until it was a feature. I wasn't a film-maker then, and I was trying to do something.

The jumping-off point was *Black Mask* magazine. Of course, it's not like *Black Mask* at all now, but that was the starting point. The thing that was cool about it is that what I wanted to do with the three stories was to start with the oldest chestnuts in the world. You've seen them a zillion times. You don't need to be caught up with the story because you already know it. The guy takes out the mob guy's wife—"but don't touch her." And what happens if they touch? You've seen that triangle a zillion times. Or the boxer who's supposed to throw the fight and doesn't—you've seen that a zillion times too. The third story isn't an old familiar story but an old familiar situation. The story starts with Jules and Vincent going to kill some guys. That's like the opening five minutes of every other Joel Silver movie—a bunch of guys show up and *pow, pow, pow* kill somebody and

First appeared in *Sight and Sound*, May 1994, p. 10. Reprinted by permission of *Sight and Sound* and the author.

then the credits start and then you see Arnold Schwarzenegger. So let's extend that whole little opening, let's hang out with them for the rest of their day and the shenanigans that follow. That's where that film came from.

It's not *noir.* I don't do neo-*noir.* I see *Pulp Fiction* as closer to modern-day crime fiction, a little closer to Charles Willeford, though I don't know if that describes it either. What's similar is that Willeford is doing his own thing with his own characters, creating a whole environment and a whole family. The thing that is so great is that those fucking characters become so real to you that when you read each new book and you find out what's going on with his daughters and his old partner, they're almost like members of your own family. I don't think I've ever felt that way about characters in a series of books before. I love J. D. Salinger's writing, but I don't go out of my way to read his stuff because it's a little treat whenever I do read it and I don't want to gorge on it. It's like a little reward I want to give myself throughout my life.

My stuff so far has definitely fallen into what I consider pulp fiction. I think *Reservoir Dogs* fits in that, *True Romance* fits in that. I always associate lurid crime fiction with pulp. Mysteries fit into that, too. If you're going to get historical, then the whole idea of pulp, what it really means, is a paperback you don't really care about. You read it, put it in your back pocket, sit on it in the bus, and the pages start coming out, and who gives a fuck? When you're finished it you hand it to someone else to read, or you throw it away. You don't put it in your library.

Pulp sneaked in through the cracks, it was made for a certain brand of reader. The pulps weren't put under any kind of critical light except in retrospect. What's cool about that is that's how I felt about exploitation movies in the '70s. I was going to see all these movies, and they weren't put under any critical light, so you made your own discoveries, you found the diamonds in the dustbin. Stephen King talks about that in his book *Danse Macabre,* about how you have to drink a lot of milk before you can appreciate cream and you have to drink a lot of milk that's gone bad before you can appreciate milk.

If I have a problem, it's that there are so many actors I want to work with and I don't feel I'm going to have time to work with them all. So I try to take care of as many as I can in the course of one movie. The casting is really important to me, I'm knocked out by the performances everybody has given. I didn't want some star-studded bullshit—they've got real characters and when they came in they had to come to play.

One of the things Bruce Willis brings to the part is that his role as the boxer Butch is similar to some of the characters he's played, except that they've never had to run the gauntlet Butch does. I wanted Butch to be a complete fucking asshole. I wanted him to be basically like Ralph Meeker as Mike Hammer in Aldrich's *Kiss Me Deadly*. I wanted him to be a bully and a jerk, except that when he's with his girlfriend Fabienne, he's a sweetheart. The jumping-off point—besides bully-asshole here, sweet guy with her—was that Bruce has the look of a '50s actor. I can't think of any other star that has that look. He reminds me of Aldo Ray in Jacques Tourneur's *Nightfall* in particular. I told him I could imagine Aldo Ray being great as Butch and he said, "Yeah, I like Aldo Ray, that's a good idea." So I said let's go for that whole look, let's get a buzz cut and just go for it.

I've been a fan of John Travolta, who I got to play Vincent, forever. I think he's one of the best actors there is. *Blow Out* is one of my favourite performances of all time, I mean of all time. But I've been very sad about how he's been used—though he has to take some blame for it himself, the movies he's been doing. But I'd sit there and look at his films of the last five years and I'd think, is this guy the best-kept secret or the best-forgotten secret out there? What is wrong with these directors? Why don't they see what they have—that if they just blew the dust off it...? And then I realised that's not going to happen. John needed to work with somebody who would take him seriously and would look at him with the love he needed.

Some parts I wrote especially for certain people. I wrote the Wolf for Harvey Keitel, I wrote the English outlaws Pumpkin and Honey Bunny for Tim Roth and Amanda Plummer. I saw them together once and it was a director's moment: I've got to put these two together in a movie. I could have been seduced by the idea of casting Tim in the Vincent role after Michael Madsen dropped out, because he would have done wonders with it; but I had so much written Pumpkin and Honey Bunny for Tim and Amanda that I would never be able to get into the roles without them.

What excites me is the idea of putting people together. I would love to put Michael Madsen and Larry Fishburne together in a movie. I would love to put Larry and Sam Jackson, who plays Jules, together in a movie. I would love to put Gary Oldman and Tim Roth together. I want to put them in a comedy. To tell you the truth, if I had rewritten the script, Gary and Tim could have played Jules and Vincent, just played two English guys. I would love to put Harvey Keitel and Christopher Walken together because they've never been together in a movie, or Al Pacino and Harvey. Then there are a whole ton of people I would like to bring back, I would like to work with Michael Parks. But again, you have to stop yourself from being a total fan boy, from just working with people because you like them. It's got to be right, and if it's right it will be fucking brilliant and beautiful.

I'm using surf music as the basic score—from the '60s, Dick Dale style. I don't understand the surfer connection to surf music. To me, surf music just seems like rock'n'roll Ennio Morricone music, rock'n'roll spaghetti Western music, that's what it sounds like. That's the basic score, that, along with the songs that are played, runs throughout the film. The big song, the one that is so fucking vivid, is Urge Overkill's version of Neil Diamond's "Girl, You'll Be a Woman Soon," which is what the boss's wife Mia is dancing to when she snorts the heroin and has her OD.

Interview with Quentin Tarantino

JOSHUA MOONEY/1994

THE OTHER NIGHT, WHILE watching the stultifying post-collegiate comedy/drama *Reality Bites*, I kept having these inspirational visions in which *Reality's* scenes of whining twentysomethings were invaded by Quentin Tarantino's quirky killers. Winona Ryder's aspiring filmmaker, sucking on a 7-Eleven Big Gulp and complaining about the sluggish job market, is blown away by *Reservoir Dogs'* Mr. Pink. Ethan Hawke's insufferably smug grunge rocker, doing a ruinous cover of a Violent Femmes song, is shot in the head by *True Romance* mobster Vincenzo Coccotti ("I haven't killed a slacker since Lollapalooza '92").

Alas, none of this happens in *Reality Bites*. Everyone lives. In Quentin Tarantino's ultra-violent crime stories, almost everyone dies. And they do not, as the poet said, go gently. Usually they have to be shot. Their blood doesn't spill so much as it gushes, spurts, splatters, soaks and coats. Sometimes it takes the stragglers an excruciatingly long time to die, but in the end, they get there too. And the really twisted part: Tarantino's movies are hilarious.

At 31, Tarantino is technically a member of the so-called Generation X; in reality, he's a one-man argument that Generation X doesn't exist. The shared habit of pop culture references does not a generation make. Tarantino lifts from the '70s like a lot of other people who grew up in that decade, but he makes his homages from deep inside his own time and place.

From *Movieline*, August 1994, pp. 51, 53, 54, 88, 90. Reprinted by permission.

I saw *Reservoir Dogs* at an early screening in 1992, as word was just beginning to filter back from the film festivals about some demented video store
clerk who'd made this sadistic yet brilliant heist flick. The opening
scene—a bunch of hoods in skinny ties and dark jackets sitting around
discussing, improbably, the semantic mysteries of Madonna lyrics—had
me hooked. And then the infamous, brutal torture scene: a psychopath
cutting off a cop's ear. It pissed me off royally because I knew it was meant
to piss me off. I had to admit, though, that the psycho talking into the
severed ear was a distinct touch.

By the time I saw *True Romance* in a theater, a year later, Tarantinomania
was growing in Hollywood—he was the latest "bad boy" filmmaker and
people were lining up to work with him. *Romance* offered yet another
notoriously offensive scene, this one verbal: Dennis Hopper proceeds to
tell a Sicilian mobster who's about to kill him that Sicilians are the descen-
dants of "niggers," explaining, in excruciating detail, just how this is so.
It's a long, bravado monologue, the most politically incorrect dialogue
heard on-screen in recent or even not-so-recent memory. The crowd around
me, stunned at first, soon began to laugh. The laughter grew because of
the sheer ballsiness of the scene, and then people in the audience were
laughing at themselves because it was so *wrong* to laugh at something like
this; but it was hilarious and they were helpless. That's when I realized
something crucial and, to the Janet Renos of this world, no doubt frightening about Tarantino: like Jack the Ripper, this guy loved his work.

Tarantino's production company is called A Band Apart Productions—a
riff on Godard's New Wave crime film, a *Bande à part*. Translated, that's
Band of Outsiders. So why am I looking for Tarantino on the Disney lot,
spawning ground for *White Fangs* and *Mighty Ducks*? Because Miramax, the
former indie company that's releasing Tarantino's new film *Pulp Fiction*,
was bought by Disney last year. I stroll past shrubbery shaped like Mickey
Mouse, take a right on Dopey Drive, enter the *Pulp* sound stage, and follow
booming gunshots to the screening room where the sound mix for *Pulp
Fiction* is being finalized. Surf music fills the air—eerie, primitive electric
guitar twangs. Tarantino, holding a blonde Barbie doll in a long black
dress, stands behind a huge bank of mixing consoles and computers with
his crew. He may be a self-professed "film geek," but he is also a big,
brawny, dangerous-looking dude. His hair's wild, his stubble appears to be

perpetual rather than intentional, and he wears a Queen Latifah T-shirt under one of those tough-guy long leather jackets favored by Shaft. If this cat came at me in a bar, I'd jump back. Tarantino and his crew are playing a word game: you say a title with the word "summer" in it, but replace "summer" with "Tarantino." "*Tarantino of '42,*" someone suggests. "*A Tarantino Place.*" "*Tarantino and Smoke.*" I resist the urge to shout out, "*Tarantino of My German Soldier.*" The director himself announces, definitively, "*The Endless Tarantino,*" and laughs. His laugh is a loud, staccato "ha-ha-ha-ha!" He laughs a lot, it turns out.

A *Pulp* scene flashes on the screen Tarantino has turned to face: hit men Samuel L. Jackson and John Travolta blow away some punks who've ripped off their boss. Tarantino decides it needs something—a gasp from one of the doomed thieves just as Jackson casually turns, mid-interrogation, and shoots the other thief on the couch. Suddenly the same scene is running backwards—the bullet is sucked out of the body back into the gun. Then Tarantino walks to the boom mike to do the overdub himself. Watching the action on-screen, he gasps on cue. Then he announces, "I want to do it again. That was too . . . breathy." This whole process is absurdly unnecessary—the gunshot is so loud and unexpected that audiences will be doing their own gasping at that exact moment. But Tarantino does it again, and then it's time for lunch.

The only person in Hollywood who might possibly talk faster than Quentin Tarantino is Martin Scorsese. It could have something to do with the endless cups of coffee Tarantino consumes. During lunch at Bob's Big Boy, he's up to at least five before I start counting. He is telling me how he's bigger in Europe than in America, "like David Hasselhoff," and so, inevitably, we segue to his new favorite TV show—*Baywatch*. "It's like, *such* a great show," he says. "I've been lamenting the fact that exploitation movies don't exist anymore, but they do—they're just on television. *Baywatch* is as good as any Crown International movie, but without the nipples. You get all the breasts, you just don't get the nipples—you can actually *see* the nipples piercing through—you just don't get to see that little red dot. I've fallen in love with that show. I really want David Hasselhoff to move to the big screen."

"You could do that," I suggest. "You have the power."

"Well, I've been thinking about it," he says. I'll bet he has. After all, this is the guy who cast John Travolta as the star of *Pulp Fiction*. Naturally,

Tarantino has a film geek's justification for this bold move: "I've always been a giant Travolta fan. His performance in [Brian De Palma's] *Blow Out* is one of my favorites of all time. Why aren't directors taking advantage? He's ripe for the picking. No one was using him the way I wanted to use him."

Here are some of Tarantino's new on-screen uses for John Travolta: He shoots heroin, discourses on foot massage and European fast food, reads *Modesty Blaise* on the toilet, dances the cha-cha, and kills in cold blood.

"Super Big Boy Combo, ranch dressing," Tarantino tells the waitress without looking at the menu. "And more coffee, please." (Mr. Pink, in *Dogs*, wouldn't tip the waitress because she hadn't given him six refills. I wonder if this girl knows the film.)

There are several scenes in *Pulp Fiction* that could vie for the title of most outrageous, but here's one that has to be in the running: a badass black crime lord named Marcellus gets sodomized *Deliverance*-style by a couple of perverted hillbillies when he stumbles into their pawnshop. Tarantino explains that he originally wanted to score the scene with "My Sharona," The Knack's 1979 powerpop classic, but he couldn't get the rights. The song turned up instead in *Reality Bites* — it serves as the musical backdrop for a scene in which recent college graduates bop around a Food Mart with cans of Pringles. "The licensing people had to decide between us and *Reality Bites*. They ultimately made the good choice," Tarantino says with a laugh. "The song ended up being too comical for *Pulp*. But it's got a good butt-fucking beat to it." Here the director stands and thrusts his hips back and forth while pumping out the song's baseline: "Da-da-dadadada-da-da-dadada..." And you know what? He's right.

A Tarantino trademark is to perversely combine comedy and gruesome violence. It keeps the audience off balance — you never know when a funny scene's going to turn a dark corner, or if a murder is leading to a punchline. This happens throughout *Pulp*. In one scene a bunch of guys attempt, with sitcom incompetence, to clean up a mess they've made before one of their wives gets home — only these men are gangsters and the mess is a murder victim, his brains and blood spattered, JFK-like, all over a car in the garage. I figure if Tarantino can explain where this weird-ness came from, I'll have some insight into where *he's* coming from. "Um — I'm not really a hundred percent sure where it came from," he says. "It was sort of like the idea of — the comedy is the reality of it. As opposed to gangsters doing what gangsters do, they're dealing with real-life concerns, which are fucking them up. They're not worried about cops, they're worried about this guy's wife coming home. It's absurd because it seems like real life." Oh yeah, real life. Right. I *hate* it when I get brains all over the backseat.

Tarantino could serve as the Janet Reno poster boy for movie violence: "Senators, here's that proof I was looking for—this poor bastard watched exploitation films as a child, and look what happened." Tarantino's been fielding questions about the blood in his movies from his earliest interviews and, well, now he has to do it again. He remains unrepentant on the subject. "It's funny because to me, I'm never—the only time I put any thought to the subject," he says a bit wearily, "is when a journalist asks me a question about it. I want to say something interesting and truthful—so I think about it. But in giving an answer I'm giving you the impression that I walk around with this philosophy of violence. I have no more problem with violence in movies than I do with dance or subtitles or slapstick. My mother doesn't like slapstick—that doesn't make her a jerk. It comes down to what some people like and don't like."

Actually, as he knows, it comes down to what some people in Washington want to ban. But Tarantino doesn't have nightmares of censors snipping away at his artfully staged mayhem. "It's just getting inflamed right now. It'll go away after a certain point. My first couple of movies have been in the crime film genre—it's *violent*. I'm not afraid of showing violence. I think it's very cinematic. I like Godard's quote in *Pierrot le Fou*: 'There is no blood in *Pierrot le Fou*. There is only the color red.'"

I ask Tarantino the film nut what his favorite shootout scenes in other people's movies are, knowing that he's probably got it all worked out. "Well, obviously *The Wild Bunch* shootout, as well as—it's almost as good—John Milius's big shootout in the last third of *Dillinger* when the G-men surround Pretty Boy Floyd. He almost manages to accomplish everything Peckinpah did without the slow motion. As far as I'm concerned, John Woo does the best shootouts of anyone, although there are a lot of people in Hong Kong who could give him a run for his money. Woo's *A Better Tomorrow Part 2* is probably my favorite shootout of all time. And—this has to be mentioned—the restaurant shootout in *Year of the Dragon*. A true masterpiece of filmmaking. It couldn't be better, actually.

When an action scene works, you forget that you're watching a movie. You forget you're breathing. Those are great, great moments that cinema can do that few other art forms can."

Movie art is one thing. But Tarantino's gleeful portrayal of graphic violence isn't just aesthetics, or for that matter, sadism. I think he wants to kick the audience's ass by giving them that "real life" he talks about. But how personal is his take on violence? Has he ever experienced violence in his own world? "Yeah," he says, quietly, then pauses. "Just bizarre things from living real life. Real-life violence is bizarre." He looks up at two young boys who are studying us curiously through the window of the restaurant. They start making faces. "Like someone looking at this kid, and suddenly giving him a smack on the face. I'd be shocked."

What about Tarantino's parents? What are they like? "I—I only have a mom," he says in a subdued voice. "My mom is an executive with a home medical organization." Period. More coffee.

"What scares you?" I ask Tarantino. "Well, it's been a long time since I saw anything in the movies that scared me—" "No," I say, "what scares you in real life?" "Oh. Well, lots of things. Rats. I have a big rat phobia. I'm *serious*." Then he launches into a detailed description of a *Roseanne* episode he just saw, in which Rosie's macho husband Dan backs out of a bar fight at the last minute because he promised her he wouldn't fight and he really just doesn't want to do it again. Later Roseanne tells him, "Me and the kids civilized you when you wasn't looking." Just as I'm wondering what this has to do with Tarantino's fears, he says, "I used to live and walk around in some of the most fucked-up areas you could ever imagine. I went out of my way to go to those areas, you know. I never once gave, like, two thoughts about it. I used to have the biggest balls in the world. I'd see a guy coming towards me. I'd look like a badass and dare him to say something."

"Just how much of a badass were you?" I ask. I know he didn't finish high school, but I'm not sure what that had to do with badassdom. Tarantino says, "Well, I—I'm not bragging about it. I'm just, you know—I don't know. I just wasn't scared about stuff. I figured I could handle any situation I was in. But oddly enough, I can't even remember the last fight I was in. Since I've been an adult. Now I'm on my guard more, and partly it's because, in a way, I've become a little civilized. Being the baddest guy in the world isn't the most important thing anymore. I think it's that I can feel the repression in the air, and the threat of violence, and it makes me a little sad and scared."

Here's some dialogue cut from the final screen version of *True Romance*. (Parental discretion is advised):

> DREXL: ... I wanna ask you a question. You with some fine bitch, I mean a brick shithouse bitch ... you're with Jayne Kennedy and you say, "Bitch, suck my dick." And then Jayne Kennedy says, "First things first, nigger, I ain't suckin' shit till you bring your ass over here and lick my bush." Now what do you say?
> FLOYD: I tell Jayne Kennedy, "Suck my dick or I'll beat your ass."

Here's some dialogue not cut from *True Romance*. (Discretion still advised): "It's a fact. Sicilians have black blood pumping through their hearts. You see, hundreds and hundreds of years ago, the Moors conquered Sicily. And Moors are niggers. They did so much fuckin' with the Sicilian women they changed the bloodline forever from blond hair and blue eyes to black hair and dark skin."

Here are young black filmmakers Allen and Albert Hughes on the subject of this crazy white boy: "We love Quentin Tarantino ... [but] he's gotta stop using that nigger shit ... That [is] straight-up racist."

I tell Tarantino about the Hughes Brothers' comments, and he says he hasn't read that interview, but that such criticism in general "doesn't bother me. That's the way my characters talk—in the movies I've made so far. I also feel that that word 'nigger' is one of the most volatile words in the English language and anytime anyone gives a word that much power, I think everybody should be shouting it from the rooftops to take the power away. I grew up around blacks and have no fear of it. I grew up saying it as an expression.

"One thing that was kinda cool," he continues, "Spike Lee called me to talk to his film class at Harvard. He and I had never spoken. He asked me, 'What's your obsession with blacks? Your films have a big black subtext and culture even when they're about whites.' He said, 'Well yeah, there's all that "nigger" shit in *Dogs*,' but he wasn't being judgmental. He was curious." Tarantino must have reached Spike on a very good day, since I just saw him on *Arsenio*, explaining how the use of "nigger" by a rap star was indefensible. Then again, maybe Spike just thinks Tarantino's a crazy white boy.

In *True Romance,* the hero interrupts his deadly confrontation with the killer pimp to set the record straight on the movie playing on the TV in the background: it's blaxploitation classic *The Mack,* he saw it seven years ago, and it stars Max Julien and Richard Pryor. That's Tarantino talking—he spent his adolescence in black movie theaters watching kung fu, exploitation and blaxploitation flicks. "I grew up around black culture and love it," he says. "Especially the '70s black culture." You can see it in his own movies: from shootouts to attitudes, plenty of moments that owe as much to hard-core inner city '70s action films like *The Mack, Coffy, Superfly,* et al. as they do to spaghetti westerns or the French New Wave. "One of the coolest perks of fame is that I've been able to track down some of my heroes growing up. I met Pam Grier, and it was so cool. I have all these Pam Grier posters in my office—*The Big Bird Cage, Coffy, Foxy Brown, Sheba Baby.* She came in and goes, 'Did you put all these posters up because you knew I was coming in?' I said, 'No—I almost took them *down* because you were coming in!'"

Waitress? More coffee over here!

When Tony Scott directed *True Romance,* he was remarkably faithful to Tarantino's script—except he gave the story of two young lovers on the run a radically upbeat ending and added a fairy tale gloss. Still, Tarantino says that, when it comes down to it, he's satisfied with Scott's movie. It seems unlikely he'll feel that way about Oliver Stone's version of his *Natural Born Killers* script, which Stone read, purportedly loved, and optioned before *Dogs* was even made. In the end, he completely rewrote Tarantino's script, and there have been reports that tension has developed between the two because of it. "I'm pretty mercurial on the subject, all right?" Tarantino says. "Because I didn't want to make the movie and I didn't want anyone else to make it. Everyone in the world is trying to get a movie made. I *didn't* want a movie made and it got made. Stone took it and completely rewrote the script. I tried to talk him out of doing the movie. I said, 'Why don't you just rip off the ideas that you like?' But he was like, 'I'd never do that.' It was out of my hands—these producers had an option on it, not given to them by me, when Stone got involved. There's still sore wounds about the whole thing. But I'm actually pretty cool about it right now. We worked out the credit situation. I'm going to get just a 'story by' credit. That's what I wanted."

Tarantino wrote *Reservoir Dogs, True Romance* and *Natural Born Killers* while working in a video store, and didn't know which one (if any) he'd get to direct first (if ever). Finally, after a few frustrating false starts, he decided to shoot *Dogs* guerrilla style, using family and friends. Then Harvey Keitel read the script and decided he was holding something hot. The rest is a quintessential Hollywood success story—or at least the first act of one. Plenty of critics and audiences didn't go for the violence of *Dogs*. The film was not a mainstream hit, but at a cost of $1.5 million, it didn't have to be. Anyway, Tarantino says he's uninterested in the "horse race" mentality that governs how Hollywood measures a film's success. *True Romance* was a flop (by Hollywood standards) and *Natural Born Killers* was eviscerated. Which brings us to Act II.

Pulp Fiction is the first pure Tarantino product since *Dogs*. Shot for less than $10 million, sporting an eclectic cast including Travolta, Uma Thurman, Bruce Willis, Eric Stoltz, Tim Roth and Amanda Plummer, it is, in Tarantino fashion, a righteously funny, yet definitely grotesque melange of oddball crooks, doomed romantics, great dialogue and crimes against humanity. It's the most original script I've read in a long time—and I have no fucking idea what the world will make of this movie.

"I don't want to be this little art house guy who does a particular kind of picture for a particular audience," says Tarantino. "That's just as much of a talent-strangling road as becoming a hack and doing every picture that comes along. I don't want people saying, 'Oh, it's the new Tarantino movie. It's just like the last Tarantino movie...'" I wait for him to tell me how he's going to break out of that mold, but he doesn't. So I finish the thought for him: "In which case, you should make something besides violent-crime genre flicks that end in Mexican standoffs." He seems to agree—to a point. He'd like to do a musical, or a kid's film like *The Bad News Bears*. Sure, why the hell not? *The Bad News Bears* in *Breaking Parole.* "*Pulp Fiction* is very much a getting-it-out-of-your-system film," says Tarantino. "But on the other hand, if I come up with a really great idea and it's a crime film, should I not do it because I've done all these others? I'm not gonna let thoughts like that dictate my life."

Tarantino likes Pauline Kael's image of Godard as a movie-mad Frenchman sitting in a café, scribbling down the poetry he discovers between the lines of American hard-boiled fiction and turning it into movies. If any young Hollywood filmmaker is attempting something comparable right now, it's Tarantino. I'll bet dimes to petrodollars that Tarantino's chapter will be longer than Kurt Cobain's. Who, incidentally, had he lived in Tarantino's world, wouldn't have had to blow his own head off. Someone would gladly have done it for him.

Interview with Quentin Tarantino

MICHEL CIMENT AND

HUBERT NIOGRET/1994

POSITIF: *The scenario of* Pulp Fiction *owes its origins to some stories by Roger Avary and you. What was involved?*

QUENTIN TARANTINO: The idea for *Pulp Fiction* was born even before I began writing *Reservoir Dogs.* I was trying to imagine how to make a film without money, so I thought of a short I'd be able to show at festivals that could be a kind of calling card. I'd be able to demonstrate what I was capable of, which would allow me to shoot a feature-length film. So I thought of the story of Vincent Vega and Marsellus's wife.

Then I realized, why not write a second short crime story, and then a third, and then shoot them one after another when I got enough money together, and then put them together? That's pretty much what Jim Jarmusch did with *Stranger Than Paradise,* showing one part at one festival, then getting the financial backing to do the second, etc.

So I phoned my friend Roger Avary to ask him to write the second story, but with the condition that it had to be the most classic story possible; and from there he could take us to the moon! And that's what he wrote: the one about the boxer who gets knocked out in the ring. The third story was going to be the one of *Reservoir Dogs.* But then our enthusiasm kind of died down, that project never got done, and I used the story of *Dogs* for my feature-length film.

Cannes, 23 May 1994. From *Positif* 405, November 1994, pp. 10–15. Reprinted by permission of *Positif* and the authors. Translated from the French by T. Jefferson Kline.

Later we came back to the project, but abandoned the idea of an anthology. What I really wanted was to make a novel on the screen, with characters who enter and exit, who have their own story but who can appear anywhere. I could get to do what a contemporary writer does: introduce into his book a secondary character who appeared in an earlier book, something like the Glass family that Salinger imagined, and whose members you find move from one novel to the next.

This is a register filmmakers simply don't work in: in Hollywood, when you make a film for, let's say, Paramount, you sell them the rights to the story. If you make the next one for Warners, you can't use the same characters because they were created for another company.

With *Pulp Fiction,* I wanted in some sense to make three films for the price of one! I liked that each character of *Pulp Fiction* could carry a film as the main hero. If I'd made a film, for example, about Butch and Fabienne and only about them, the character played by John Travolta probably wouldn't have had a name. He'd have been called "Bad Guy No. 1." But as *Pulp Fiction* is conceived, he is Vincent Vega. We know his personality, we have an idea of his way of life, he's not simply a minor character. So then when they shoot him, the spectator feels something.

POSITIF: *So, when going to write* Pulp Fiction, *the feature, you already had two stories, Vincent Vega's and the boxer's?*

QT: Right, and I didn't know what the third story would be until I was half way through the scenario. While rewriting the story of the boxer, I said to myself: "Why not end the morning with Jules and Vincent instead of having them separate after the shooting?" Their characters seemed to me to have rounded out a lot and I felt that with them I had my third story. So I followed them instead of leaving them there. I also knew that at the end I would reintroduce Pumpkin and Honey Bunny to wrap up the story. I had created a universe of a certain dimension, into which I was going to integrate the story of the boxer which Roger Avary had written.

There are a bunch of ideas that belong to him: the hillbillies, the pawnbroker. He had invented the watch, for example, but I had to make up the history of this watch. I also made Fabienne into a French woman. These pieces of the puzzle came together during the writing of the scenario, but during the editing, we continued moving the pieces around.

When I start writing, I know more or less where I'm going. It's not like I have a map, but instead as if I were following tips that a friend had given me for my itinerary and that I had noted down. You go by McDonald's, and then you drive for a few miles and then you see a big tree. Then you know you're going in the right direction. Then you get to a mountain with a sculpture carved in the rock, so you have to turn left. You go over several hills, and finally you reach a very long stone bridge.

This analogy is a pretty good indication of how I work: with a series of markers. I set out on a trip in my car, and my characters never stop telling stories, and moving the scenario along, while I keep glancing out the window to pay attention to the route markers. The strange thing is that, working in the organic way I do, knowing my story as I do, I still discover it as I write it. I could never write the sequences separately and then distribute them through my scenario. I need to clear a path through the material, each episode leading to the next. I overlap things, make connections, bring things together in a process which I experience simultaneously as emotional and intellectual.

POSITIF: *Your dialogue has a very particular vitality and rhythm which one associates with comic actors like the Marx Brothers, W. C. Fields or Woody Allen, who would try them out in nightclubs. How did you go about gauging their impact?*

QT: I know they're going to work by measuring their impact on me, on their ability to make me laugh! If I think they're funny, I think others will have the same reaction. But giving them to an actor is a good test. You can write a line of dialogue you think is side-splitting, but acted it won't work at all. But in general I'm my own guide. If I read my script to someone else, I can immediately tell what's not working. It's pretty much the same thing with directing.

I don't believe at all in test screenings or sneak previews where you hand out questionnaires to the viewers to get their reactions. Although I like to show my films to the public, we didn't do any research of this kind, on certain ages or groups, for *Reservoir Dogs* and *Pulp Fiction*. I had it put in my contract that there would be no marketing studies. Any director will tell you that you don't need questionnaires to find out what spectators are feeling. When you see your film for the first time surrounded by all these unknown viewers, you know immediately all you need to know: if it's funny or not, if it's too slow or too fast, if it's moving or not, if you've lost your viewers and if you'll find them again.

I don't give a damn about the specific problems such and such a viewer will have with a particular scene or character. I don't care what they think as individuals, what interests me is how they react as an audience. At that moment, there is no critic who could be more severe than myself towards my work.

POSITIF: *The story of the watch as told by Christopher Walken gets its particular force from being filmed in a single take. Was that your conception when you were writing the scene?*

QT: A single shot, that was my first idea, but it was too intellectual, too theoretical, so I changed my intentions when writing, and when I was on the set.

When I wrote it, given the length of the monologue, I rethought it as a series of shots. When I was shooting this scene, I wanted the flexibility of being able to choose among several shots of Chris, who is such an amazing actor. I also added several shots of the little boy which I liked, because he looks a bit like Chris. I also have a close-up of the watch. So in fact there were several cuts, though you get the feeling in memory that it is a single shot.

I chose from among these shots according to the three stages of the story: the great grandfather's, the grandfather's and the father's. And for each section there was a different connotation which corresponded to the various interpretations offered by Christopher Walken. For the great grandfather, I chose a lighthearted interpretation. For the grandfather, when he's talking about himself on Wake Island, I made a sea-green, sort of hard tonality. For the third section, the beginning was more matter-of-fact and informative. I think that gives a very strange rhythm to the monologue.

POSITIF: *While you were creating the characters did you think about the actors who would play them?*

QT: In some cases, yes, but not always. I wrote the part of Jules for Samuel Jackson, and of course Honey Bunny and Pumpkin for Amanda Plummer and Tim Roth, who is one of my best friends. They are friends in real life, and when I ran into them one night at a party I was struck with a director's intuition: their size, their look, their energy, everything about them made me want to use them together in my film. I've also always been a fan of Sam's. I knew he gave off an incredible feeling of power and that, if given the possibility, he could express this Richard III side of himself that he has in the film. There are not a lot of actors who can dominate a scene, move people around the room like pawns in a chess game without even standing up, just sitting there. And that's what Sam does in *Pulp Fiction*.

POSITIF: *Where did you get the idea of having him quote the book of Ezekiel?*
QT: This quote had a funny origin. I heard it for the first time in a kung-fu film, *The Bodyguard,* where it appeared in the prologue. Then I located it in the Bible in a slightly different version. I'd also seen a Japanese ninja series on TV called *Shadow Warriors* which is the best cartoon I've seen on the screen. The action takes place in ancient Japan, between the good guys who want to open the country to Western influence and the bad guys who are isolationists. There's this group of ninjas who answer to no one and who, during the day, are complete imbiciles working as waiters in a restaurant, but at night, they are fearsome warriors.

At the end of each episode, there was a mortal combat where the chief of the Shadow Warriors, before killing his adversary, would make an interminable speech about the necessity for exterminating evil. The guy who had to listen to this speech was sure to die in the end! My friends and I were always fascinated by these endings, which we found cool and poetic. It was in this spirit that I put the quotation from Ezekiel in Jules' mouth. When I was writing the scenario, I realized that in the final scene in the coffee shop, Jules couldn't say this religious epiphany in the same way as he's said it before. After using it for ten years, for the first time he realizes what it really means. And that's the end of the film.

POSITIF: *Did you always see John Travolta in the role of Vincent Vega?*
QT: I'd written this very specific character without thinking of any particular actor. When I was wrapping up the scenario, I wanted to meet John Travolta simply for the pleasure of it and because I knew that some day I'd like to work with him, without thinking of any film in particular. While talking with him, I discovered his personality. I thought he could take the

character of Vincent in an exciting direction. He has character traits that coincide with Vincent's analytical side, when he talks about foot massages. John always wants to get the the root of the matter, to investigate things. But when you sign on someone like John Travolta, you have to realize that the film is not going to be the same as the one you wrote.

What's funny is that the dance scene was written before I thought of John! If I'd thought of this sequence after having chosen him, it wouldn't have been as good an idea, or as powerful.

As for Bruce Willis, for me he's the only star of today who evokes the actors of the '50s, guys like Aldo Ray, Ralph Meeker, Cameron Mitchell, Brian Keith, and to some extent Robert Mitchum, all the tough guys of that era. He's made of the same stuff. I told him that and he liked it, he understood the register he was going to act in. Then I showed him *Nightfall* by Jacques Tourneur, with Aldo Ray *and* Brian Keith! That was the link that allowed him to really get into his character.

POSITIF: *The tonality of* Pulp Fiction *is a bit that of mystery novels as illustrated by Rauschenberg or Roy Lichtenstein!*

QT: I see what you mean! The tone is close to the novels of Elmore Leonard, especially the first and third stories where the humor comes from putting characters from crime novels into situations that are taken from daily life. I'm thinking of a novel like *Miami Blues* by Charles Willeford.

The best scene from that book was cut from the (1990) movie adaptation. A guy enters a pawn shop by disabling the alarm system. He grabs the money and jewels and is standing there with his hands on the counter when this huge woman who owns the store appears brandishing a machete and cuts off his fingers. He kills her, runs out in the street, and then realizes that he has to go back to get his fingers which will reveal his identity. But it's too late, the door has locked behind him! You couldn't imagine anything more brilliant from the point of view of writing. It's a criminal situation which suddenly becomes crazy and operatic, but the very absurdity of the event brings it back to reality. That's a bit the spirit in which I worked, this back-and-forth between day-to-day problems and unexpected dissonances like the appearance of Harvey Keitel in a role à la James Bond.

POSITIF: *We mentioned some pop-art artists. Did they influence you, in particular the dance hall at Jackrabbit Slim's?*

QT: I love visual pop art and that's why I love the big screen, which does it justice. My idea of color is that you make a color film which is really *in colors,* where the red is red, blue blue and black black. Primary colors. But I don't like flat lighting. For my two films my head cameraman, Andrzej Sekula, and I used 50 AMC film which has the slowest emulsion there is. It requires a huge amount of light, but it's not the least bit grainy and the image is as clear as crystal. I'm happiest with the results in *Pulp Fiction.* The colors are so bright they jump right out at you!

In the dance hall, there's an explosion of color with all those lyrical posters of '50s films, the convertibles and the shots of Los Angeles streets on the video monitors. And also the fake Marilyn Monroe and Mamie Van Doren. It was like a huge cinematic effect within the film. This set was built entirely in a warehouse in Culver City. My set designer, David Wasco, oversaw every detail in this scene from the menus to the drinks they served, even the matches. We spent a good part of the film's budget on this scene.

Of course, the danger is to fall so much in love with the set that you get entirely caught up in it rather than paying attention to the relationship between Vincent and Mia. That's why I initially wanted to follow Vincent's entrance with a travelling shot so he could discover the restaurant at the same time we did; then he sits down and talks with Mia for twenty minutes. The subject of the film is not Jackrabbit Slim's but what happens between these two characters. That's why during their conversation there are no shots of the set.

POSITIF: Reservoir Dogs *also begins with a scene in a bar-restaurant.*

QT: I thought it would really be cool to begin *Pulp Fiction* that way as well. I thought the idea of a robbery in a restaurant would be funny; it was also the ideal place to wrap up the story, with other characters in the film ending up there. There are restaurant scenes in all of my scenarios, and I think every viewer can identify with this kind of scene. I often go to restaurants and just like to sit there and talk with friends. My characters talk a lot, and you open up in this kind of conversation. I like these kind of scenes. If I were to make *D'Artagnan's Daughter* or even a prehistoric film, there would definitely be a scene in a restaurant!

I also liked developing my own personal mythology by having the first scene in a coffee shop and the second with Jules and Vincent in black suits, like the gangsters in *Reservoir Dogs*. It's like wearing armor, when you see them for the first time. They really look sinister and mean, like really bad guys, like the ones in *Dogs*. Then I spend the rest of the film deconstructing these characters. When you follow them through the rest of their morning, you see their clothes are dirty, bloody, and wrinkled. These tough guys end up looking a little stupid with their T-shirts and their sloppy dressing. They literally decompose right before your eyes.

POSITIF: *How do you answer critics who think that your generation, with Tim Burton, the Coen brothers, or even an older person like David Lynch is just making borrowed, post-modern, self-reflexive art with no connection to reality, just a kind of formalist game?*

QT: I'm never bothered that people say I don't make films "from life" and that I have "nothing to say." I don't try to *say* anything but to create characters and to tell stories out of which meaning can appear. What's more, I think I make films about life since I make films about *me*, about what interests me.

The only artistic training I had was as an actor. An actor has a very different aesthetic conception from a director or a writer. He uses what works. Without betraying the truth of my style, my rhythm or voice, when I saw something I liked in Marlon Brando or Michael Caine, I'd use it in my own acting. Actors work like this: they steal from others and make it part of themselves.

I don't consider myself just as a director, but as a movie man who has the whole treasure of the movies to choose from and can take whatever gems I like, twist them around, give them new form, bring things together that have never been matched up before. But that should never become referential to the point of stopping the movement of the film. My first concern is to tell a story that will be dramatically captivating. What counts is that the story works and that viewers will be caught up in my film. Then movie buffs can find additional pleasure in getting whatever allusions there are.

But I never try for an exact copy or a precise quote or a specific reference. Carbon copies give me headaches. I like mixing things up: for example that golden watch story begins in the spirit of *Body and Soul* and then unexpectedly ends up in the climate of *Deliverance.* What I most enjoy are space-time distortions, jumps from one world to another. You don't need to know the two films to appreciate the story of the watch, but if you know them it's even more surprising and fun.

Sometimes I have an idea for a film which I carry around in my head for five or six years, without writing the scenario, since the right moment hasn't hit. But when I sit down to write, everything that's going on in my personal life finds a place in the film. When I've finished a scenario, I'm always astonished by what it reveals about me. It's as if I were disclosing a bunch of personal secrets, even though people don't notice, and I don't really care if they notice or not!

Again, if an actor is driving to the theater or to a film set and hits a dog, like Irene Jacob did in *Red,* well, it's going to affect the acting, no matter how well the scene has been prepared. What happened is going to show up on stage or on the screen. Anyone able to keep strictly to what had been planned isn't really creative. At least that's how I think about my work. Whatever happens to me, even if it's completely unrelated to the subject I'm doing, will find its way into the scenes I'm shooting, because I want my characters' hearts to really beat.

If you really knew me, you would be surprised by how much my films talk about me.

Hollywood's New Hit Men

GODFREY CHESHIRE/1994

IT IS ALREADY THE stuff of movie legend, New Hollywood-style. Quentin Tarantino and Roger Avary meet as clerks at Video Archives in Manhattan Beach, California. They rent movies, watch movies, talk movies, fantasize avidly of making their own. Tarantino, after an abortive first effort, is aching for the plunge when he meets fledgling producer Lawrence Bender. Bender asks for a year to raise the money to make Tarantino's latest script; Tarantino gives him two months. With luck and a little help from Harvey Keitel, it flies.

The movie, *Reservoir Dogs* (1992), coins the '90s definition of cult glory. Though only an indiescale success, it seems to hit every critic, cinephile, and aspiring filmmaker on the planet like a smart bomb from the B-movie id. Tarantino is established, as are his trademarks: tough-guy killers, wise-guy dialogue, jackknifed plots, pop-culture in-jokes, scalding ultraviolence played out in stylish spasms that reference everyone from Godard to Leone. A movieholic's coup, *Dogs* only begs the question of whether such knowingness might curdle into a postpomo shtick.

Flash-forward to 1994. Tarantino's *Pulp Fiction*, produced by Bender with story contributions by Avary, shoots the sophomore jinx between the eyes when it wins the Cannes Film Festival's grand prize. Retaining the trademarks while adding bigger stars (John Travolta, Bruce Willis), the movie wraps lush wide-screen visuals around a three-compartment crime story that foregrounds Tarantino's increasingly assured audacity as a talespinner.

From *Interview*, November 1994. Reprinted by permission of *Interview* and the author.

Its mix of chills and hilarity reaches an unnerving apex when Travolta and Eric Stoltz attempt to revive an OD'd Uma Thurman with a hypodermic to the heart — a scene to place alongside Michael Madsen's ear-chopping frug in *Dogs*.

Meanwhile, like a battalion-devouring blob from '50s sci-fi, the Tarantino-Bender-Avary vortex continues its centripetal spiral. Pre-*Dogs* Tarantino scripts come to light in Tony Scott's *True Romance* (1993) and Oliver Stone's *Natural Born Killers* — the latter heavily rewritten, to its author's dismay. Bender also produces first-time director Boaz Yakin's *Fresh*, a bracingly inventive tale of crime and redemption in New York's ghettos, and he and Tarantino join forces to executive-produce Avary's directorial debut, *Killing Zoe*.

Avary's film stars Eric Stoltz as Zed, basically the same character he plays in *Pulp Fiction*, and abounds in bloody criminal excess, but its account of a Parisian bank heist gone fatally awry is as coolly naturalistic as Tarantino's films are unabashedly pop. Comparisons to the Sidney Lumet of *Dog Day Afternoon* (1975) should suit Avary fine, since they remove him from his friend's shadow while acknowledging a parallel set of cinephilic concerns; in a less obvious way than Tarantino's films, *Killing Zoe* bristles with movie mania.

Do these guys know something that Hollywood forgot sometime during the '70s, Avary and Tarantino's favorite movie decade? Is their work the mark of a decisive forward turn in a form that desperately needs one, an anomaly founded on friendship, or a regression to that age-old place where boys play with movie cameras in order to play with guns? Meeting the two directors and Bender in Hollywood in June, I'm momentarily stunned when Tarantino declares topic number one — violence — off-limits. I regroup by wondering whether, for all of us, childhood's earliest fascinations link movies with mayhem.

GODFREY CHESHIRE: *One of my primal movie memories is the killing that climaxes John Ford's* The Man Who Shot Liberty Valance *[1962]. After seeing that, three friends and I would enact it over and over. Coincidentally or not, this was the first time I ever noticed a director's name and thought, "This is really good. I'll have to go see his next movie." Any similar memories?*
ROGER AVARY: When I was really young, *Dawn of the Dead* [1978] made a big impression on me. When it first came out and we used to go play

guns, we would have a rule that once you were shot and died you'd come back as a zombie and be unstoppable. Me and a friend got this big piece of wood and actually built a mall and a big forest, and we'd get little H-O-train guys and bust their arms off and paint them red and make them look like zombies. The game was you've got to get into the mall and get to the helicopter before the zombies eat you alive.

LAWRENCE BENDER: My first real thing was with *Dirty Harry* [1971]. My parents were divorced, so my dad had us on the weekends, and he took me and my friends to the movies. I remember we'd come out shooting at each other and jumping over the turnstiles and banging through the doors.

QUENTIN TARANTINO: I remember the first movie I saw on television when I was, like, "Oh wow, you can do *this* in a movie?" was *Abbott and Costello Meet Frankenstein* [1948]. That was my favorite movie when I was five years old. The Abbott and Costello stuff was funny, but when they were out of the room and the monsters would come on, they'd kill people! And the big brain operation when they take out Costello's brain and put in Frankenstein's Monster's brain was *scary*. Then this nurse gets thrown through a window! She's dead! When's the last time you saw anybody in a comedy-horror film actually kill somebody? You don't see that. I took it in, seeing that movie. Then I saw *Abbott and Costello Meet the Mummy* [1955] and I remember thinking, these are the greatest movies ever made. You get a great comedy and a great horror movie—all together.

GC: *Your films obviously do something similar. How do you look at combining laughter and terror? Is it a balancing act where at times you can get too funny?*

QT: I don't think there's any such thing as "too funny," or that there's any such thing as "too hard." But I don't do it like *Abbott and Costello Meet Frankenstein,* where you're at the funny part, then you're at the scary part, then you're at the funny part again. To me, all my stuff is the funny part. If you were to tape an audience watching *Reservoir Dogs* and play it back, you'd swear you were listening to people watching a comedy. But oddly enough, it's not a situation where I'm being *strategic* about how I put this and that together. Part of the way I think is having you laugh, laugh, laugh, laugh until I *stop* you from laughing. That's what I did on *Dogs. Pulp* is different; in a way you never stop laughing, right? You have the same [*morbid gasp*] from time to time, and particularly in the needle scene with Uma Thurman. That's actually my favorite sequence as far as the reaction

I've had so far, because you have half the theater giggling like hell and the other half diving under their seats. That's really cool.

GC: *Roger, where did the idea of* Killing Zoe *come from?*

RA: Lawrence called me up when they were scouting locations for *Dogs* and said, "Oh my God, we've found this great bank, and you've gotta come down and check it out. We have no use for it in *Dogs,* but it's a great location." So I went down, and he said, "If you have any scripts that take place in a bank, we could kick together a hundred or two hundred thousand dollars and make a movie here."

LB: Roger didn't even skip a beat. He goes, "Oh yeah, I was just thinking about an idea that takes place in a bank." I was, like, "Really?"

RA: So I drew a map of the bank and went home and wrote the script in about a week, week-and-a-half. I brought it back to Lawrence and said, "Here it is." Slapped it on his desk.

QT: It got you going.

RA: Yeah. It's like what Roger Corman used to do: "Oh, we've got a prison set and we've got the Tropicana girls — we should do a women-in-prison film!" He'd find a young Jonathan Demme or Jonathan Kaplan or Joe Dante or Francis Coppola or Martin Scorsese, and just because they were so hungry to make a movie, they'd make the best women-in-prison film ever. A lot of Corman films are exploitation films, but they're also art-house films. When I started writing *Killing Zoe,* that was what I really wanted to do. I wanted to do a movie that was an art-house film for the coffeehouse crowd and then for the exploitation crowd. The movie that really first got me thinking about that was *Platoon* [1986].

QT: We saw that together, didn't we?

RA: We did. And when we were sitting in the audience, there were all these Vietnam vets who had come to see the movie in their wheelchairs, you know, to go through some kind of cathartic experience. At the same time, there were a bunch of kids who were there to see all the Vietnam action stuff. The thing about the movie is that it really pays off for both. There's a scene where Kevin Dillon is busting open the head of a Vietnamese person with the butt of his gun, and it's very, very intense. After it happens he's laughing, and some kid in the audience started laughing, and a Vietnam vet in the back was going, "Shut up, it's not funny!" It occurred to me at that moment that the interactivity in the audience was much

more intense than what was going on on the screen. I mean, all great
movies begin when you leave the theater, and when I made *Killing Zoe*
what I really wanted was people to leave the movie talking about it,
whether they loved it or hated it.

GC: *I wonder if, as filmmakers, you think about audiences at all.*
QT: I think about the audience all the time, but not a specific audience.
Mostly I think in terms of *me*. I'm the eternal audience.
LB: You always make a movie for yourself before anybody. If you don't,
all you're doing is feeding a machine.
QT: Exactly, but I don't mean just me as a filmmaker, satisfying myself. I,
of course, am totally doing that. But I'm thinking of me as an audience
member. What would I like? If I hadn't made *Reservoir Dogs*, and someone
else had made it and I went and saw it, I'd think it was the best fuckin'
movie of the year. With these two movies I've done so far, I've enjoyed
giving the audience a real ride. But it's not a roller-coaster ride like *Speed*.
It's more the fact that you're confounding the audience's feeling about
how to watch a movie. Everybody's a film expert these days. We all know a
lot about movies, particularly because the movies of the last ten years have
been so much the same. But you can take the audience another way, and I
do this. The only problem here is that I sound like some manipulative wise
guy, which I'm not. I *am* having fun telling stories this way, but what
makes my movies special, if they *are* special, is that—even though they're
wild genre movies—they're connected to a human heart. The people in
them are not puppets; they're characters, living out their lives doing what
they do. That is very important to me.

GC: *In terms of defying conventions, another good example is* Fresh, *which
basically shifts genres about two thirds of the way through. That gives audiences
something they want, I think, and the surprise is primarily on the level of form.*
LB: I think that's one reason why foreign companies and people from
Europe and Asia especially like what Roger and Quentin and Boaz [Yakin]
do. It's because their movies do have all these twists and turns, and that's
where Europeans come from. It's a sudden revitalization of a way of
thinking.
QT: My only problem with talking about the technique of playing around
with film forms and the audience is that this aspect is like the jokes in the

movie—it's not the *whole* movie! The most important thing is the story and the characters. It exists on a completely human level. The thing that you get in our stuff, I think, is something that's otherwise lost in American cinema right now. Also, I'm not one of these independent filmmaker guys that just bashes Hollywood, because I don't believe that—

RA: I love Hollywood.

QT: Me, too. At the end of the year, there's usually at least ten really good, straightforward, no-apology Hollywood movies that come out of the studios. I think that's a pretty good average. So the system, while it could be better, still functions. Enough good work gets done by people who care. But the thing that's really missing from the overall output, and that really comes home when you look at films of the '70s, is that we have lost the art of telling a good story well. There is no storytelling going on right now in 85 percent of the movies that are made.

GC: *What you just said leads to what I really wanted to ask you about violence. If your primary gift is storytelling, how do you feel when people just look at the blood and go, "Oh, Quentin Tarantino—violence"?*

QT: Well, it's a big fuckin' drag, all right?

GC: *How do you react, though? Are you tempted to let go of the violence to prove what you're really about?*

QT: No, no, I knew what I was stepping into. But the thing about it is, what do I do? Do I relish it and want to go even further in that direction? Or do I say, I'm gonna show you what I can do with a bedroom comedy— same kind of dialogue, same basic movie, but without the violence? Well, I think you're kind of a fool going with either of those things. You just, you know, "To thine own self be true."

RA: I'll tell you a passing thing about me. I don't intend to ever make another movie with guns in it, because whenever you fire a gun on a movie set it sucks three hours out of your day that you could spend working with actors, and that's the real fun of filmmaking. I can't imagine making *Last Action Hero,* for example. It would be my worst nightmare. And had I known how frustrating it would be and how much time it would take to have guns on a set, *Killing Zoe* wouldn't have had any guns in it.

G C : *I've talked to people who consider the violence in* Killing Zoe *really objectionable. What struck me is that it feels violent because the movie is so intimate. You don't see that much violence, but what's there hits hard because the characters are real.*

R A : You see a hell of a lot less in *Killing Zoe* than you see in *Cliffhanger* or *Demolition Man* [both 1993]. The reason people get freaked out about violence in movies is because obviously it touches them somewhere. As far as I'm concerned, we have equal amounts of good and evil in us, and it's important to know that we are partially evil as people. But we're also good. I think it was Joseph Campbell who said that the only real thing is the center, and everything else is just an apparition. Good and evil, right and wrong, black and white: Those things are apparitions. But you have to know your extremes before you can find the center. That's partially what I'm about and why I made the film I made. Some people have told me I'm a nihilist. But I'm not a nihilist at all; I'm an optimist.

G C : *I didn't feel* Killing Zoe *was nihilistic.*

R A : The people who get it think, "Oh my God, it's such a moral movie." The people who don't get it say, "God, you're so immoral."

Q T : I always thought I didn't have any big moral bounds when it came to so many things. But if you look at my movies, they almost follow the old Hays Code. Violence was never a major issue in the old days of Hollywood. You could have as much violence as you wanted as long as the bad guy dies in the end, or denounces his sins. The thing those films specialized in is what I specialize in when it comes to violence. It's not so much about graphic violence, but there's a brutality to it. When Raoul Walsh or Howard Hawks shot violence, it was brutal, man.

L B : That's how violence should be, isn't it? Is it supposed to be candy-coated?

Q T : No, that's like saying a dance sequence should be acrobatic or it should be poetic. It can be *anything*.

L B : But in a dance sequence you should be able to see people's feet.

Q T : Maybe yes, maybe no. It depends on how you shoot it. There is no "can't," no "have to." But what I'm doing is like in *The Big Sleep* [1946], where there's a guy waiting outside the door for Bogart, and Bogart makes this other guy go out. The guy is, like, "I'm not gonna go out," so Bogart shoots him in the leg. He's still not going, so Bogart shoots him in the hip, in the hand. Finally, the guy goes out and he gets shot, all right? It's tough stuff, and that's what I'm trying to do with my violence. It really annoys me to see an action movie like *Patriot Games* [1992], which is just so obvious in its structure that you can feel the committee behind every choice the hero makes. And then they end it in this awful way where the hero, who has been fucked in the ass for the whole first half, gets in a fight with the villain, who falls down and impales himself! Anyone who makes a movie that way should go to movie jail and not be allowed to make movies for a while. The only reason to do a revenge movie is to have the hero kill the guy at the end; otherwise, it's like watching a Zalman King movie and never seeing any sex.

LB: In *Fresh,* it's not that the kid in the story gets revenge, but that in getting it he destroys himself morally. That's what's so bittersweet about the ending. The kid gets what he wants, but he has to lose a part of himself to get it. Everything has a price.

RA: Exactly. Which in *Patriot Games* the hero doesn't have to pay.

LB: The other thing about talking about the violence and racism in, say, *Reservoir Dogs,* is that there are so many things about the movie that are revealing about who we are as people. To me it's antiviolent because it shows our dark side.

QT: It's funny. You guys thought I wasn't gonna talk that much about violence, but we're having a semi-intelligent discussion about it. My feeling is, I like violence in movies. I enjoy watching it and I don't take it seriously one iota—unless the filmmaker takes it seriously, and then I'm happy to go down that road with him. If he wants to take it down a comic-strip road, I'm happy to go down that road with him as well. But I have no more of a problem with violence than I do with people who like bedroom comedy versus slapstick comedy. It's an aesthetic thing. People will attach a moral thing to it, but that's bullshit. It's just one of the things that movies can do.

When You Know You're in Good Hands

GAVIN SMITH/1994

IT MAY BE THAT writer-director and sometime actor Quentin Tarantino is to videostore clerks what the French *nouvelle vague*, Peter Bogdanovich, and Paul Schrader were to several generations of movie critics—proof that it's possible not only to slip through the looking glass of film history and go from spectator to participant, but also to have a decisive influence on that history in the process. Tarantino's 1992 debut *Reservoir Dogs* will, I think, prove pivotal in the history of the American independent film, for legitimizing its relationship to Hollywood genre.

Tarantino's new film *Pulp Fiction* consolidates his reconciliation of the American hardboiled pulp tradition since the Forties with the post-Pop idiom that dates from the Sixties. Films like Robert Altman's *The Long Goodbye* and Jim McBride's *Breathless* anticipate Tarantino's sardonic contemporary pop-pulp fusion, and share Los Angeles/Hollywood coordinates and drug-culture comic elements. But unlike either Altman or McBride, Tarantino ultimately redeems genre morally; even in *Reservoir Dogs'* world of simulation and identity-projection, betrayal is still betrayal. *Pulp Fiction* attaches scant irony to the conceit of a professional killer's spiritual conversion and renunciation of crime.

Far from succumbing to easy cynicism, Tarantino achieves the remarkable feat of remaining a genre purist even as his films critique, embarrass, and cross-breed genre. Like the critics-turned-directors named above,

From *Film Comment*, July–August, 1994, pp. 32–43. Reprinted by permission of *Film Comment* and the author.

Tarantino can't or won't entirely go native; instead he retains both the sensibility of the profound cinephile and a palpable, almost innocent faith in cinema, a movie idealism that frees him to approach writing and directing on one level as an almost intoxicating play of formal and grammatical adventures and inversions and reinventions of code.

In *Pulp Fiction* one such excursion is the sequence at Jackrabbit Slim's, a restaurant/club that inverts the archetypal waitress-to-superstar legend by using lookalikes to reduce dead Fifties idols (Monroe, Dean, etc.) to table staff; the menu meanwhile collapses film history into pure consumption, offering Douglas Sirk steaks and Martin & Lewis shakes (junk food is a Tarantino motif). Vincent Vega (John Travolta) escorts his boss's girl Mia (Uma Thurman) to this pop mausoleum, and the two connect. The scene unexpectedly achieves a kind of abandon that reminds me of Leos Carax: Mia and Vincent pairing for a cool, beyond-chic twist on the restaurant's dancefloor, their ultrastylized choreography the very image of the genre rhetoric of attitude, manners, and gesture that Tarantino seems to thrive on. He finds a Juliette Binoche in Uma Thurman here—and in the next scene as she dances alone in her house: it's an almost transcendent moment.

Tarantino's semi-mischievous reclassification of the crime movie as art film, begun in *Reservoir Dogs* and carried through in *Pulp Fiction,* is accomplished partly through the introduction of improbably elaborate narrative architecture that obliges the viewer to contemplate the usually invisible mechanisms of narrative selection. But more crucially, in Tarantino's oeuvre, spectacle and action paradoxically take the form of dialogue and monologue. The verbal setpiece takes precedence over the action setpiece, particularly in *Reservoir Dogs,* where, after all, the film's central, defining absence is the much-discussed but never-shown jewelry store holdup. As Mr. Orange's carefully rehearsed and Method-acting-perfected anecdote about a drug deal and a men's room full of cops demonstrates, truth, even reality, become merely verbal constructs. More than what they do, what the characters say—and they never stop talking.

Both *Pulp Fiction* and *Reservoir Dogs* push genre convention towards dissonance, not only by saturating them in pop self-referentiality but by staging philosophical and metaphysical questions latent in genre itself. *Reservoir Dogs* confronts crisis of meaning and the limits of the knowable, from the opening argument about Mr. Brown (Quentin Tarantino)'s reading of Madonna's song "Like a Virgin," to undercover cop Mr. Orange's deceptive text (does that make him a sub-tec?), to the final negation of meaning faced by the betrayed Mr. White, who, falling dead, leaves an empty frame to express final, definitive denial of meaning's presence.

But if *Reservoir Dogs* implies truth and fiction alike are acts of both will and faith, in *Pulp Fiction* verbal and narrative monopoly over truth shows signs of breaking down. Now there are three interdependent stories, far less determinist in character and not imperiled by *Dogs'* narrative crisis of confidence; and now the spoken word, though potent, isn't absolute — as Vincent says of a rumor about Mia, "It's not a fact, it's just what I heard."

Pulp Fiction shares its predecessor's fetishes — violence as grammar; styling over pathology; plot as farcical, sadistic game; a hermetic, atemporal-yet-retro sense of the present — but is a far more adroit, nuanced work. Its short-story format, complemented by an anthology of period styles from the Fifties, the Seventies, and Forties noir, liberates its fondly regarded characters from genre's fatal maze. In place of *Reservoir Dogs'* mounting crescendo of confrontations, *Pulp Fiction* against all expectation resolves its narrative threads with a series of negotiated settlements. The film is rife with amicable partings, terse exchanges of bygones, acts of generosity and forgiveness; all the stories furnish lucky escapes from nightmarish, no-win predicaments. If it's Tarantino's *Short Cuts,* call it *Close Shaves.*

But Tarantino ventures further. By opting for a structure that scrambles chronology without flashbacks, he grants centrality to the transformation of the character of killer Jules (Sam Jackson), who survives death through "divine intervention," is blessed and cleansed by Harvey Keitel's debonair angel, and discovers mercy. Jules is the beneficiary of the film's accumulated grace, and Tarantino, revising the image of void that ended *Reservoir Dogs,* frees him to exit the film's last shot.

GAVIN SMITH: *Both* Pulp Fiction *and* Reservoir Dogs *pull in different aesthetic directions simultaneously — realism on the one hand, artifice on the other.*

QUENTIN TARANTINO: That's this mix that I've been trying to do. I like movies that mix things up. My favorite sheer cinematic sequences in *Pulp Fiction,* like the OD sequence, play like, Oh my God, this is so fucking intense, all right; at the same time, it's also funny. Half the audience is tittering, the other half is diving under the seat. The torture scene in

Reservoir Dogs works that way, too. I get a kick out of doing that. There's realism and there's movie-movie-ness. I like them both.

The starting point is, you get these genre characters in these genre situations that you've seen before in other movies, but then all of a sudden out of nowhere they're plunged into real-life rules. For instance, in *Reservoir Dogs* the fact that the whole movie takes place in real time: what would normally be a ten-minute scene in any other heist movie ever made—all right, we're making the whole movie about it. That's not ten minutes, it's an hour. The movie takes place in the course of an hour. Now, it takes longer than an hour to view it because you go back and see the Mr. Orange story. But every minute for them in the warehouse is a minute for you. They're subjected to not a movie clock but a real-time clock. So you've got these movie guys, they look like genre characters but they're talking about things that genre characters don't normally talk about. They have a heartbeat, there's a human pulse to them.

GS: *One of the things that struck me about* Reservoir Dogs *was that it felt very theatrical in terms of mise-en-scène, especially the section between Steve Buscemi and Harvey Keitel before Michael Madsen arrives, where you film them as if they're on an empty stage.*

QT: That was actually a problem [when] trying to get the film made. People would read it and go, "Well, this isn't a movie, this is a play, why don't you try and do it in an Equity Waiver house?" I was like, "No, no, no, trust me, it'll be cinematic." I don't like most film versions of plays, but the reason I had it all take place in that one room was because I figured that would be the easiest way to shoot something. To me, the most important thing was that it be cinematic. Now, having said that, one of the things I get a big kick out of in *Reservoir Dogs* is that it plays with theatrical elements in a cinematic form—it is contained, the tension isn't dissipated, it's supposed to mount, the characters aren't able to leave, and the whole movie's definitely performance-driven. Both my films are completely performance-driven, they're almost cut to the rhythm of performance.

GS: *Performance being a key theme in the film—Mr. Orange's onscreen construction of his fictitious persona obviously suggests that the other characters do much the same thing.*

QT: Exactly. That's a motif that runs through all these gangster guys. Jules

[Sam Jackson] has the line in *Pulp Fiction,* "Let's get into character."
They're a cross between criminals and actors and children playing roles. If
you ever saw kids playing—three little kids playing Starsky and Hutch
interrogating a prisoner—you'll probably see more *real,* honest moments
happening than you would ever see on that show, because those kids
would be so into it. When a kid points his finger at you like it's a gun, he
ain't screwing around, that's a gun where he's coming from.

It was never a conscious decision, playing on the idea of big men are
actually little boys with real guns, but it kept coming out and I realized as I
was writing *Pulp,* that actually fits. You can even make the analogy with
the scene with Jules and Vincent [John Travolta] at Jimmy [Quentin Taran-
tino]'s house, they're afraid of their mom coming home. You spilled shit
on the carpet—clean up the mess you made from screwing around before
your mom gets home.

G S : *The opening scene of* Reservoir Dogs *with the characters at the diner to
me isn't naturalistic, but rather sets up the illusion of naturalism.*
Q T : It has that cinéma-vérité give and take, and yet: it has one of the
most pronounced camera moves in the whole movie, that slow-moving
360° where people get lost and then you find them again. But while I've
got this big camera thing happening—and believe me, it was a big pain in
the ass to shoot that—at the same time the camera is just catching whoever it happens to catch at the time. It's not choreographed so that it's on
Mr. Orange and it hits Mr. Pink as he says his line and then finds itself on
Mr. Blonde as he says his line—no, it's not doing that at all, people are
talking off-screen and the camera's just doing its own independent thing.

One of the things I like doing is incorporating many different styles of
shooting in the course of making a movie. I never shoot in one specific
cinematic language. I like using as many as are appropriate. Part of the fun
of that opening sequence is that there's three different styles of shooting.
The whole first part, the Madonna section, is just the camera moving
around—even when you go to a closeup, the camera's still doing its move
around. Then when it gets into the Harvey Keitel—Lawrence Tierney
thing about the address book, you stop and do two-shots, and then when
it gets into the tips part, we've got the geography of the table now, so the
whole thing is done in these massive closeups. Whenever you do a scene
that long, you have it break it down into sections. Ten minutes for your

opening sequence is a real long fucking time, especially if they're doing nothing but sitting down talking. Why did I shoot the third section in closeups? I don't really have an answer—it just felt right.

G S : *So what do you do if it's ten minutes of one person talking in a room, not moving about?*
Q T : I kind of do that with the Christopher Walken scene [in *Pulp Fiction*]. Three pages of monologue, this long story. And I'm not Mr. Coverage. Unless I know I want to shoot a lot of different things so that I can play around with it in the editing room, I shoot one thing specifically and that's all I get. I never cover myself.

G S : *What kind of coverage did you do in the Walken scene?*
Q T : I shot maybe 13 or 14 takes of the basic shot that you see in the movie, the kid's point of view. Then I did five or six takes of him doing it in closeup, and then I just had the little kid. Chris would do one take this way and one that way. He's telling a three-part story about the First World War, the Second World War, and then Vietnam, and all three beats are very different. So I could use the more humorous take on the First World War and then the Second World War story where he's talking about Wake Island, which is more tragic, I took his darkest take, and then for the Vietnam story I took his most irreverent one, which is the funniest. The whole thing with him is take it and run with it. He's just so great at doing monologues, about the best guy that there is at it, and that's why he did the movie, because he doesn't get the chance to do three-page monologues in movies knowing it's not gonna be cut.
One of the fun things about making a movie is, there's a whole lot of vocabulary, so this scene I'll shoot in one long take, this scene I want to do through forced perspectives, this scene I want to do with very minimal coverage, like the bathroom scene between Bruce Willis and Maria de Medeiros.

G S : *What do you mean, forced perspectives?*
Q T : The camera's taking some odd point of view.

G S : *For instance, in* Reservoir Dogs *when you film Buscemi and Keitel in the bathroom from way down the hallway?*
Q T : Exactly. Or the perspective outside the doorway during the scene

between Bruce and Maria, which is set up that way so you feel like you're a fly on the wall, observing these people alone together acting like people act when they're alone. The sequence when they're in the hotel room, it should be somewhat almost uncomfortable and embarrassing being in the room with them because they're madly in love with each other and they're at that uppermost honeymoon point of a relationship so they're talking all this babytalk. You're watching something you shouldn't really be seeing, and you don't know how much you want to see it because there's an extreme level of intimacy going on. When he first comes in, that whole sequence is just made out of three cuts, three long sections; there's very little intercutting in the entire motel sequence. And the shower sequence is just one shot. The third section with the big argument about the watch was done with zooms slowly creeping in. Focusing in but not moving: a dolly up to somebody has a whole different feel, a zoom is more analytical. Also, there's a tension when actors have to pull the scene off in one shot. If you try to get too smart with it, you shoot yourself in the foot, but there's something about getting together with the actors and saying, "Look, this is the deal, we're gonna do these-many takes and the best one is gonna be the one in the movie." Good actors rise to the occasion.

G S : *Have you ever been forced to patch a scene or moment together in the cutting room because it didn't work the way you shot it?*

Q T : Part of my job if I do something like that is to know I got it when we're on the set. If you get to the editing room and it absolutely didn't work, then you'll still make it work. Sometimes you have a great sequence but with a stumble, and you got to fix that stumble.

Other scenes I know that I'm gonna shoot from a zillion different angles because in the editing room I want to be able to completely pop around and cut to performance. People think you shoot a lot of different angles just because you're doing action. That's true, but the thing is, it's also a big performance thing. When you look at the way Tony Scott did the Christopher Walken-Dennis Hopper scene in *True Romance*, a million different angles, but it's all cut to a performance rhythm.

G S : *I tend to associate that kind of coverage with a lack of directorial point of view.*

Q T : When Tony does it, it's not a willy-nilly thing, that's just how he shoots. His whole style is to have a cut every 15 seconds.

GS: *Can't stand that.*

QT: Yeah, but when you say you can't stand that, you're reacting against his aesthetic—but that's what he wants to do. Me, I like to hold for as long as I can before I have to cut, and then when I do cut, I want it to fucking mean something. At the same time, I love how Tony does it. The whole sequence in *Pulp Fiction* where Sam Jackson and John Travolta come to the yuppies' apartment is covered in that style, because I'm dealing with Sam's big monologue and I've got all these guys all over the room. We're popping all around.

GS: *Was that the most covered scene in the film?*

QT: That and the whole [coffee shop] sequence at the end is covered from this side and that side so that I can pretty much cross the line at will, depending on the action. Far and away, forget what anyone else says, the biggest problem with making movies is that fucking axis line. I always thought that would be a major fucking problem that I would have, because I never quite understood it; if you tried to explain it to me, after a certain point I would glaze over. I realized that I actually did grasp it, instinctually. In that sequence you start out with the guys here, and I'm coming this way [*Sam Jackson left/Tim Roth right*], and I want to get over this way [*right of Roth*], and just as we were shooting I figured out the exact line, the exact setup, and the exact cut that would bring me over here— OK, great! I've got a really good script supervisor, and his number-one thing is the line. And from the moment that I established that I can cross the line, I know I can go back—I got over there the way you're supposed to, it's not crossing the line, it just gets me over to the other side. And once I got over there, I can go back and forth between the two. I figured that out on my feet, and it's one of my prouder moments.

GS: *A moment that really stands out in* Reservoir Dogs *is the cut to Tim Roth firing the gun at Michael Madsen at the end of the torture scene. It's one of those cuts that just knocks you out. Is there a secret to a cut like that?*

QT: It's a great emotional cut. Like after all those long takes in *Rope*, all of a sudden you cut to Jimmy Stewart. They fucked up, they said something wrong, and it cuts to Jimmy Stewart's reaction, you've never seen a reaction shot the whole movie—whoa! I figured out what was important was watching Mr. Orange empty out his gun. It wasn't BLAM—cut to Michael Madsen—BOOM. More shots. It wasn't going back and forth between Mr. Blonde getting shot and Mr. Orange shooting. It looks like he's gonna set the guy on fire and BOOM—he's blown out of frame and we see the guy who you forgot was even in the room, by this time he's become a piece of furniture. And as he's emptying the gun, the camera goes around him and reveals Mr. Blonde blown all the way across the warehouse. It was realizing that the visceral dramatic impact of the piece was not Mr. Blonde getting shot but Mr. Orange doing the shooting.

G S : *Because it's Mr. Orange finally doing something. The whole movie he's lying there and suddenly he acts.*

Q T : One of the things about *Reservoir Dogs* that really came off was how after a certain point you just forgot Orange was in the room. You can see him, he's there, but his presence becomes this lump. It wasn't like we even cheated by framing him out constantly so you get the illusion of being alone—Blonde actually goes over to him and still he doesn't make the impression. So when Orange shoots him it's a real jolt. They're always referring to him, too—he's the reason they don't leave. The whole thing as a writer was to constantly throw something new in their path that they have to deal with too. The trick was to keep them in the warehouse. Why would they stay? When all of this stuff starts becoming clear? Because something new keeps happening. Harvey can't take him to a hospital but Joe's supposed to be there, Joe can get a crook doctor like that; all right, if we just sit here and wait for Joe at this rendezvous—that's what he's saying to Mr. Orange. The irony is, when Joe shows up, he shows up to kill Orange. Then Mr. Pink shows up and says, "No, this was a setup." Mr. White never thought of that, now he's thinking about that. And Mr. Pink is saying, "No one's showing up, we're on our own, we gotta do something."

G S : *And Pink and Blonde have no emotional investment in Orange, unlike White.*

Q T : Oddly enough, though, me and Steve have talked about this quite a bit. People write off Mr. Pink as being this weasely kind of guy who just cares about himself, but that's actually not the case. Mr. Pink is right throughout the whole fucking movie. Everything he says is right, he just doesn't have the courage of his own convictions. However, there's a moment that nobody ever talks about, nobody catches, it's there but they don't see it: he says, "Look, Joe ain't coming, Orange was begging to be dropped off at a hospital. Well, since he doesn't know anything about us, I say it's his decision—if he wants to go to a hospital and go to jail afterwards, then that's fine. That's better than dying." So then Mr. White does something different than he's done throughout the entire movie. His whole thing throughout the whole movie is, What about Orange? What about Orange? But now he says, "Well, he knows a little bit about me." His one moment of self-interest in the whole movie. If all he gave a shit about was just saving Mr. Orange, he might have kept his mouth shut and taken the consequences. But he says it. And Mr. Pink says, "Well, that's fucking it. We're not taking him." And now it's not on Mr. White's shoulders anymore, now Mr. Pink is drawing the line, and they get into a fucking fight about it. White conveniently lets Mr. Pink be the bad guy now and then actually slugs him out of righteous indignation. Faced with that one little moment where he could be completely selfless, White doesn't rise to the occasion, which in some ways even highlights what he does later on when he actually does rise to the occasion. I never make a big dramatic moment about that. White's hesitation is very human.

G S : *Jean-Pierre Melville's films are maybe the primary influence on* Reservoir Dogs—*I think* Le Doulos *particularly, with its emphasis on structure and mannerism. Yet there are big differences:* Le Doulos *is so minimalist and nonverbal, Melville applies a less-is-more principle;* Reservoir Dogs *is ruled by verbal excess. And* Le Doulos *has a very steady, even tone, where* Reservoir Dogs *is all peaks and valleys. I think the relationship is fascinating.*

Q T : I do, too. *Le Doulos* has always been probably my favorite screenplay of all time—just from watching the movie. I just loved the wildness of watching a movie that up until the last twenty minutes I didn't know what the fuck it was I was looking at. And the last twenty minutes explained it all. I was really fascinated by how, even though you don't have any understanding about what's going on in that first hour, you're emotionally caught up in it. I know when I go see a movie and I start getting confused, I'm emotionally disconnected, I check out emotionally. For some reason I don't in *Le Doulos*.

G S : *The film's power is that it's genuinely mysterious.*

Q T : But the first time you see it you have no idea that mystery is gonna be solved as well as it is. That's the joy of it — I've had faith in this movie all this time and I had no idea my faith was gonna be paid back so well. [*Laughs.*]

G S : *You feel the director at play with the material and with you — that's the emotional thread, his feeling for the genre.*

Q T : I think you've hit the nail on the head — 99 percent of the reason that when a film starts confusing me I check out is because I know it's not intentional. I know whoever's at the helm doesn't have firm control of the material and it's a mistake that I'm confused. When you know you're in good hands, you can be confused and it's okay, because you know you're being confused for a reason. You know you'll be taken care of.

G S : *Were you concerned about what unified* Pulp Fiction *as you wrote it?*

Q T : In a way yes, in a way no. The most organic stuff when you're writing something like this, taking all these separate pieces and trying to make one big piece out of it, the best, richest stuff you find as you're doing it, you know? I had a lot of intellectual ideas, like wouldn't it be great if this character bumped into that character? A lot of it was kind of cool, but if it just worked in a cool, fun, intellectual way, ultimately I ended up not using it. It had to work emotionally.

As opposed to *Dogs,* which is a complete ensemble piece, [*Pulp Fiction*] works in a series of couples — everybody's a couple all the fucking way through. It starts off with Tim Roth and Amanda Plummer, then it goes to Sam Jackson and John Travolta, then John Travolta and Uma Thurman, then it goes to Bruce Willis and the cab driver, then it's Bruce and Maria de Medeiros — and then for a moment after he leaves her he's the only character in the movie who's viewed completely alone. Then he makes a bond with this other character and they become a team. It's only when they become a team that they can do anything. Circumstances make them a couple.

G S : *Your characters are all social beings situated in their own private culture. The only other loner is Madsen in* Reservoir Dogs. *He's not on the same wavelength as the other guys.*

Q T : But him and Chris Penn are just as close, if not closer, as the others.

GS: *But there's a side of Madsen that nobody knows about. Nobody really truly knows him.*

QT: Even Chris doesn't know about it. Some switch got flipped in prison.

GS: *[The screenplay for]* Pulp Fiction *opens with the title "Three stories... about one story." What does that mean?*

QT: I thought I was writing a crime film anthology. What Mario Bava did with the horror film in *Black Sabbath* I was gonna do with the crime film. Then I got totally involved in the idea of going beyond that, doing what J. D. Salinger did with his Glass family stories where they're all building up to one story, characters floating in and out. It's something that novelists can do because they own their characters, they can write a novel and have a lead character from three novels back show up.

GS: *That's why all your films have references to characters from one another. The characters in* Reservoir Dogs *refer to Marsellus, who is the hub of all the stories in* Pulp Fiction.

QT: Very much so, like Alabama. To me they're all living inside of this one universe.

GS: *And it isn't [pointing out the window] out there.*

QT: Well, it's a little bit out there, and it's also there, too [*points at his TV*], in the movies, and it's also in here [*points to his head*]. It's all three. I very much believe in that idea of continuing characters. So what I mean when I wrote "Three stories... about one story," when I finished the script I was so happy because you don't *feel* like you've seen three stories—and I've gone out of my way to make them three stories, with a prologue and an epilogue! They all have a beginning and an end. But you feel like you've seen one story about a community of characters, like *Nashville* or *Short Cuts* where the stories are secondary. This is a much different approach— the stories are primary, not secondary, but the effect is the same.

GS: *I interpreted "Three stories... about one story" as being a comment on genre: that these three stories are all ultimately about the genre invoked by the title,* Pulp Fiction.

QT: The story of a genre. The three stories in *Pulp Fiction* are more or less the oldest stories you've ever seen: The guy going out with the boss's wife and he's not supposed to touch her—that's in *The Cotton Club, Revenge.* The middle story, the boxer who's supposed to throw the fight and doesn't— that's about the oldest chestnut there is. The third story is more or less the opening three minutes of *Action Jackson, Commando,* every other Joel Silver movie—two hitmen show up and blow somebody away. Then they cut to "Warner Bros. Presents" and you have the credit sequence, and then they cut to the hero 300 miles away. But here the two killers come in, BLAM-BLAM-BLAM—but we don't cut away, we stay with them the whole rest of the morning and see what happens to them *after* that. The whole idea is to have these old chestnuts and go to the moon with them.

G S : *You also combine these archetypal movie genre narratives with incidents straight out of pop-contemporary urban legends—the date who ODs or the S&M torture chamber in the basement.*
Q T : If you talk to anybody who was a heroin addict for any period of time, they all have stories about someone who OD'd, they all have their own version of that story. If you talk to any criminal, they all have their own version more or less of The Bonnie Situation, some weird fucking thing that happened that they had to deal with.

G S : *On the one hand you're making films in which you want the audience emotionally involved, as if it's "real." On the other you're commenting on movies and genre, distancing the viewer from the fiction by breaking the illusion. On one level your movies are fictions, but on another level they're movie criticism, like Godard's films.*
Q T : One hundred percent.

G S : *Does your movie consciousness prevent you from doing a movie—*
Q T : —straight.

G S : *Right.*
Q T : Your way of describing it makes what I'm doing sound so incredibly impressive. That's one aspect of Godard that I found very liberating— movies commenting on themselves, movies and movie history. To me, Godard did to movies what Bob Dylan did to music: they both revolution- ized their forms. There were always movie buffs who understood film and film convention, but now, with the advent of video, almost everybody has

become a film expert, even though they don't know it. My mom very rarely went to movies. However, now that there's video she sees everything that comes out—I mean everything—but on video, six months after the fact. What I feel about the audience—particularly after the Eighties where films got so ritualized, you started seeing the same movie over and over again—intellectually the audience doesn't know that they know as much as they do. In the first ten minutes of nine out of ten movies—and this applies to a whole lot of the independent films that are released, not the ones that can't find a release—the movie tells you what kind of movie it's gonna be. It tells you everything that you basically need to know. And after that, when the movie's getting ready to make a left turn, the audience starts leaning to the left; when it's getting ready to make a right turn, the audience moves to the right; when it's supposed to suck 'em in, they move up close . . . you just know what's gonna happen. You don't know you know, but you know.

Admittedly, there's a lot of fun in playing against that, fucking up the breadcrumb trail that we don't even know we're following, using an audience's own subconscious preconceptions against them so they actually have a viewing experience, they're actually involved in the movie. Yeah, I'm interested in doing that just as a storyteller. But the heartbeat of the movie has to be a human heartbeat. Now, if you were to walk out of the theater after the first hour of *Pulp Fiction,* you really haven't experienced the movie, because the movie you see an hour later is a much different movie. And the last twenty minutes is much different than that. That's much harder to do than when you're dealing with a movie about a ticking bomb like *Reservoir Dogs. Pulp Fiction* is much more of a tapestry.

Again, a lot of things that seem unusual for films—for instance, the *Reservoir Dogs* characters' offhanded brutality, their commitment to their coldbloodedness—are not unusual in a novel in the crime genre. The characters have a commitment to their own identity, as opposed to action movies or big Hollywood movies where every decision is very committee-ized and the whole fear is that at some point the character might not be likeable. But people find John Travolta's character in *Pulp Fiction* not only likeable but very charming—considering the fact that he's first presented as a hitman and that's never taken back. He is what he is, he is shown plying his trade, but then you get to know him above and beyond that. The reverse of never breaking that hitman mode in Hollywood movies is, Wow, he can't fucking do that, he can't kill the villain with his bare hands, why don't we have him punch him and have the villain fall on something—so then he killed him but he didn't really mean to so he can go back to his family and everything is cool, we can still feel good about liking him. That kind of bullshit I can't abide. But you have to be engaged in the character in a human way or else it becomes an intellectual tennis game.

G S : *But once a film starts breaking itself down, commenting on itself, exposing the illusions of fiction, you open a Pandora's box. When Madsen makes the Lee Marvin joke in* Reservoir Dogs *or Uma Thurman draws a square out of thin air in* Pulp Fiction, *once you reposition the viewer like that, can you get away with reverting to straight storytelling later in the film as you seem to?*

Q T : I think I do. What makes that whole square so exciting is you hadn't seen anything quite like it in the movie up until that point. There are little moments like that—you see the black-and-white behind Bruce Willis in the cab, the car process shots in general—but they never disconnect you emotionally. Because after the square, you dive into one of the more realistic sections of the movie. You go on a fucking date with them, that's not a quick "They talk—babababababa—and get to the point". The movie almost stops for you to get to know Mia [Uma Thurman].

G S : *But the device of giving genre characters like hitmen unlikely conversational topics inevitably draws attention to the fictive basis of what's onscreen.*

Q T : That's putting your preconceptions about what you think people who do that for a living talk about.

G S : *No, on a behavioral, emotional level you're making choices that go against naturalism. When Sam Jackson has all that business with the hamburger and delivers that long spiel to Frank Whaley in the apartment before killing him, the only naturalistic justification is because his character has some need to do that—but you don't make that choice. So where's it coming from?*

Q T : To me, it's coming from the fact that he's taking control of the room: you walk in like you're gonna cut off everybody's head, but then you don't cut off their heads. He's never met these guys before, he's improvising, he's gotta get that case. So he's like a real nice guy, he's cool, he's kind of playing good cop/bad cop and he's the good cop, he's the guy who sucks you in. He says that speech before he kills him because . . . that's what he does.

He explains that later in the movie—"I have this speech I give before I kill somebody." That's Jules's thing, to be a badass. It's a macho thing, and it's like his good-luck charm. He's playing a movie character, he's being the Green Lantern saying his little speech before he does what he does.

GS: *That's what I mean—that's where it stops being a character and starts being a commentary.*

QT: To me, they don't necessarily break the reality. You hear stories about gang-bangers doing routines from movies before they do a drive-by.

GS: *Why do you think neither of your films adheres to the classical principle of single-character point of view?*

QT: I've picked two projects where it's very organic and almost imperative to do it that way. I keep applying to cinema the same rules that novelists have when they come to writing novels: you can tell it any way you want. It's not just, you have to tell it linearly. It's inherent in the stories. *Reservoir Dogs* and *Pulp Fiction* would be dramatically less interesting if you told them in a completely linear fashion.

GS: *And the* True Romance *screenplay is linear.*

QT: *True Romance* wasn't written in a linear fashion originally. It started off with the same first scene of Clarence talking about Elvis, then the next scene was Drexl killing all his cronies, and the third scene was Clarence and Alabama at Clarence's father's house. And then you learn how he got what he got. Tony made it all linear, and it worked that way.

If you break it into three acts, the structure they all worked under was: in the first act the audience really doesn't understand what's going on, they're just getting to know the characters. The characters have far more information than the audience has. By the second act you start catching up and get even with the characters, and then in the third act you now know far more than the characters know, you're way ahead of the characters. That was the structure *True Romance* was based on, and you can totally apply that to *Reservoir Dogs*. In the first section, up until Mr. Orange shoots Mr. Blonde, the characters have far more information about what's going on than you have—and they have conflicting information. Then the Mr. Orange sequence happens and that's a great leveler. You start getting caught up with exactly what's going on, and in the third part when you go

back into the warehouse for the climax you are totally ahead of everybody—you know far more than any one of the characters. You know more
than Keitel, Buscemi, and Penn because you know that Mr. Orange is a cop
and you know more than Mr. Orange does because he's got his own little
ruse he's gonna say. But you know Mr. Blonde's lineage, you know he went
to jail for three years for Chris Penn's father, you know what Chris Penn
knows. And when Mr. White is pointing the gun at Joe [Lawrence Tierney]
and saying, "You're wrong about this man"—*you know he's right.* You know
Keitel's wrong, he's defending a guy who's actually selling him out.

To me, 90 percent of the problem with movies nowadays lies in the
script. Storytelling has become a lost art. There is no storytelling, there's
just situations. Very rarely are you told a story. A story isn't "Royal Cana-
dian Mounted Police officer goes to New York to capture a Canuck bad
guy." Or, "White cop and black cop looking for a killer but this time
they're looking in Tijuana." Those are situations. They can be fun. I just
saw *Speed* the other day, a totally fun movie, had a blast. The last twenty
minutes gets kind of cheesy, but up until then it was totally engaging. Situation filmmaking at its best, because they really went with it. *Speed* works.
Most of them don't work. The only thing is, I used to ride a bus for a year
and I know that people aren't as gabby on a bus as they're portrayed. They
were kind of doing an *Airport* thing. But on a bus you're getting to work
and people do not talk.

I watched *Macon County Line* again a few months ago. Cool film. And I
was shocked at how much of a story it told. Not that complicated a story,
but it took me to different levels in the course of the story. *One False Move*
was a story; they didn't tell you a situation, they told you a story. However, *Groundhog Day* is one of my favorite movies of last year, if not my
favorite, and that's a totally situation movie, but they went way beyond
the situation and told a story. A friend of mine said action movies are the
heavy metal of cinema, and that's not that far off. Action movies have
become the mainstay for young male cinemagoers, and they don't have
the Good Housekeeping Seal of Approval. However, you're so used to seeing weak-assed action films that don't deliver. Even a mediocre action
movie has a couple of good sequences that you can enjoy to some degree
while you're watching, but then it's gone by the next day. *Speed* stayed
with me. I'm kind of interested in seeing it again. What other action
movies have you seen recently that you look forward to seeing again?

Fox approached me for *Speed.* I didn't read it, my agent didn't give it to me because I was doing *Pulp Fiction.* I was sent a script this weekend that's gonna be a big movie and they want me. It was an interesting idea. I don't read many scripts but I read this one. And it's a fun movie. I'll see it on opening night. But it's not what I want to spend a year making. And it's an action movie, wall-to-wall action scenes. And I don't do wall-to-wall action movies.

GS: *Do you think* Pulp Fiction *represents the start of a partial retreat from genre?*

QT: The entire time I was writing *Pulp Fiction* I was thinking, This will be my Get-It-Out-of-Your-System movie. This will be the movie where I say goodbye to the gangster genre for a while, because I don't want to be the next Don Siegel—not that I'm as good. I don't want to just be the gun guy. There's other genres that I'd like to do: comedies, Westerns, war films.

GS: *Do you think your next film might not even be a genre film?*

QT: I think every movie is a genre movie. A John Cassavetes movie is a genre movie—it's a John Cassavetes Movie. That's a genre in and of itself. Eric Rohmer movies to me are a genre. The thing that I came up with a little bit after that was, If you come up with something that falls into that same crime/mystery genre and it's really pure and really organic and it's what you should do, well, if you really want to do it, do it. Because I'm basically lazy, and to get me to stop enjoying living life it's gotta be something that I really wanna do. I'm gonna take almost a year off. I remember when I was younger I was, like, I want to be like Fassbinder, 42 films in ten years. Now that I've made a couple, I don't want it.

Quentin Tarantino, Master of Mayhem

HILARY DE VRIES / 1994

PERHAPS IT IS GENIUS at work—an audible whir that is evidence of synapses plying their magic in a West Hollywood apartment complex. But no.

"I'm in the kitchen!"

It is here that Quentin Tarantino lives, 31 years old and a legendary filmmaker with just a pair of movies—*Reservoir Dogs,* his 1992 cult hit, and now *Pulp Fiction,* the winner of this year's Palme d'Or at Cannes. Already he is the stuff of myth and currently at work—over a blender.

"I'm on this diet," Tarantino sings out over the whirring, slinging a fistful of ice. "I've already lost twelve pounds."

Even the diet, penance for a lifetime's devotion to Denny's, Tarantino imbues with his own zealous stamp. "It's the best, because you make it with any kind of diet soda," he says, cracking a Mountain Dew, dumping its telltale luridness and a packet of mysterious pink powder into the icy slush. The blender glows like neon.

"God," he says, snapping off the machine, pouring himself a glass and holding it aloft to admire his creation. "I would never go on anything disgusting like Slim-Fast."

It is, to be sure, a fine distinction but indicative of the deep idiosyncratic taste that has propelled Tarantino into the forefront of a new generation of filmmakers. With his playwright's ear for dialogue and a

From the *Los Angeles Times, Fanfare,* 2 October 1994, pp. 9–10. © 1994 by the *Los Angeles Times.* Reprinted by permission, and by permission of the author.

penchant for violent, structurally complex narratives, the self-taught director — a former video store clerk and high school dropout from Los Angeles'
working-class South Bay area — has parlayed a fan's fascination with pop
culture into one of the most promising and controversial film careers
going, a move he describes almost disingenuously: "I'm a guy who makes
movies you either like or you don't."

That divisiveness certainly attended his debut film, *Reservoir Dogs*, a stylish, low-budget crime drama about a jewelry heist gone awry that both
mocked and exploited the genre's conventions with its *Rashomon* narrative
techniques. After sweeping through the Toronto, Sundance and Cannes
festivals, the film earned Tarantino comparisons to Sam Peckinpah and
Martin Scorsese. In the words of one producer, "It was the best film debut
in twenty-five years."

Like the other young, culturally diverse directors to whom he was initially compared — John Singleton, Gus Van Sant and Abel Ferrara —
Tarantino had arrived with an agenda: to revive and personalize an art
form he saw as more than due for generational overhaul.

As a post-baby boomer raised on a cultural diet of videotape movies,
MTV and "reality-based" tabloid news shows, the filmmaker brought a
puckishly postmodernist sensibility as well as a cineaste's rigorous esthetic
evident not only in *Reservoir Dogs* but in his scripts for last year's *True
Romance* directed by Tony Scott, and *Natural Born Killers,* Oliver Stone's
controversial drama, which opened in August.

"Because movies are so characterless these days — basically film versions
of situation comedies — I like to work in a genre while subverting it from
the inside," Tarantino says. "I like to work against an audience's usual
expectations."

Not everyone sees his work in those terms. Many critics decried *Reservoir
Dogs,* which contained a controversial 10-minute torture sequence, as
overtly violent, needlessly profane, racist and possibly misogynistic, a
showy calling card as much as serious artistic endeavor. Siskel and Ebert
gave the film a resounding "two thumbs down." Given that *True Romance*
was hailed as a *Bonnie and Clyde* for the '90s, and *Natural Born Killers*
opened only after a protracted struggle with the ratings board over the
film's violent content, Tarantino would seem to have a lock on what he
calls "the guy with the gun."

That simple perception is already being tested with *Pulp Fiction,* Tarantino's much-awaited second directorial effort that will arrive in theaters October 14. A crime drama that blends seemingly banal pop cultural references, explosive violence and an absurdist style of humor in a rich, twisting novel-like narrative, the movie stars John Travolta, Samuel L. Jackson, Bruce Willis and Uma Thurman. The film won the honored slot to open the New York Film Festival in September and received four-star reviews from local critics. Then there was that Palme d'Or.

"Oh, the Palme d'Or? I'll give you the real answer to that question," says Tarantino, flopping onto a chair in his living room, which seems largely furnished with a massive television set and mountains of laserdiscs. "It hasn't changed my stature in the industry, because my stature in the industry couldn't be better. But it has given me the Good Housekeeping Seal of Approval, so if you don't like my work now, it has to do with your own taste and not my material."

His feckless self-confidence not withstanding (he already has termed *Pulp Fiction* "a great film"), Tarantino faces the larger issue of determining what his career means for Hollywood as a whole. In an industry that has, with few exceptions, seldom been comfortable producing edgy, iconoclastic films, and in the current economic climate even less inclined, the question lingers: Exactly how mainstream will Tarantino become?

So far the signs appear to be mixed. Despite the cult-hit status of *Reservoir Dogs,* the film was regarded within the studio system as largely "a *succès d'estime*" as one producer put it, a perception that was not altered when *True Romance* failed to generate much more than controversy. As early as last year, one studio, TriStar Pictures declined to produce *Pulp Fiction* despite its modest $8-million budget.

Even now, when the movie is arriving with the Cannes imprimatur and the marketing savvy of Miramax Films (the producers of *Pulp Fiction,* with whom Tarantino has a development deal), the anticipation is not one of guaranteed box-office success.

Yet *Pulp Fiction* is arriving at a perhaps crucial time when studios have begun to re-examine their formulas. When difficult, downbeat films like *The Crow* gross a surprising $50 million at the box office and *Natural Born Killers* scores an unexpected $10-million opening weekend—a figure that caught several studio heads unaware—the possibility exists that *Pulp Fic-*

tion may further tap into that growing segment of the audience that appreciates dark, even violent, films done in a classy, art-house way.

"If *Natural Born Killers* and *Pulp Fiction* are commercial as well as critical successes, Tarantino can write his own ticket," says the former executive, "because he will have shown not that he is mainstream but that he can bring mainstream audiences over to his vision."

Indeed, amid all the pre-release hype surrounding *Pulp Fiction,* there is the growing perception that Tarantino's rise to prominence has been far more calculated than the guileless ascent by some idiot-savant filmmaker that the media have so far reported. Rather, colleagues say, Tarantino's career has been a carefully orchestrated, frankly self-serving campaign that not only speaks to his abilities as a director but also to his talent for creating himself in the public eye.

"Quentin is a brilliant guy, and he is brilliant in a lot of ways, and one of those is managing his career," says a longtime friend, screenwriter-director Roger Avary. "He is a completely self-taught guy, a writer, director and actor who has closely studied the lives of other filmmakers, and he knows exactly how his career should go."

"Everyone is waiting to see how this film does," says Lawrence Bender, the producer of *Reservoir Dogs* and *Pulp Fiction* and Tarantino's partner in their film company, A Band Apart. "But even before *Dogs* we had an overall plan—we knew the second movie would be more important than the first one—and we deliberately set out to build our careers."

Yet, all of this has begun to take its toll, not only on some of Tarantino's key professional relationships—notably the fraying of his longtime association with Avary, who recently directed his own first film, *Killing Zoe,* and who shares story credit with Tarantino on *Pulp Fiction*—but also on the filmmaker himself. According to some reports, he is struggling with the ramifications of having become "too big too fast," as one colleague puts it. As Tarantino recently confided to one old friend: "I still feel like that kid in the video store and that some studio guy is going to tell me to get out."

But in conversation, particularly one for the record, Tarantino seems far from any display of insecurity. With his lantern jaw, rumpled hair and stocky build, he has the slightly menacing look of an overgrown kid—an impression only abetted by his college-dorm approach to domestication and his swaggering conversational style, a school-yard bravado that would be off-putting if he were less catholic in his enthusiasm. As Julia Sweeney, the former *Saturday Night Live* actress and one of the filmmaker's closest friends, characterizes it: "Quentin is totally into his own opinions."

Or as he describes himself: "People keep on me for all the violence and the pop culture stuff," he says, downing the last of his homemade brew. "But if that's all that I really had to offer, well, my movies would be boring, and they're not."

It was supposed to be simple, as its title suggests, a film noir homage to the crime novels of the 1930s. Crime stories are one of Tarantino's favorite narrative styles—he has used variations of the genre in all four of his screenplays—and he finds inspiration for his work in such diverse sources as Howard Hawks films, Elmore Leonard novels, and black exploitation and kung-fu movies.

"I just thought it would be really cool in *Pulp Fiction* to do like a *Black Mask* style of crime anthology where you made one movie out of three separate stories." His intentions were not "gimmicky," he adds, but literary, a way to infuse genre filmmaking with some of the creative latitude he saw in novels. "Fiction writers," he explains, "have a freedom that filmmakers have yet to enjoy."

Perhaps it was the scope of those ambitions or the film's unusually long gestation period in a foreign locale (Tarantino spent more than a year, most of it living in Amsterdam, writing a 500-page first draft) or his collaboration with Avary, who had written a full-length script called *Pandemonium Reigns* that eventually became the film's middle story. Or perhaps it was simply that Tarantino was wary of being permanently labeled "the gun guy." Whatever the reasons, the resulting 2½-hour gangster movie is the director's most mature, complex and accessible script to date.

"You hear the same voice in this, the same playing around with humor and [violent] intensity as in my other scripts," Tarantino says, "but basically this is a totally different kind of movie, a much more laid-back tapestry where the humor takes center stage."

It is all part of his boldly immodest ambitions to not only write a film "that I want to see" but also to lay down something of a gauntlet to American moviemakers, whom he sees as languishing under a lack of imagination.

"There are so many films out there now that are just carbon copies of what we've seen—this version of the action movie, that version of a comedy," Tarantino says. "I want to see a return to storytelling, which is what American films did best — tell stories, but we can't even do that anymore."

He wants to challenge rather than appease an audience, which is one reason he says he uses violence with such a liberal hand, to keep the audience on its toes and off-balance.

"You usually don't hear a music cue when something horrible is about to happen," he says. "Real-life violence isn't that way. It's more like one minute you're waiting for a bus and the next minute people are chasing each other with baseball bats. That's how I try to play it in my movies."

Yet, for all his protestations about his genial ambitions, *Pulp Fiction* narrowly avoided an NC-17 rating with its numerous gunfights, stabbings and, in one particularly memorable sequence, an S & M anal rape scene — the kind of content that troubled, at least initially, some of the film's cast.

"I wasn't sure that I could morally or ethically align myself with this kind of movie," says John Travolta, who plays a heroin-addicted hit man. After discussions with Tarantino "helped me realize that he is portraying crime and drugs in a very unglamorous way," Travolta signed on.

It is an incident that speaks to Tarantino's continuing frustrations with what he sees as misperceptions of his work. Most of the objections to his films, he says, "are from people who haven't even seen them." As for the violence tag, he says, that has more to do with perception than reality. "It's not that something graphic is happening every minute, but the threat of violence is in the air all the time, so the audience sits there with its gut all scrunched up."

That's one reason Tarantino remains touchy about *Natural Born Killers*, a film about two serial killers that he wrote several years ago as "a dark, satiric comedy" about violence and celebrity. Although he had written the script intending to direct it, Oliver Stone wound up directing and substantially rewriting it.

The question of authorship clearly rankles Tarantino and was a major reason the release of *Pulp Fiction* was pushed from August to October.

"I didn't want to go head-to-head with *Natural Born Killers*," he says, "because I didn't want the two films compared, because Oliver basically took my script very seriously, which, as dark as it was, was also pretty playful. I like audiences to make up their own minds, but Oliver Stone has to get the big idea across, and if one person doesn't get it, he thinks he's failed. I would rather the film never got made and that my script remained pure."

Harvey Keitel and Steve Buscemi, *Reservoir Dogs*, 1992

Harvey Keitel and Tim Roth, *Reservoir Dogs*, 1992

Christian Slater and Patricia Arquette, *True Romance*, 1993
(Photo credit: Ron Phillips)

Woody Harrelson and Juliette Lewis, *Natural Born Killers*, 1994
(Photo credit: Sidney Baldwin)

Quentin Tarantino on the set of *Pulp Fiction*, 1994
(Photo credit: Linda R. Chen)

John Travolta and Samuel L. Jackson, *Pulp Fiction*, 1994
(Photo credit: Linda R. Chen)

John Travolta and Uma Thurman, *Pulp Fiction*, 1994
(Photo credit: Linda R. Chen)

Uma Thurman, *Pulp Fiction*, 1994
(Photo credit: Linda R. Chen)

Bruce Willis, *Pulp Fiction*, 1994
(Photo credit: Linda R. Chen)

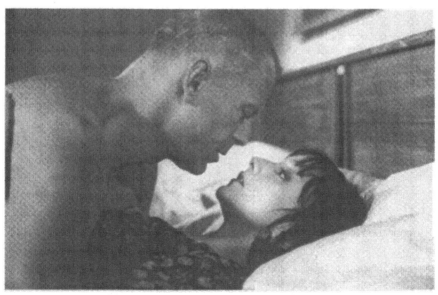

Bruce Willis and Maria de Medeiros, *Pulp Fiction*, 1994
(Photo credit: Linda R. Chen)

Salma Hayek and Antonio Banderas, *Desperado*, 1995
(Photo credit: Rico Torres)

Quentin Tarantino, *Desperado*, 1995
(Photo credit: Rico Torres)

That issue of authorial purity, however, has never been a clear-cut one for Tarantino, who freely concedes his collagelike techniques impel him to "steal from every movie I see." With his almost encyclopedic knowledge of film, an apparently photographic memory, as well as the kind of easy access afforded by videotape, Tarantino has a wealth of movie sequences at his fingertips.

Indeed, many critics noted the similarities between *Reservoir Dogs* and Joseph Sargent's *The Taking of Pelham One Two Three* and Stanley Kubrick's *The Killing*. Such stylistic homage is increasingly common among young filmmakers such as Tarantino, Sam Raimi, and Joel and Ethan Coen.

"Every generation has its blessing and curse," says Avary, who has known Tarantino for more than 10 years. "Ours is being such a media-literature generation."

For Tarantino, however, the issue has become something other than a theoretical one. Already one film journal, *Film Threat,* has accused him of lifting entire scenes as well as the basic framework of *Reservoir Dogs* from an obscure Asian film, Ringo Lam's 1987 *City on Fire*—a charge Tarantino publicly dismissed at Cannes.

Tarantino's pugnacious attitude is perhaps no surprise, given that he took the hard-knocks, rather than the film-school, route to Hollywood. Tarantino, an only child born in Knoxville, Tennessee, in 1963, moved to Los Angeles when he was 2, after his mother, Connie Zastoupil, a nurse who was part-Cherokee, separated from Tarantino's father. "I never met my real father," he says coolly.

The two settled in Torrance, where from the very first Tarantino was something of a film buff, attending movies several times a week accompanied by his musician stepfather. By the time he was 8, Tarantino had seen films ranging from *Bambi* to *Carnal Knowledge*.

Not surprisingly, he originally planned on becoming an actor. A poor, almost dysfunctional student—one story has Tarantino not learning to tell time till he was in sixth grade—he dropped out of school after the ninth grade to study acting full-time. Although he eventually would become proficient enough to land a guest shot playing an Elvis impersonator on *The Golden Girls,* as well as cameo roles in his own films, Tarantino quickly realized writing was his forte and directors were his real heroes.

Looking to create the kind of splashy, attention-grabbing script that would lure investors, he penned *True Romance, Natural Born Killers* and

Reservoir Dogs as somewhat flamboyant writing samples while supporting himself by working at a video rental store, the now-fabled Video Archives in Manhattan Beach.

It was there that he first met Avary and began to establish his reputation as a walking library of film, the kind of self-described "movie geek" who knew every camera angle in all of Sergio Leone's films but who couldn't be bothered to keep his car registration current. A legendary story has Tarantino spending 10 days in L.A. County Jail when he wouldn't pay the more than $7,000 in parking fines he incurred on the chance that he might pick up some dialogue useful in his screenwriting.

"Quentin was the kind of guy who had such a limited education I don't even think he knew how to write—he printed everything—but no one could hold a candle to him when it came to his knowledge and enthusiasm for movies," recalls Dennis Humbert, a co-owner of Video Archives.

After five years, Tarantino left Video Archives to take a job in CineTel, a small Hollywood production company, where he finished writing *Reservoir Dogs* and, more important, met Bender, an actor and aspiring producer. Using Bender's contacts from acting school, the two were able to get *Reservoir Dogs* to Harvey Keitel, who had a history of working in venturesome films. After Keitel agreed to star (he also has a cameo appearance in *Pulp Fiction*), Bender was able to raise the $1.5 million for Tarantino's debut film.

Today, Tarantino makes almost that much as a director. Although he lives relatively modestly in his apartment—"I like this place," he says defensively. "It reminds me of an apartment in Paris"—and drives his tiny Geo Metro, the car he bought after he sold *True Romance,* he has acquired a few trappings of success.

He works out with a private trainer now, more freely indulges his insatiable appetite for acquiring books and videos, and he has begun to travel, not just to film festivals where his work is screened but also for pleasure, such as the four-day trip he took to Ireland this summer with Sweeney, a nonromantic friendship, they both say.

"Quentin kept saying this is like being in a Merchant-Ivory movie," the actress says. "I think it really opened his eyes to different kinds of lifestyles he might lead."

Perhaps most significant, Tarantino says he has no immediate plans for his next movie. Other than a brief segment he will direct in *Four Rooms,* a

Miramax-produced collaboration that also features the work of directors Allison Anders and Alex Rockwell, two of Tarantino's close colleagues—he plans to spend the year in relative repose, riding his new mountain bike and acting in other people's movies while he waits "for that organic idea for my next film" to germinate.

"That's the lamest thing about making a movie, because you don't have a personal life," Tarantino says. "Right now I just want to totally chill, and maybe in, like seven months, I'll have any idea for my next movie."

Meanwhile, he can be seen in cameos in two small movies, *Sleep With Me* and *Destiny Turns on the Radio,* which begins filming this fall. "I have the coolest part," he says, speaking almost as much about himself as his role. "I play Destiny."

Quentin Tarantino, Violence and Twisted Wit

DAVID WILD/1994

QUENTIN TARANTINO PROVED HE was no one-shot
wonder with *Pulp Fiction,* but is he a true craftsman of film violence or a trainspotter whose films are a patchwork of B-movies,
comic strips and crime novels? David Wild interviews the film
censor's Public Enemy Number One.

Quentin Tarantino, madman of movie mayhem, has a mother. How's that
for a shocker? And she's seen *Reservoir Dogs,* the 1992 heist film that made a
cult sensation of her writer-director-actor son and raised the stakes on
movie gore with a ten-minute torture scene featuring the severing of an
ear. "That happens to be my mother's favorite scene," says Tarantino, 31, a
high-school dropout who has gone from video-store clerk to genius
"auteur du jour" in just a few feverishly busy years. Mom has just checked
out *Pulp Fiction,* a wildly ambitious and darkly comic crime anthology
about Los Angeles low-life that won the Palme d'Or at Cannes, opened the
prestigious New York Film Festival and put her son in the hot-contender
line at next year's Oscars. Although the film includes shootings, stabbings,
S&M, homosexual rape and a drug-overdose sequence that leaves audiences reeling, Mom doesn't flinch. Tarantino's West Hollywood, California

From *Rolling Stone,* 3 November 1994, pp. 78–81, 110. Reprinted by permission of Straight
Arrow Publishers Company, L.P. 1994.

bachelor apartment is another matter. "That's not particularly my decorating style," she says with a laugh.

Chez Tarantino is hardly the sort of glitzy home in the Hills one might imagine to house a ballsy Generation X-rated triple threat on the verge of becoming his own one-man genre. Rather, the homey—OK, messy—pad looks like a kitschy pop-culture Valhalla. Movie posters, videos, laser discs, albums, fanzines, books and assorted film artefacts fill every available inch. Along with memorabilia from his own movies—including that razor used in the famous ear-slicing scene—there's a frighteningly life-like head of B-movie diva Barbara Steele, a pack of genuine Texas Chainsaw chili, a Zorro knife given to him by Jennifer Beals, a Robert Vaughn doll, cases by the dozen of bottled Pepsi and what must be the world's most impressive collections of film and TV-related board games.

"I've been collecting all this shit for years," says Tarantino, who is wearing a Racer X T-shirt today. "Then I finally decided I wanted to start collecting something new. At first I chose lunch boxes, but they really rape you on lunch boxes. They're just too fuckin' expensive. And as for dolls, well, you can't have much fun with them! You have to keep them in the box. So, I started with board games." Proudly, he shows off his collection, which he has broken down by genre. *The Dukes of Hazzard,* he reports is a particularly fine game. Two of his most impressive acquisitions are *Dawn Of The Dead* and *Universe,* which he claims is "the closest they ever came to an official *2001: A Space Odyssey* game". He also owns a *Platoon* game, of which he's joked: "I really would love to play with Oliver." Stone, apparently, would be only too happy to take up the offer. The bedroom is dominated by a personal collection of tapes. The fare here ranges from art-house classics to *Ma Barker's Kill Brood* and a healthy number of vintage blaxploitation flicks.

You also can't help noticing the shrine to John Travolta about the ledge of Tarantino's fireplace. Certainly part of the satisfaction of making *Pulp Fiction* for Tarantino came from the chance to work with Travolta, aka Vinnie Barbarino, head Sweathog on one of Tarantino's TV faves from the '70s, *Welcome Back, Kotter.* In a film of stand-out performances, Travolta scores a stunning comeback as the henchman, hot dancer and heroin junkie Vincent Vega. Tarantino will happily expound for hours on the "total brilliance" of the actor's work 13 years ago in Brian De Palma's *Blow Out.* "John's a real sweetheart, and we became friends," he says. "I just gave John a role like the ones he used to do, and I took him seriously. But getting to know John, I can sort of see why he did all those *Look Who's Talking* movies, because that character is similar to who he is in real life— a charming, goofy kind of guy."

Travolta was also charmed. "I've been doing this for 20 years now, and I've never seen anyone have more fun on a movie set than Quentin," he says. "And it's contagious. You think: If this guy can get off as much as he does, then I definitely want to get on board. Quentin's knowledge of film is acute. His joy of film is acute, and just the pure wattage of Quentin as a human being is extraordinary. And his willingness to accept criticism as well as admiration and not get introverted by it just floors me. I'm so envious of it. I can't find his fear."

So what did Travolta make of Tarantino's deep appreciation of his past work? "How can you not respond to that?" Travolta says. "It was clearly articulated to me what I meant to him growing up and what I meant—in certain performances—to a generation." Travolta lets out a chuckle, then adds: "I realized that Quentin represents how a lot of people feel about me, only now it's OK to say it."

All of this mutual admiration begs a question: when Tarantino first met with Travolta before casting him, did he mention that he had a shrine to the actor? "No," Tarantino says. "But I did bring along my Vinnie Barbarino doll so he could sign it for me."

The success of *Pulp Fiction* tastes sweet to Tarantino. Not so long ago, the most high-profile credit this engagingly intense wannabe could boast was playing an Elvis imitator on an episode of *The Golden Girls.* He made his first splash with *Reservoir Dogs,* a heist film with an unseen heist, and returned a year later as the writer of Tony Scott's underrated *True Romance.* More recently, Tarantino was in the public eye for writing the story that, shall we say, evolved into Oliver Stone's controversy-raising *Natural Born Killers.* He even found the time to help out pal Julia Sweeney (who has a cameo in *Pulp Fiction*) with the movie *It's Pat.*

But for all this activity, Tarantino is definitely not your average Hollywood careerist. Extremely confident yet decidedly unpretentious, he remains very much a fan with strong and exceedingly far-flung tastes. He's the guy who loved Kevin Costner's megaflop *Wyatt Earp.* An avowed *Bay-*

watch watcher Tarantino is happy to ponder the frightening issue of David Hasselhoff's big screen potential. He's also the rare and brave aesthete able to make the qualitative judgment that *Look Who's Talking Too* represented the creative apex of the cinematic Travolta trilogy.

Tarantino's pop-culture freak status has even informed and colored his own performances. In *Reservoir Dogs* he made a memorable appearance as Mr. Brown, arguing passionately with Mr. Pink (Steve Buscemi) over the true meaning of Madonna's "Like a Virgin." Mr. Brown insists that the lyric is "a metaphor for a big dick," while Mr. Pink suggests that the song is about love. Her Blondness settled the matter. "Madonna liked the movie a lot, but she said I'm not right," says Tarantino. "She signed my *Erotica* album: 'Dear Quentin, it's about love, it's not about dick. Madonna.'" In *Sleep With Me*, Tarantino nearly steals the show with a cameo as a party-goer lecturing passionately on the homosexual subtext of *Top Gun*.

Even the Tarantino kitchen — with it's apparent lifetime supply of Yoo Hoo displayed next to a big box of Cap'n Crunch — suggests a sort of glee-fully arrested development. But after some years where he had trouble getting arrested in Hollywood, Tarantino has established himself as a mature and much-in-demand talent. Still, it wasn't long ago that Taran-tino was a clerk toiling at Video Archives, a cineaste-run video store in Manhattan Beach, California. "People ask me if I went to film school," he says. "And I tell them: 'No, I went to films.'" The clerk Christian Slater played in *True Romance* was based on Tarantino's younger days living near the Los Angeles airport. "All day long he just sees people taking off and leaving," says Tarantino. "And he's going nowhere. I'm not that guy any more. That guy is someone who's never had a girlfriend, he's very inexpe-rienced and naive. He's only had failure in his life." In the hands of director Tony Scott (who also happened to direct *Top Gun*), the film became a hyperviolent but highly romantic theme-park ride. "Tony did a great job," he says admiringly. "The movie was really cool. Of course, the whole thing was bizarre for me to see — like watching a big-budget feature of your home movies."

Admiring would not be the word to describe Tarantino's feeling regard-ing what became of his *Natural Born Killers* screenplay, which Oliver Stone chose to substantially rework with his collaborators. Tarantino declined a credit, taking responsibility only inasmuch as the movie was based on a story by him. Bringing up *Killers* is the single easiest way to quiet this otherwise affable chatterbox. Asked if he has seen the film, Tarantino turns strangely silent.

"No," he says, finally.

According to Tarantino, he was invited to a preview screening of *Killers* but declined, saying he would catch it in the theatre. "It's just kind of out there, and it doesn't have anything to do with me," he says after being coaxed to elaborate. "I think people pretty much know that I have distanced myself from the film. I don't think I'll get much credit, and I don't think I'll get much blame. I'm definitely not looking for either. If you like it, then that's Oliver. If you don't like it, that's Oliver, too."

In fact, the release date of *Pulp Fiction*—a film substantially closer to his heart—was pushed back in America by Tarantino, producer Lawrence Bender and Miramax Films, partly to distance it from *Killers*. "At first we were going to open it in August, and at first my attitude was, fuck it, let's open it the same day. But in the end, I don't want that association. I could just see all those double reviews in *Rolling Stone, Time* and *Newsweek*. You know, a photo from it next to a photo from *Pulp*. We'd be forever linked."

Pulp Fiction began with a 500-page first draft. For Tarantino, "the only strange thing about writing *Pulp Fiction* was that, for once, I knew what I was writing was going to get made," he says. "It's not so ethereal anymore. And if it's going to be made, it ought to be worth making. That's a harsh magnifying glass." Certainly, Tarantino bit off a lot with the intricately plotted *Pulp,* a film he early on described as "an anthology about a community of crooks." In writing the film, he says he was influenced by the writings of J. D. Salinger. "When you read his Glass family stories, they all add up to one big story. That was the biggest example for me." Some writer pals advised Tarantino that he might have difficulty following up his *Dogs* debut. "Callie Khouri, who wrote *Thelma and Louise,* and Richard LaGravenese, who wrote *The Fisher King,* both told me I was going to have trouble," he recalls. "Fortunately, it really wasn't that difficult."

Even having the *Pulp* script put in turnaround by TriStar ended up helping Tarantino to make the film for a lean $8 million at Miramax—part of the reason the movie's already out of the red in pre-sales. "I enjoyed making *Pulp* even more than *Dogs* because this time I sort of knew what I was doing," Tarantino says. "Back when we were making *Dogs,* Lawrence and I used to joke that we were the least experienced guys on the set. Because we were. This time around, we'd been there, which made it a lot more fun."

Tarantino has nothing but raves for all the cast, including Harvey Keitel, who makes a dramatic appearance — alongside Tarantino — as The Wolf, a resourceful Mr. Fix-It. This seems to be typecasting, since Keitel proved a savior when he helped kick-start Tarantino's career by signing up to be a reservoir dog.

To hear Tarantino tell it, the hardest part since *Pulp* is getting down to work with all the Hollywood distractions. "A lot of young directors get a little success and turn into phone junkies," he says, with a slight tone of disgust. "All they do is talk. My attitude is, fuck all these phone calls, forget all these meetings, you have work to do! Eighty percent of the people calling you, their job is to make phone calls all day. That's not our job."

On a sunny Hollywood afternoon, Quentin Tarantino is in his natural habitat: the movies. Lately, making them can get in the way of watching them, but this isn't one of those days. This afternoon he's one of the few non-OAPs attending a lunchtime screening of *Mad Love* at the Los Angeles County Art Museum. "I think most of the people here saw it when it came out in 1935," he says. *Mad Love* — later adapted as *The Hands of Oriac* — is a nicely twisted Karl Freund film starring Peter Lorre as a crazed physician who's driven by love to undertake some rather misguided surgery. Tarantino is psyched finally to see it. Somehow he has always missed the film, but he's already well versed in its lore. "The director was the cinematographer of *Metropolis*," he explains excitedly. "And in Pauline Kael's famous essay *Raising Kane,* she claims that this was what the cinematographer Gregg Toland did before *Citizen Kane* to try things out for *Kane* later." He sits back and smiles as the theatre darkens.

After the movie lets out, Tarantino walks out into a blindingly sunny LA day. Over lunch at nearby Johnnie's, a no-frills diner that served as a *Reservoir Dogs* location, he's asked if it's unusual for him to be coming out of a film in the middle of a beautiful day. "Not at all," he says. "I go to movies whenever I can. I mean, I've done a few interviews where people have said they want to hang out with me on an average day and do what I do. And I always think they're waiting for me to take them horseback riding or something. They've got the wrong guy. I go to movies, sometimes more than once a day, and I watch TV with friends. Occasionally, I go to coffee shops. That and work. That's what I do."

This state of affairs is not a recent development. It has pretty much been the same routine since Tarantino grew up in LA's South Bay in the shadow of the International Airport. His parents had already split up when a two-year-old Quentin and his mother, Connie, moved west from Knoxville, Tennessee, where she had been a student. According to Connie, who later remarried, Quentin was already demonstrating an insatiable appetite for movies. "Some people describe me as a permissive mother," she says. "I took Quentin to every movie I saw. I didn't censor his material." Soon, the young auteur's bedroom was beginning to resemble his current apartment. "I kept a pretty tight rein on Quentin in the rest of the house," she says, laughing.

"My mother worked very hard to supply me with a nice house to live in," Tarantino recalls. "We lived in Harbor City, which is middle-class but a little rough." Connie describes the area as upper-middle-class—"even if that doesn't fit in with the rags-to-riches story some people want to tell about him." But she adds that, "even early on, Quentin was drawn to some rough neighborhoods." The attraction, it goes without saying, was the movies.

Young Quentin—who both mother and son agree hated school—had found his refuge. "See, Harbor City's positioned between Torrance, which is an OK neighborhood, and Carson, which is rougher," he explains. "I spent a lot of my time in Carson because that's where the Carson Twin Cinema was. That was the theatre that showed all the kung-fu movies and the Allied International movies like *The Van*. The first time I met Danny DeVito, I said: 'Oh yeah. Danny, you were in *The Van* and *Pom-Pom Girls*.' There was also the Del Amo mall theatre, where all the real Hollywood stuff played, and I went there, too. Basically, I spent my life at the movies.

"I grew up going to the grind houses and to the art houses and loving them both," Tarantino adds. "That sort of defines my aesthetic. I mean, it's not like I'm some arty guy just getting off on myself. Studios are afraid of one thing—that someone's going to make a boring movie. My stuff may not be obvious, but it's not esoteric. I'll never write a movie about sheep herders contemplating God and life."

Tarantino broke into movies professionally as a teenager by ushering porn watchers at the Pussycat Theater in Torrance. He'd already tried his hand at writing his first screenplay, penning something called *Captain Peachfuzz and the Anchovy Bandit*. At 22—around the time he started shooting a never-completed 16mm film called *My Best Friend's Birthday*—he got a much more satisfying and educational job working at Video Archives, a relatively small operation that Tarantino proudly calls "the best video store in the LA area." It was there that he met up with like-minded movie freaks such as fellow clerk Roger Avary, for whose recent directorial debut, *Killing Zoe*, Tarantino served as an executive producer. "Now Video Archives is like LA's answer to the *Cahiers du Cinéma*," Tarantino says with a laugh. "At William Morris they'll be telling agents: 'You've gotta check out the scene at that video store.'

"I basically lived there for years," he continues. "We'd get off work, close up the store, then sit around and watch movies all night. Other times Roger, our friend Scott and I would take a Friday and plot things out so we could see all four new movies we were interested in. We always took whatever we got paid and put it right back into the industry."

"Quentin was always a great talker," Avary recalls. "The difference now is that everybody's listening." At first there was some tension between the two. "We were a little competitive about who knew more about movies," says Avary. "Eventually, we realized that despite being very different people, we had the exact same tastes. It was kismet." Avary—who contributed to the story of *Pulp Fiction*—sees himself and Tarantino as part of a whole new out-of-the-stores-and-on-to-the-screens movement. "Film schools have become completely franchised," Avary says. "There's a fresh generation of filmmakers, and they're coming out of the video stores. All of us have the advantage of a data base of thousands of movies."

Unsurprisingly, then, a few naysaying critics have called Tarantino's work derivative. Some saw *Reservoir Dogs* as borrowing heavily from earlier movies, including Kubrick's *The Killing*. "Generally, I've been treated really well by the press," says Tarantino, who still regrets that famed *New Yorker* critic, Pauline Kael—"one of my biggest influences, my Kingsfield"—retired before *Dogs* came out. "But a few critics have said, ironically enough, that *Dogs* felt like a film-school movie—that it's a film more about movies than about experiences. I don't agree. I think one of the strengths of the film is that it's realistic. It does give you a glimpse into the criminal life. But I like the idea of my films commenting on film itself. A lot of directors I love have done that." Suddenly Tarantino breaks into a wild grin. "And the fact of the matter is, the shots I actually did rip off no one has caught yet.

"Part of the fun of making movies is that you're on ground that's been covered before," he says, "and you can used that as a jumping-off point for all the weird places you want to go. I'm trying to make a combination of a movie movie and a real movie. I want to make movie movies with real consequences."

One consequence of the artful brutality that has marked the movies Tarantino has made so far is the reputation it has earned him — like Peck-inpah before him — as the thinking man's poet of violence. Some audiences still may be having flashbacks to the ear-amputation scene in *Reservoir Dogs*, which Tarantino — a pop-music lover of extremely catholic tastes — played out to the cheerful strains of Stealers Wheel's '70s classic "Stuck In The Middle With You." "It never bothered me when people walked out," Tarantino says. "It just meant that scene worked. Go to a video store, and nine out of ten films in the action section are more graphic than mine. But I'm not interested in making a cartoon. I'm interested in making the violence real."

Still, when Tarantino showed the film early on at a horror festival in Spain — where it followed a splatterfest called *Brain Dead* — he figured he'd found an audience that wouldn't be thrown by the sadism. "So we show the movie, and, like, 15 people walk out during the torture, including [cult horror director] Wes Craven and [horror special-effects artist] Rick Baker," says Tarantino. "Wes Craven — the guy who directed *Last House on the Left* for God's sake — walked out of my movie. Stuart Gordon, the guy who did *Re-Animator*, was one of the judges, and he was burying his head in his hands. It was hysterical." Tarantino later ran into Baker, who told him: "Quentin, I walked out of your movie, but I want you to take it as a compliment. See, we all deal with fantasy. There's no such thing as werewolves or vampires. You're dealing with real-life violence, and I can't deal with it." *Pulp Fiction* offers no shortage of scenes for its exhausted audience to talk about on the way out, including that memorable male S&M rape scene. "Well, *Deliverance* did it," he says. "And there's three butt-fucking scenes in *American Me*. That's the one to beat in that particular category!"

As it turned out, nobody beat *Pulp Fiction* at Cannes. The victory of the Palme d'Or surprised many observers, but not Tarantino himself. "I thought it was in the realm of possibility," he says, smiling. "Basically, it was like no one knew about our movie, then it was like boom! It's like people who really shouldn't know what the Palme d'Or is, they all of a sudden knew that I won. I guess it's sort of like *Sex, Lies and Videotape* just coming out of nowhere. After Cannes was over, I went to Paris to chill out. Let me tell you, when you win the Palme d'Or, don't go to Paris to chill out. Cannes is their Oscars, so everyone was coming up saying: 'You're the American who won the big award.'"

Today, Tarantino—who doesn't have a girlfriend at the moment and who has apparently failed to develop the habit of having torrid affairs with his actresses—says that he wants to take a break. "I've got to take some time to have a life," he says. However, his addiction to cinema runs too deep to allow much time lounging by a pool. Ahead of him is a starring role as Jimmy Destiny in director Jack Barar's *Destiny Turns On the Radio*. After that he'll direct one segment of an anthology movie called *Four Rooms*, which also calls on the talents of Allison Anders, Alexandre Rockwell and Robert Rodriguez.

Tarantino, who was thanked by Kurt Cobain in the liner notes for *In Utero*, seems to be on the verge of turning into a cinematic slacker icon. But his mother—who is boycotting *Natural Born Killers* out of respect for her son—says success hasn't spoiled him yet: "No, I haven't seen any change in Quentin. He's just as self-confident as he's always been."

In terms of the long run, Tarantino explains that he simply wants to stay on the treacherous career path that he has set for himself. "When you look at a career in Hollywood, it seems like there's two roads," he says, as he sits back happily among the clutter of his home. "There's the studio-hack career or the art-film career. They're both dangerous roads. Nobody wants to turn into a hack. But the art-film trip is just as bad because you get lost and start disappearing up your own ass. But there is another road, I think, where the budgets of your film depend on what type of movie you really want to make and that someone might really want to see. All I have to do is stay on that road."

The Boy Wonder's Favorite Films:

RIO BRAVO (1959)
Director: Howard Hawks
Starring: John Wayne, Dean Martin
"When I'm getting serious about a girl, I show her *Rio Bravo* and she better fucking like it."

TAXI DRIVER (1976)
Director: Martin Scorsese

Starring: Robert De Niro, Jodie Foster
Scorsese's classic set the blueprint for Tarantino's fascination with ultra-violence.

BLOW OUT (1981)
Director: Brian De Palma
Starring: John Travolta, Nancy Allen
De Palma is probably Tarantino's favorite director (he cites De Palma's *Casualties of War* as "my favorite war movie"). This, before *Pulp Fiction*, also marked John Travolta's best screen performance.

ABBOTT AND COSTELLO MEET FRANKENSTEIN (1948)
Director: Charles T. Barton
Starring: Bud Abbott, Lou Costello, Bela Lugosi
"When I was a little kid that was my favorite movie of all time. It's not like they make comedy now. The scary parts are really scary and the funny parts are really funny. Frankenstein actually kills people. He throws the nurse through the window, and she's *dead*."

BIG WEDNESDAY (1978)
Director: John Milius
Starring: Jan-Michael Vincent, Gary Busey
"I don't like surfers; I didn't like 'em when I was growing up. I lived in a surfing community, and I thought they were all jerks. I like this movie so much. Surfers don't deserve this movie."

WHERE EAGLES DARE (1969)
Director: Brian G. Hutton
Starring: Richard Burton, Clint Eastwood
"This is my personal favorite guys-on-a-mission movie. I'm gonna do a guys-on-a-mission movie one day."

FANDANGO (1985)
Director: Kevin Reynolds
Starring: Kevin Costner, Judd Nelson
"Kevin Reynolds is going to be the Stanley Kubrick of this decade. *Fandango* is one of the best directorial deubts in the history of cinema. I saw *Fandango* five times at the movie theatre and it only played for a fucking week, all right?"

BREATHLESS (1983)
Director: Jim McBride
Starring: Richard Gere
"Here's a movie that indulges completely all my obsessions — comic books, rockabilly music and movies."

DAYS OF THUNDER (1990)
Director: Tony Scott
Starring: Tom Cruise, Nicole Kidman
"It's like a fucking Sergio Leone movie with cars."

ROLLING THUNDER (1977)
Director: John Flynn
Starring: Willian Devane, Tommy Lee Jones
"Most movies let you down, but this is ass-kicking Nirvana."

Celluloid Heroes

CHRIS WILLMAN / 1995

IN 1994, IT SEEMED, you might have been classified as either a *Forrest Gump* person or a *Pulp Fiction* person, just as once upon a time you might have been asked whether you were a Beatles person or a Stones person. This was the year's Rorschach that presumably would determine whether you tended toward naughty or nice.

And these were the two pictures that, above all others, captured America's adult imagination in the last year. With both sleepers-cum-smashes up for many of the same crucial Oscar categories, it was easy to posit some sort of moral competition, *Gump*'s triumph of dumb virtue being pitted against *Pulp*'s wages of venality.

Their directors, Robert Zemeckis and Quentin Tarantino, will have none of this handy polarization. They will, if prompted, point out that their pictures have as much in common as not: a hugely ironic sphere of reference; sudden, shocking shifts in tone between comedy and tragedy; a kind of epic-scale intimacy, and a sensibility steeped in the quirky dialects and rhythms of real life, but also informed by a century of all the razzle and dazzle the big screen has to offer.

With that in mind, the *Times* asked Tarantino and Zemeckis — real film *fans* as well as makers — to get together and interview each other about nothing more or less than "the movies." They did, gladly. Tarantino showed up at Zemeckis' office on a hot afternoon with a bottle of champagne in a bucket of ice, and Zemeckis supplied the sushi. (There were no chocolates or Royales with cheese in sight.)

Not very long ago, Tarantino, 32, was just another young rank-and-file fan of Zemeckis, 42—and, charmingly, still acted like it; the elder director wasn't above gushing in turn over his upstart Oscar competitor's preternaturally accomplished auteurism. Mostly, though, these excerpts show, they unpretentiously shared some common crushes, two guys who really did (per Pauline Kael) lose it at the movies.

Zemeckis' and Tarantino's conversation began with the usual what've-you-been-up-to's. Tarantino mentioned that he was planning to executive-produce a picture that pal Robert Rodriguez will direct, from an old script of Tarantino's, a vampire film to be titled *From Dusk Till Dawn*. Coincidentally enough, it turned out, Zemeckis also has some old bloodsuckers he's dusting off.

ZEMECKIS: Actually, the very first script that I wrote with Bob Gale is being made. And it's a vampire movie, *Bordello of Blood*.
TARANTINO: No kidding! Really?
RZ: Yeah, we're making it as a *[Tales from the] Crypt* movie.
QT: Now, did Brian De Palma use your title? Was that a homage to you, in *Blow Out*? That's one of the horror films that John Travolta is doing the sound on.
RZ: It wasn't a homage; he stole it. *[amazed]* Now, do you see all that background stuff when you watch movies, or do you just see 'em so many times. . . .
QT: I tend to notice stuff like that. And I do see 'em a bunch of times. But actually, *Bordello of Blood* stands out. If I just saw the movie once, I would probably remember that. I always pay attention when they have a title for a nonexistent movie in a movie. Because they always have it too outlandish; it never sounds like a real title.

I thought one of the first victories I ever had in that regard was in *True Romance*. The name of the Vietnam movie that the cocaine dealer was the producer of was a thing called *Coming Home in a Body Bag.* And I thought, that's cool! See, I'd go see that!

RZ: Favorite movie lists are impossible for me to do.
QT: I've now got it broken down to my top three. One is *Rio Bravo.*
RZ: I *love* that movie.
QT: I adore that movie. And *Taxi Driver,* and Brian De Palma's *Blow Out,* which we were just talking about.
RZ: Really?
QT: Yeah, I love *Blow Out* I really, really do. He's one of my very favorite directors. I always thought that was his best movie.

One of the things that really cracks me up in that is, De Palma had been working for a while on *Prince of the City* which he was going to do with John Travolta. And then they took it away from him and hired Sidney Lumet. And he's got that great sequence in the middle of *Blow Out* where you find out that what Travolta did before he was a sound man was wiring people for a committee to stop corruption on the police force, and they have a flashback to it — and it's just like De Palma got the chance to do, like, a few seconds of the material that he put together on *Prince of the City!*

But I've actually always said that one of my favorite movies of the '70s was *Used Cars* [a Zemeckis film that actually came out in 1980].
RZ: Really? Did you see it when it came out?
QT: I saw it in a drive-in. I absolutely adored it. It's one of my favorite comedies of the last 20 years. And when I say that, you have to understand that when you work at a video store for five years and you have a favorite comedy, you get to *know* the movie.

We always put on *Used Cars* and watched it as we were working. It was like putting on a record album. There's quite a few comedies that we knew every line of dialogue. It becomes part of your vocabulary. Whenever the appropriate moment comes, you can just say, "Well, what do you want to do, put roller skates on those boys?" [*laughter*]
RZ: You know, I've got to tell you, of all the movies that I've made, that's the movie that people compliment me the most on. And when that movie came out, I was so disappointed, because it wasn't even released in half the nation. It just dribbled out. There was no real distribution plan at the studio. But what amazes me is how many people, at the end of the decade, have seen the movie.

QT: It was so much different before video. Now some movies that didn't do so well have entered the consciousness completely, even as little as five years later. I always had a theory that if they had ever done a sequel to *Buckaroo Banzai*—not now, but four years or so after the first release—that film could've done really well, because by then a lot of America knew who Buckaroo Banzai was!

I had a theory about what I hoped would happen with *Pulp Fiction*. I had had some success overseas with *Reservoir Dogs,* and people talked a lot about it, but in America it did art-house business. And then *True Romance* came out and didn't do that well, and I remember thinking, "Oh my God, I guess what I do doesn't get a large audience. I guess that's that."

But with *Pulp Fiction,* I knew we would make our money and do OK for-eign-wise—but I *hoped* that by the time it came out, anyone even remotely inclined to like my stuff probably would have seen *Reservoir Dogs* on video after three years. I was hoping that the ticket sales when *Reservoir Dogs* came out were not a correct judgment of my audience now.

RZ: I'm in a constant conflict about having to make a movie for the big and the small screen at the same time, stylistically. So I just basically make it for the large screen. And I actually have a hard time watching videotapes at all. I can only watch laser discs now. Because it's getting that I can't stand . . .

QT: The pan-and-scan?

RZ: And just the degradation of the image.

QT: I feel the exact same way. Except if I'm looking at an old exploita-tion film that I have on videotape, that doesn't bother me, because more than likely, when you were having the theatrical experience on that, it was with a one-light projector anyway, and a big hole in the screen. [laughter]

RZ: But you don't get the experience of the wine bottle rolling down underneath the seats.

QT: No, you don't have that. And you don't have the audience going "*Yes!* Punch him again! Blow his head off!" It's funny, though, because while I'm so almost sanctimonious about the whole theatrical experience, it was after I'd made my first movie and I saw how in actual fact it's the *projectionists* who have the final cut—after I had my film screwed up by lame projectionists—that I actually started really appreciating that laser disc. That there'll be one thing that exists where all the reel changes work and the print is good and I approved the color timing on it. From beginning to end, it's gonna be a good showing.

R Z : The other thing that I'm wondering about is, I have a 9-year-old son, and when he was really small, he would watch videotapes over and over and over again. And so do all the kids that we know. And you don't know why they're so infatuated with a certain cartoon or whatever it is. We all talk about how we grew up with television. But imagine if when you were 3 and 4 years old, you watched a particular movie 50 times, and nothing else, over and over again?

Q T : We never had an opportunity.

R Z : Of course. No one ever did.

Q T : When I worked in a video store, I heard parents complain about that, and they'd get mad at their children in the store: "You've seen that already! Try something new!" And I would take on the psychology of the kid. Where the children are coming from, they're not *blasé* about the movie experience. They're [thinking], "Well, why should I try something that I might not like? I *know* I'm gonna like *that*!" And it actually makes me wish I could be them in a way, that you could watch a movie 14, 15 times in a row—and they laugh through it every time!

Tell me if you ever had this thought when you were a kid when you went to the movies. My dad took me to *It's a Mad, Mad, Mad, Mad World*. We missed the first 15 minutes of it, so we stayed to see the first 15 minutes of the next show. And I remember consciously thinking to myself, "You mean, for the same price of admission, they just keep showing them over and over again? Well, when I'm an adult and I go to the movies, I'm gonna watch it *four* times!" It didn't seem crazy to me, when I was a kid.

R Z : But I did that, and I remember the movie. It was *Swiss Family Robinson*.

Q T : [shouting] I did it on *Swiss Family Robinson* too!

R Z : I sat all day in that movie theater and just watched it, because I thought that was the coolest way to live your life, to be shipwrecked and live in a treehouse and kill a bunch of pirates. . . . So that was the same experience, but, having the video, it's much more extreme.

R Z : So would you ever consider directing something you didn't write?

Q T : I'm sure I will eventually, but right now I'm just too comfortable— but I think comfortable in a good way—doing my own stuff. Was it a big deal when you finally did somebody else's script?

RZ: No, it wasn't a big deal. I found myself being a lot more open to other people's suggestions. Because when someone would say, "What color should we paint that door?" and I had written it, it was like, "Well, it's gotta be red, of course! It's obvious!" But of course it wasn't obvious to the department head. But when you do somebody else's material, you say, "Well, let's talk about this." I found that directing other people's scripts improved my writing.

QT: The only movie that I've seen in the last couple of years where I thought, "If I had been offered that screenplay, I might have done that," was *Hero*, written by David Peoples, who did *Unforgiven*.

RZ: Huh! That's interesting.

QT: Not that Stephen Frears did a bad job, but I would have tackled it in a different way. So far, it's the only one, when I think back on all the films I've seen in the last few years, that might have made me take the bite of the apple. I don't want to criticize the movie, but something about the cleverness of the screenplay inspired me, and I thought, "Oh, I would have gone this way with that, where he went that way."

RZ: Right, right. Did you ever get the screenplay and read it?

QT: No, I'm dying to. I remember when I met John Milius. See, one of my favorite screenplays of all time is *The Life and Times of Judge Roy Bean*...

RZ: It's the greatest. Now *there's* a movie that I would've made different [than the version John Huston made].

QT: I know, exactly, you can't help but feel the movie was made with the guy's left hand, compared to what was on the paper. But the thing is, saying it's one of my favorite screenplays was based on the *movie* that I saw.

RZ: Oh, really?

QT: And then Milius told me how different it was, and then I read it, and it was just like, whoa! It's hard for me to even look at that movie now. But yet, when I saw the movie, John's [Milius'] voice just sung like an opera singer.

RZ: Yeah. Just like you can hear John's voice in *Jeremiah Johnson*, it's in there. That is a brilliant, brilliant screenplay.

The last movie where I saw the movie and had to read the screenplay was *JFK*. Because the movie was *so* different and exhilarating, I had to see whether this was something that was constructed in the editing room. And what was of course amazing was that it was all in the script.

QT: Speaking of *JFK*, I had a very interesting experience, because apparently, Oliver Stone's initial idea was to have an intermission in the middle of the movie, just the way they used to do in the '60s. Then I met him and was talking to him about it: "So, you didn't do the intermission idea." He goes, "Yeah, if you do it, just know that you're throwing money *away,* because it's costing you major show times."

Well, I saw it with an intermission. I saw it in Holland. And in the city of Amsterdam, every movie has an intermission. *L.A. Story, Camp Nowhere,* they all had intermissions in the middle—well, you *hope* in the middle—of them.

RZ: You ever see a movie in Mexico? They have one between every reel change!

QT: Are you serious?

RZ: Every 20 minutes they stop the movie and then vendors walk up and down and sell you stuff in the theater. [*laughter*] I never knew they put an intermission in in Amsterdam. So where'd they put it in *JFK?*

QT: They put it where I would guess would be where Oliver Stone wanted it, right in the middle. The movie was *even better* with an intermission. It was so terrific. The first half of the movie played, and there was this big emotional moment. It felt like a '60s intermission. And then you go outside, and all the people that are in the theater are drinking coffee and buying ice cream, and you're sitting there assimilating all the information you've taken in for the first half of the movie. You have about 10 minutes to do that. Then you go back in, then the rest of the drama starts. I mean, it was *perfect.*

QT: You actually said something in *Film Comment* that I wanted to talk to you about, because I totally agree with you. One of the things that I'm considering doing, of the dancing projects in my head, is the genre that I call World War II Movie—Bunch of Guys on a Mission. Thinking about intermission made me think about it, because I was watching the laser disc of *Where Eagles Dare,* which is my favorite of the Bunch-of-Guys-on-a-Mission movies.

RZ: Isn't that the one where Clint Eastwood kills more guys than anybody else in movie history?

QT: He's the Terminator in that movie. He has no other personality, other than that he's killing people all the time!

R Z : Of course, the Terminator didn't kill anybody. Well, in the second one.

Q T : Just shot them in the kneecaps so they can't walk right ever again.... No, Eastwood would just stand at the top of the stairs and wait for the Nazis to congregate, and then mow them down!

But it was great, because in that *Film Comment* article, you're questioning: "I love that type of movie—can it still be done?" And my thinking on it is, I *think* so. Simply because I think there's been so much focus on the victims of World War II—and not ignoring any of that, but that's where we've been for so long—I think it could be considered a breath of fresh air to get back into that kind of adventure story where you've got the *greatest villains ever.*

R Z : Right. Well my concern is that the Vietnam War screwed up the World War II genre, because war movies of any kind can't be fun anymore, because war is presented, as it probably should be, as this ugly, horrible thing. Nowadays, if you did *The Dirty Dozen,* I don't know if you could have most of the guys get killed and not have it be this heart-wrenching thing.

Q T : I think you can, and I'll tell you why. Could you make a fun movie about a famous battle in World War II or any war now? Possibly not, though you could make it an *exciting* movie. But could you make what we were talking about—potboiler movies? If you're going to do a *Von Ryan's Express* or [*The*] *Great Escape* or [*The*] *Guns of Navarone* kind of thing. I think it could be done. Because it's about The Mission. So it's not just the futility of war.

And the fatalities that happen, I actually think that's part of the staple of the genre, that they one by one are gonna start dying. I never liked it when they all just got away scot-free at the end of it. Because you want that pain, of the ones that died and the ones that survived, and trying to figure out who that was gonna be.

I guess the way I would do it would be try to do what I've done with my characters and their dialogue in the crime films that I've done, and just try to bring that over to men in war.

R Z : Right. And have'em speak the way they probably really spoke, instead of saying lines like "Pipe down, you foul-ups!" [*much mutual laughter*]

Q T : "OK, you goldbrickers!"

R Z : "C'mon you goldbrickers, let's get a move on here! Get the lead out!"

There's probably some obscure World War II movie that I haven't seen, but I just *devour* World War II movies.

QT: Really? I didn't know that! See, I would imagine that if I were to ask
you, "Who are some of your favorite directors?," Frank Tashlin would be
who I would think would be one of your favorites....

For me and my friends, you were always one of our favorite comedy
directors. At one of the market research screenings that you had for *Who
Framed Roger Rabbit*, in Redondo Beach, a friend of mine went. He's both a
cartoon fan and a comedy film fan. He's kind of a big guy, and he was driving a moped to the theater, and he said he was in the parking lot
unlocking his moped afterward, and then, he recognized you.

RZ: I know what this story is! Go ahead.

QT: We were such fans of your work, and he had to tell you. And he said
he got on the moped and just made a beeline right toward the group of
people, and here's this crazed guy barreling toward you out of the blue
at midnight, just so he could say, "Keep up the good work!" [*hysterical
laughter*]

RZ: I thought we were gonna get killed! I remember exactly. I was standing there with my agent, doing the debriefing of the evening, and all of a
sudden there's this roar and this headlight, and I thought some dis-
gruntled moviegoer was gonna run me over! Was that him? I remember
that distinctly! I think I jumped 10 feet.

Right, right. I have a story like that. I saw one of the early previews of
Jaws at the Dome...

QT: Oh really? At the *Dome*? Oh my God, wow.

RZ: Before it came out. And I had known Spielberg, and I was so blown
away by that movie. It's one of the greatest movies ever made. And there
was so much publicity about the mechanical shark, remember? And it was
just so filmic and terrifying, and I was so wildly in love with the movie,
because Steven was able to create this terror without showing the shark. I
loved that so much that I was nervous that, when it came time at the end
to show the shark, it was going to look mechanical. And then when the
shark ate Robert Shaw, it was done so brilliantly that I applauded in the
theater.

Cut to the next day. I came into Steven's office to congratulate him, and
he hadn't been there that night, but they had taped the audience reaction
for him. And I was going on and on about how the movie's great, and he
said, "Yeah, but I'm a little upset. When Robert Shaw got eaten by the
shark, somebody was *applauding*!" I said, "No, that was me!" [*shouting*] He

said, "It was *you*? But weren't you sad that Robert Shaw got eaten?" I said, "Yes, I was! But it was done so great! It's not like I had any problem with the Robert Shaw character!"

ΩT: *[laughing]* It was just, cinematically, you had to go bravo!

By this point in the conversation, the champagne and cumulative effect of decades of moviegoing seemed to have collectively kicked in. Tarantino, who had started the meeting at a zealous pitch, was now even more in hyperdrive, and the much lower-key Zemeckis had slowly but surely taken to enthusiastically shouting much of his end of the conversation, too. Sometime deep into the mutual reverie on *Jaws*, personal assistants conspired to pull them apart. But before they did, reporter Chris Willman entered the directors' hermetically sealed environment to ask them to comment directly on each other's pictures, and whether they might not make a decent double-bill after all.

CALENDAR: *People naturally have set your movies up as points of polarization, but do you think there are points of commonality? After the Oscar nominations were announced, Quentin was quoted as saying* Gump *was comedically in the same ballpark as* Pulp.

ΩT: They've been making such a tremendous deal about the fact that, "Oh wow, *Forrest Gump* is the exact opposite of what *Pulp Fiction* is," and vice versa. But I don't see them as being as drastically different or right and left. If you're familiar with Bob's work, actually there's a tremendous amount of acid running through it. I actually think it's a black comedy.

RZ: Well, I think that some of the black comedy and the tragedy *and* the irony in *Forrest Gump* is what makes it palatable to a larger segment of the audience, because it's not a melodramatic, saccharine story. It's balanced. It's got very emotional and moving moments in it, and it's got some very, very dark and fun moments in it as well.

ΩT: To me, when I was watching the movie, the moving moments and the touching moments, they are meant to be moving and touching, and they are. But the comedy element running through there—subversive is the wrong word—but there is a big edge to it. A movie about *that* guy as the No. 1 guy of America of the last 20 years has got a bite.

RZ: I think that's why the two films have found large audiences: Because they're not just the manipulation or moving of one emotion. And I think that's what audiences want to experience: They don't want to know that they're just gonna be in a laugh riot, or that they're just gonna see gore and nothing else. Hitchcock was always doing that. I mean, I'm not comparing us to the master, but if you look at the movies that you love, he was always releasing the tension with humor...

QT (to Zemeckis): OK. Now if you owned a video store, what section would you put *Forrest Gump* in?

RZ: You know what, I can't answer that. I don't know. Comedy? Drama? Adventure? They should have a video store section that's unclassifiable movies.

QT: I was thinking, if I was working at the video store, I would imagine my boss would put it in the drama section, and I'd be making fun of him for doing that, saying, "People might look for it in the drama section, but you should make a *stand* and put it in the comedy section!"

For any video store owners out there, when *Pulp Fiction* comes out, I want it in the comedy section! If I come in and *Pulp Fiction* is in the drama section, that'll be the last time I go into *your* closed-minded video store!

RZ: Well, would you put *Pulp Fiction* in the action section?

QT: There's not that much action in it!

RZ: See, but you know, you can understand why they would put it in there—

QT: Oh, I can totally see.

RZ: —because they would think it's like a caper movie.

QT: See, one of the things that I think about both of the two movies is the fact that, whether you like them or not—and both of our movies are movies you either embrace or you put at arm's length—when you saw them, you saw a *movie*. You've had a night at the movies; you've gone this way and that way and up and down. And it wasn't just one little tone that we're working to get right—

RZ: —over and over and over for 90 minutes. It's trying to weave something a little more dense. And I think that with the amount of images and information that people are bombarded by, it's not a problem. They can assimilate this, and enjoy it. And I think that's the level of density that modern stories have to have.

CALENDAR: Conversely, *Pulp* might be said to have some of the—for lack of a better term—"life-affirming" elements that most people think *Forrest Gump* stands for. Albeit in, uh, smaller doses.

RZ: Yeah, well—redemption! In its own way, it's a redemption story.

QT: That's not a drum that I'm necessarily trying to bang, and as a writer, I'm never out trying to get a message across. But I feel that in my heart. I never said, "I'm gonna write a redemption story." But if I'm writing this big passel of characters and weaving it in, that's what ended up coming out, because that's what I really believe in.

But it is different when you don't set your mind that that's the tune you're gonna play for the next two hours. All the notes end up adding up to that tune. I think it's very meaningful that Jules [the character played by Samuel L. Jackson] comes to that. At the end of the movie, for all the talk about the film being violent and this, that and the other, the guy who actually becomes the lead character after the movie's over with is a killer who has a religious epiphany! And it's played straight. It's not a big joke. That's supposed to be meaningful—and not in a sanctimonious way.

But when you try to do it and not make fun of it but yet not be self-serious about it, some people get it, some people don't, some people misread it—but in a way that's kind of cool, and that's one of the things I like about it, actually. And I think you can say the same thing about the Forrest Gump character.

RZ: Well, the way I like to describe it—I think for both movies—is, you have to bring a little something to the party.

Four X Four

PETER BISKIND/1995

CHECK INTO THE FOUR ROOMS hotel, and you'll discover what happens when four of the hottest independent directors around test their friendship by making a movie together.

Four Rooms is an unusual experiment in collective filmmaking. It was made by Allison Anders, Alexandre Rockwell, Robert Rodriguez, and Quentin Tarantino. Each directed a "room" in a fictional hotel, and all four collaborated on a wraparound story featuring a bellhop, played by Tim Roth, who appears in every room.

PREMIERE: *Anthology films rarely work. Why did you want to torture your-selves?*

QUENTIN TARANTINO: The funnest thing about doing it is to do a movie that, one, doesn't take that long to do, and, two, the weight of the world isn't riding on it. If they like your story, great, and if they don't, too fuckin' bad.

ROBERT RODRIGUEZ: I love short films. *Desperado* is like a series of short films. Most of my room is setup, until the last five minutes when it builds to a tremendous pace that you can't ever sustain in a feature film.

ALLISON ANDERS: It's exciting when you're just starting to make films, and you first learn about the French New Wave or New German Cinema — those guys all hung out together and they made films together and they were all part of a time. Filmmakers, especially young filmmakers, really

From *Premiere,* November 1995. Reprinted by permission of *Premiere* and the author.

want to belong to something. We were all sort of the Sundance Class of '92 and '93.

PREMIERE: *What are the stories about in* Four Rooms*?*
ANDERS: There were not really any rules, except that all the action had to take place in a hotel room on New Year's Eve, and we had to use the bellhop. We called him Ted. I wanted to put chicks in my room. I was, like, They're in a bad—no, they're a bunch of midwives. No, no, no. Finally, it was, like, They're a coven! And what do they need out of Ted? What do I need? Sperm! I found myself writing this story about how they're trying to resurrect this goddess who was turned to stone 40 years earlier because she was cursed on their wedding night, before she could give her virginity. And I had just turned 40. I was raped when I was young and I was never able to give my virginity. So for me, it became this incredibly heavy thing that I hadn't even realized.
ALEXANDRE ROCKWELL: Mine is kind of a weird psychodrama. It's like *Days of Our Lives* on crack or something. I once heard a story about how Sean Penn tied Madonna up on New Year's Eve, so the idea is, a jealous husband with a gun ties up his wife.
RODRIGUEZ: I figured Quentin and Alex would be really dramatic. So I thought I'd go the other way, do a family comedy.

PREMIERE: *Quentin, your story, about an out-of-control star and his entourage, has personal overtones, doesn't it?*
TARANTINO: The character started off being comical, because I thought I could play a character like that really well, and then he ended up shouldering some of my own baggage as—for want of a better word—a celebrity. I am totally teeming with anticipation about how people are gonna react. The media is fucking sick of me. It's never been more evident than in reading the reviews of *Desperado*. Because every review—I think I'm really funny in that movie, I think I kick ass in that scene—is not about me being bad, but "We're sick of this guy. We just don't wanna see his face anymore." They're not gonna give me a break for another couple of years on this. They almost resent the fact that I want to act. Until I keep doing it and doing it and shoving it down their throats, then maybe they'll look at it for what it is. I just got through reading three, count 'em, three, biographies of my life. It's a peyote-like experience. They're

questioning my character—I'm really a bad person, I've fucked all the Video Archive guys, Roger Avary is the true genius behind all my work. All these questions about what an asshole I've become, what do I do? I come out with a movie where I play an asshole! I play more or less myself in the worst light I could.

PREMIERE: *What was the most difficult thing about making the movie?*
ROCKWELL: In the beginning, it was pretty much Allison and me, because Robert was doing *Desperado* and Quentin was doing publicity for *Pulp Fiction*. But no one wanted to make a decision without Quentin's approval. And here I was, one of the executive producers, and if I wanted to have a toothpick or a coffee cup in the lobby, there would be this "We'd better check with Quentin." I would find myself negotiating with Quentin's third assistant. But when I finally got through to Quentin, it was fine.

PREMIERE: *Quentin almost dropped out at the very last minute?*
ROCKWELL: I had knee surgery, major reconstruction, and I'm lying in bed with a machine moving my knee. I was high as a kite on a morphine derivative, and I get this phone call. It was Allison. She said, "Guess what? Quentin's backing out!" It was one week before she had to start shooting. "Why?" "He's just totally overstressed. He told me, 'I'm just not excited about it and I don't want to do something I'm not excited about.'" I said, "You know what? He can't back out. That just not one of the choices. If he checks that box, I'm going to get a gun and shoot him, and then he'll experience violence firsthand. He won't have to watch it in a John Woo movie." Allison appealed to his sense of loyalty. And humiliated and embarrassed him. Very good motivators. So next time I saw him, he was, like, "You know what? I was riding on the airplane and I read it again, and I really started getting excited about it again."

PREMIERE: *When you saw the rough cut for the first time, what was your reaction?*
ROCKWELL: I'm the last guy you want to go to a rough cut with. I wanted to jump out of a window afterward. We all went out to Denny's in LA, and we're sitting there ordering taco pizzas or sloppy joes and huge RC Colas. I said, "Well, personally, I think the movie really sucked." It was more than two and a half hours long, at least 45 minutes too long. Robert's

was the tightest, 24 minutes, but I felt the rest of our stuff was unbearably long. Quentin said, "No way, man, come on. We all just have to go back and rethink this thing." Allison was second-guessing herself, and she's really self-critical. It's a female thing. She's like a human mood ring. With Quentin you know exactly what he's thinking, but you don't know exactly what he's feeling. Robert is the extreme opposite of Allison. You never know what Robert is thinking or feeling. You can't tell if someone shot his dog. If he tells you anything, it's in a very curt sentence, like "It's too long."

PREMIERE: *Why didn't you turn over your room to someone else to edit?*
RODRIGUEZ: Editing is too subjective. If Alex had turned his picture over to me to cut down, I would've cut it my way, which wouldn't necessarily be right for the film or for his style. In my room, there are 600 cuts in twenty minutes. Quentin's room has three cuts in the first ten minutes. If someone else is telling you to cut something down, you end up with something that's not really yours, and not really all theirs.

PREMIERE: *What was Miramax's attitude?*
ROCKWELL: The biggest challenge to our friendship and the feeling of goodwill about the film was less about ourselves and more about the powers that be. I'm not pointing a finger and saying they tried to divide us. It's just—that's their job. This is a comedy. Put yourself in the shoes of the distributors. You're saying, "A comedy should run about 90 minutes, 100 minutes or something." They're saying, "we want you to cut it." You really couldn't cut Robert's, it's like a comic strip. I don't think Robert has changed a frame since his rough cut. Quentin shot his in long takes so it's hard to cut his. So the pressure was building on me and Allison. Look, I love Quentin's work and Robert's work and Allison's work—but the bottom line is, I have to rally my troops around my film. I said to Bob and Harvey [Weinstein, who run Miramax], "Well, okay, everyone is going to do some cutting right?" And Harvey and Bob crack up and say, "Who's going to tell Quentin he has to cut?" Harvey says, "Well I'll tell him Alex is cutting, but then he's going to think he can add the minutes to his room."

PREMIERE: *Was it hard to criticize Quentin?*
ANDERS: Quentin at one point wanted to direct one last piece, the very last piece in the movie. And I said no. He asked why. I said, "Because I

wrote it. It's the end of my story, even though it comes at the end of the end credits." He was, like, "Well, so what?" And I said, " 'So what?' What do you mean, 'So what?' " And he said, "You know, you're always saying we're like a band, like the Beatles, where everyone bickers—'No, I want to sing lead,' 'No, I want to sing lead'—and just makes one record and then splits up." And I said, "Well, there are other kinds of bands that make one hit and disappear like the Buckinghams, where everybody kisses each other's ass." And he said, "Well, I would like a little more of the ass-kissing model right now." And I said, "Yeah, as long as it's your ass being kissed." I won that one.

PREMIERE: *Will the pressure of "making it" corrupt you all, destroy your friendships?*
ROCKWELL: I was sitting there talking to Quentin about how you have to protect your integrity. Look at the '70s. Hollywood co-opted a lot of those directors. A lot of friends stopped being friends. A lot of people lost their visions. Sean Penn once asked Brian De Palma, "What is it with you guys? What happened?" And Brian said, "Well, after a while people start to second-guess you so much that their voices get inside your head, and you start second-guessing yourself. And once you do that, you can't do anything right." So I said to Quentin, "Believe me, they're going to descend on you like wolves on meat," which, you know, they did. Quentin was looking at me, like, So? I felt like a shmuck. I thought, Oh my God, I'm Mr. Paranoid New York. And here's Mr. That's a Great Opportunity for Me LA—he relishes the challenge of being a pop figure in the middle of the pop cycle.

PREMIERE: *Was it all worth it? Would you do it again?*
ANDERS: Even if we had failed and ended up hating each other's guts, we tried something that had not been done. But, of course, we all feel like the movie works as a film, and that our friendships are actually much better as a result of having gone through this together.
TARANTINO: I don't know. The big problem in making a movie like this is that as far as audiences are concerned, it's a popularity contest: who did the best one, who did the worst. Which is not where we were coming from. I won't do it again right away. I don't want to do anything right away. Anyhow, we're all still friends, better friends than when we started.

Interview: Quentin Tarantino

J. HOBERMAN/1996

HAS SUCCESS SPOILED QUENTIN Tarantino? Not since Steven
Spielberg made *Jaws* and *Close Encounters* back to back has an American
director uncorked anything comparable to the one-two punch of *Reservoir
Dogs* and *Pulp Fiction*. What's more, the self-taught, thoroughly attitudi-
nous 32-year-old filmmaker has rewritten the formula for Hollywood
success. The only child of a teenage single mother who brought him up
while putting herself through college, high-school dropout Tarantino per-
sonifies American independence — or, at least, the new face of American
independent movies.

Tarantino, who grew up in Los Angeles and wanted to star in movies
since childhood, has invented a style we might call "talk-talk, bang-
bang" — an actor-driven shoot'em-up in which each character has a rap or
a riff, if not a full-fledged theory of life. The language is as calculatedly
brutal and as much a tour de force as the action — full of baroque racial
invective as well as continual profanity. "Being the baddest-assed guy in
the room isn't necessarily a noble ambition," Tarantino says, although he's
clearly enjoying his reign as king of the wild frontier. The past year has
brought a flood of faux Tarantino movies from both Hollywood and the
independent sector — from every place but the man himself. Since com-
pleting *Pulp Fiction* in early 1994, Tarantino has directed only an episode of
ER and a 25-minute segment of the anthology film *Four Rooms*, while

From *US*, January 1996, pp. 54, 56–59. Reprinted by permission of *US* Magazine Company,
L.P. 1996, and the author.

appearing, sometimes quite briefly, in *Sleep With Me, Destiny Turns On the Radio, Desperado* and next month's *From Dusk Till Dawn,* directed from a Tarantino script by fellow indie Robert Rodriguez (*El Mariachi, Desperado*).

Filmmaker as rock star, celebrity as pop-culture connoisseur, Tarantino has redefined the essence of Hollywood cool (to use one of his favorite words). Only six years ago, he was turning the customers of the Manhattan Beach, California, emporium Video Archives on to the films of Eric Rohmer. These days, Tarantino's good friend Steven Spielberg is giving him career advice, and perhaps vice versa. Sylvester Stallone has dinner with Tarantino; Pauline Kael sends him an inscribed copy of her published movie reviews.

"It seems to me that people should be patting me on the back and giving me cigars because I have not started thinking about myself in the third person," Tarantino says. He still drives the red Geo he bought after his first script sale and maintains a relationship with his longtime girlfriend, Grace Lovelace, an instructor and Ph.D. candidate at the University of California at Irvine. Tarantino lives modestly in a pleasant, if cluttered, West Hollywood garden apartment—a trove of movie posters, movie board games and movie action figures that suggests an imploded, funky version of the night spot where John Travolta and Uma Thurman go dancing in *Pulp Fiction.* The fact that it's the same apartment Travolta rented when he came to L.A. to make *Welcome Back, Kotter* only enhances its historic luster.

No less than his characters, Tarantino is full of opinions at our first meeting—all the more for being primed with many cups of coffee served at an appropriately seedy Thai joint on Sunset Boulevard. When I see him next, in his apartment—the morning after he and Rodriguez have taken in a midnight screening of John Woo's *Bullet in the Head*—he is no less effusive, listing Rodriguez among the three best directors who edit their own footage, after Soviet montage master Sergei Eisenstein and skinflick pioneer Russ Meyer. Be that as it may, listening to Tarantino talk, watching him pace and gesture to make his points, you figure he has to be one of the three best directors in history at pitching a story.

To spend time with Tarantino is to observe the violence of his own imagination as well as to appreciate that, more than anything else, this artist is a spinner of tall tales. There's a sense in which Tarantino's ascension—a legend burnished by three quickie biographies, all published this past fall—is his own greatest whopper. Act 2 begins with the hero on top of the world wondering, perhaps, how it happened. "He's smart," says

Rodriguez. "He's waiting to feel what the next thing is. He's not like me—I just jump right into the next project. It comes to him in a different way."

Devotees of *Pulp Fiction* need consider the possibility that Quentin Tarantino may never make another movie like it again. But then, success has made it possible for Tarantino to be Tarantino—not least, on the screen. This 6-foot-2 man-child is still growing. If there's anyone who can top *Pulp Fiction*...

J. HOBERMAN: *Tell me about* From Dusk Till Dawn.
QT: Me and George Clooney play brothers, Seth and Richie Gecko. I'm a complete live wire, but I'm very much his little brother. I'm psychotic. During the course of the movie, I rape and kill an old lady—I have my reasons. I've just broken Seth out of jail, and we're trying to get to Mexico, and on the way we rob a bank. We kill Texas Rangers, we kill civilians. So, it's like everybody is after us now. The FBI and the *federales* are waiting for us in Mexico. The way we decide to get across the border is to find a family in a motorboat, and it's Harvey Keitel, who's an ex-preacher who lost his faith, and his daughter, Juliette Lewis.

JH: *Hmm.*
QT: We take over the motorboat! We take over the family! We get across the border, and then we go to our rendezvous, which is this Mexican titty bar, and, much to our surprise, find out that the bar is a haven for vampires!

JH: *Did you write Richie's part for yourself?*
QT: Not really.

JH: *Did you think of some other actor or a type?*
QT: I really wasn't visualizing anybody. I wrote an exploitation film. It's a head-banging horror film for horror-film lovers! It's not a horror film for people who never go see horror films. Probably the horror fans will see it six times. I would [*laughs*].

JH: *You're in a position now to write roles for yourself.*
QT: Yeah. I want to adapt [Elmore Leonard's] *Killshot*, but I don't necessarily want to direct. There are two parts that would be terrific for me and Harvey Keitel.

JH: *Are you working on a script?*

QT: I play around in a notebook. I'll write out titles or characters or just kind of explore ideas—make little posters.

JH: *Where did you get the idea for the adrenaline shot to the heart that brings Uma Thurman out of her heroin overdose in* Pulp Fiction?

QT: Every junkie in the world has their own version of that story. An old junkie trick is to do the same thing with salt water.

JH: *Were you ever in that kind of scene?*

QT: I have a lot of different friends who've done f---ing everything. I've never taken heroin myself.

JH: *How did you direct Uma Thurman to respond to the injection?*

QT: What I had in mind was that we stab her, and then she just— voom!—bolts up! It took another turn when we rehearsed it. Before I told her how to do it, she just flew! She was like a Tasmanian devil! She told me she had done a movie—I think it was *The Adventures of Baron Munchausen*—where they had this leopard knocked out and transported. When it woke up, it was f---ing pissed and it just jumped up. That's what she was doing. I said, "Wow, that looks f---ing great!"

JH: *So, what's your next project?*

QT: I'm offered all kinds of things, but I'm not looking for a job. After *Pulp Fiction*, I never really have to work again if I don't want to, which is kind of a cool position. I've spent a year acting, leading up to *From Dusk Till Dawn*, which is the performance I'm proudest of.

JH: *Some of your previous performances have come in for negative critical attention.*

QT: A lot of critics resent me for trying to go this route. They're not even seeing the work. It's like they're sick of seeing me. Roger Ebert was particularly vocal, like: "We don't want to see this guy as a character actor. We want to see him direct movies." Well, I don't love anything right now. It's like saying, "Why don't you get married?" I'm going into my sabbatical. I want to just live life with my girlfriend.

JH: *Is that Grace Lovelace?*

QT: Yeah. Read books, reacquaint myself with friends, just have a good time. I don't have the itch right now to be on a set. I just had a major artistic breakthrough on *From Dusk Till Dawn*. I realized that everything I had done before had been pretty much what you do in an acting class. I had never, you know, completely become another person before.

JH: *How did you relate to the rest of the ensemble?*

QT: Everybody was different. Me and George [Clooney] were like brothers. We had this bond, and part of the bond was George taking care of me, like Seth takes care of Richie. He was always encouraging me: "F--- those a--holes ʼbout *Destiny Turns On the Radio*! F--- them! You were the best f---in' thing in that movie, man! You got my respect, and you got the respect of other people, and you're going to be great in this movie!"

Now, Harvey Keitel is almost like my father. And in the movie, me and George have to dominate Harvey. I'm thinking Harvey is just going to show up and have a fun time doing a groovy monster movie. But he's in for a whole different thing with me. I was totally prepared that if we do a scene and I got a gun on Harvey and if he's not giving it to me, I would take him aside and say, "Hey, look, man, you're not f---ing giving it to me, so why don't we put a loaded clip in this gun and do the scene again— let's see if it f---ing changes!" I was prepared to do that. I was prepared to go there. Now, I never had to, because Harvey was—*voom!*—he was there, and we were working!

JH: *So, you're committed to acting?*

QT: As an artist, I'm going to do the time that it takes to work this muscle. It doesn't matter to me if critics look at it like a celebrity turn. Acting peers and directors respond very favorably. There are a lot of actors I would like to work with who would like to work with me. I remember talking to Spielberg, and he said: "I don't want you to lose that—there's a spontaneity to what you did in *Sleep With Me*. I had never seen it before. It was a special thing. In *Desperado*, you're like a cinema raconteur."

JH: *He's right.*

QT: I have a critic guy in me, and I also have a comedian guy in me that wants to go out and be funny on the talk shows—not be a boring f---ing director up there talking about his navel, but go out there and f---ing *kill!* I've got a relationship now with Jay Leno. I don't do a preinterview any- more because I f---ing know what I'm doing. I'm a good guest!

JH: *Who are your favorite stand-ups?*
QT: George Carlin. The fight I'm trying to do in my movies as far as the use of language, he's been doing forever. Words are words. To give any word too much power—whether that word be *f---* or *nigger* or whatever— is to give a word too much power. Richard Pryor's *That Nigger's Crazy* is the closest to a perfect comedy album ever. It's the great American novel done as a comedy routine.

JH: *Any favorite actors?*
QT: I'm a big fan of wild behavioral actors. I think Michael Parks [*The Hit- man*] is one of the greatest actors that's ever been produced in our lifetime! He ruined most of the breaks he got. He's in *From Dusk Till Dawn*.

JH: *How about your generation?*
QT: Sean Penn, Tim Roth and Nick Cage. Tim because of his versatility and ferociousness. He's got this chameleon quality. Sean out of sheer sexual- violence charisma. And Nick Cage just for fearlessness. I don't think that I've ever seen another actor in the history of film that made a career of being miscast and rising to the occasion.

JH: *You've expressed admiration for Mickey Rourke.*
QT: I'm a big fan, but to tell you the truth, I find it hard to get excited about working with somebody who just says, "Ah, f--- acting, it don't mean s--- to me." Well, acting means everything in the world to me. I studied for six years, but I never got any work. I could never get the audi- tion. I tried for years to have a career and couldn't get anywhere. Acting taught me everything I know about writing and directing. I didn't go to film school, but I studied acting. Most directors don't know s--- about act- ing. Actors are used to dealing with directors that don't really understand what they do or how they do it or how to talk to them about it.

JH: *How closely did you work with John Travolta and Uma Thurman in* Pulp Fiction—*for example, in the dance scene?*

QT: I choreographed him. I had a very specific, severe twist in mind — a little bit roboticized. I had a whole list of different dances, and then I just threw them out: Watusi, hitchhike, Batman! John has a really great memory for a lot of that stuff. In particular, I wanted them to do a cha-cha-cha. I wanted Uma to dance like this moment in *The Aristocats,* where Eva Gabor's cat dances.

JH: *Did she know she was being modeled on an animated character?*
QT: I never showed Uma *The Aristocats.* I would just imitate it — hands pointed down and everything.

JH: *Is there anything in particular you've learned about stardom in America?*
QT: The single weirdest thing about being a celebrity, for lack of a better word, is that you meet other celebrities and they're strangers to you, but it doesn't seem like it. It feels like you already know them because you know so much about them.

JH: *Are there any you haven't met?*
QT: I'd really like to meet Michelle Pfeiffer.

JH: *I just read an interview with a bunch of guys you used to work with at Video Archives, and they say that you've mellowed.*
QT: I had much more of an edge before I was successful because I felt I was as good as I am now then and I wasn't being recognized. I'm not talking about this star s---. I'm just talking about respect for what I do. From the moment that I moved out of my mom's house and was living on my own, I was hassled by the cops. I looked like white trash. I never went anywhere. I never left Los Angeles County all through my 20s. When I went to [the Sundance Film Festival], it was the first time I'd been in snow.

JH: *There were three Quentin Tarantino biographies published this fall.*
QT: It's kind of mind-bending.

JH: *Did you read all three?*
QT: Yes. I didn't realize there were controversies until people started writing books about my life. I don't think about the people who have a bone to pick with me. I don't go public, because that empowers them. It gives

credence to the argument. It's not a classy thing. When I was younger, I'd be kicking down their door and kicking the s--- out of them. But when I became a man, I gave up childish things. If they want their careers to be talking bad about me—well, have a nice career.

JH: *Whom do you mean?*
QT: Roger [Avary, co-writer of *Pulp Fiction*] was my best friend, and not to get too melodramatic about it, I've never been more betrayed by anybody that I was close to, that I loved and that I was surprisingly unselfish toward. Because I'm kind of a selfish guy. Not in a horrible way but, like, only-child s---—since my stepfather walked out on me when I was 10.

JH: *You mean the fact that Avary feels he deserves credit for your explication, in* Sleep With Me, *of* Top Gun *as a gay movie?*
QT: He just keeps talking about these things. Now I'm not hurt anymore. I'm just mad.

JH: *Do you feel like you've been misrepresented in the press?*
QT: There are a couple of misconceptions about me that are starting to get me angry. One is that I just completely live my life through movies—like that's the only thing I relate to. It's so not true! I feel I've lived a life more than most of the people I bump into!

JH: *So, what are some of your nonfilm activities?*
QT: Just before *From Dusk Till Dawn*, I took up boxing with a trainer, and I really like it. I was doing it, like, five days a week. But to tell you the truth, my real interest is to grab time by myself. I was an only child. I spent almost all of my 20s by myself. I really need to be alone. I'm known for just going underground for four days—just unplugging the phone. I like to read. It's almost like sex in a relationship—you have to keep on it, or you won't do it.

JH: *What are you reading now?*
QT: Right now I'm going through Elmore Leonard's *Rum Punch* to see if I were to adapt it, how I'd go about that. Grace got me the Molly Haskell book about her relationship with Andrew Sarris when he was sick [*Love & Other Infectious Diseases*]. She read it, and she liked it.

J H : *You got back with Grace after* Pulp Fiction?
Q T : Right. The first thing that we did together was go to the New York Film Festival.

J H : *Grace knew you when you were a clerk at Video Archives.*
Q T : Oh, yeah. She was a clerk, too. I completely trust her, and more importantly, it's nice to still be close to somebody that I have a history with. You don't lose your friends when stuff like this happens. It's the exact reverse. My friends are more weirded out by me than I am by them. I have an open invitation to have dinner with Arnold Schwarzenegger. I've met Warren Beatty, and I really like Warren Beatty, and I'd like to hang out with Warren Beatty. I don't have the time. The bottom line is, I'm busy, and when I'm not busy, I want time for myself or I want it with Grace.

J H : *Did you put your relationship with Grace on hold while your career took off?*
Q T : Well, it wasn't this conscious decision. We actually broke up. She was with somebody else. And I kind of got my wild oats out of my system. Then, you know, we were drawn back together again. I was raised by a strong woman, and I've always assumed other women would be as strong as my mother. That's not necessarily the case.

J H : *President Clinton was also brought up by a very independent-minded single mother who married several times. Can you identify with him?*
Q T : He married Hillary! He didn't want a weak sister. When you're raised by a strong woman, you think of a girlfriend as a partner. It's equal. You expect them to live their own life at the same time you're together.

J H : *Grace has her own work apart from your career.*
Q T : She always thinks of me as Quentin. She doesn't know who this "Quentin Tarantino" is.

J H : *How do you feel about being "Quentin Tarantino"?*
Q T : Zillions of people have said it before me, but it's the truth: As far as fame is concerned, if it had an on-and-off button, it would be the greatest thing in the world. And I mean, people coming up to me never say anything rude. I never get anyone saying, "I think your stuff sucks." People

are really positive, but I'm going to live a regular life. I went to a screening of *Get Shorty* recently, and I didn't sit in the reserved section. I sat down in front with the rest of the kids. And then, like, this one guy came up to me and asked for my autograph. I said: "Not when I'm in a movie, man. I'm here to see the movie like you, and you got to respect that, you know?" You tell me if I'm wrong about this, but I guess I don't have the fame of a director in America. I have the fame of a movie star.

JH: *I would say that it's a combination.*
QT: Spike Lee is about the only director that they would probably ask to host *Saturday Night Live* because he's that famous.

JH: *They asked you.*
QT: For *From Dusk Till Dawn*. But they didn't ask me before.

JH: *You have a cameo in Spike Lee's upcoming* Girl 6.
QT: I did something I said I would never do. I said I would never play a director in a movie. I just felt I wanted to do it for Spike. I have the first scene in the movie. It's this white-boy hip-hop director making this black movie, and it starts off with a screen test for Theresa Randle. The whole idea of the scene is for me to get her to take her clothes off.

JH: *How did Spike tell you to play it?*
QT: He didn't—it was just pretty obvious in the script. He took me and Theresa into a room [to do our scene]. It was a tiny touch intimidating because he was like the boss, you know? His set is kind of tough. Him and his AD, they're like [*snaps fingers four times*]. They didn't bark any orders to me, but.... My sets are like a big f---ing party.

JH: *He's said how much he admires* Pulp Fiction, *but he also said in* US *that he wishes you would stop using the word "nigger" as much as you do.*
QT: He's had the opportunity to bring that up to me in person, and he's never brought it up, ever. I don't think he has a problem with it. I think that's more political. And he didn't like *Pulp Fiction*—he loved it!

JH: *Would you ever make a documentary?*
QT: I'm producing one now about the making of *From Dusk Till Dawn*. We were going to have this big fight with the union—take on IATSE

[International Alliance of Theatrical and Stage Employees]. I thought, We should do a movie [about this], because I don't want this reduced to sound bites. This is a big issue.

J H : *How so?*

Q T : The way independent productions work in L.A.—if you're making a movie for $3 million, you're praying that you're under IATSE's radar. Not only were we *not* under their radar, we were on their board with red flags.

J H : *Did IATSE try to organize your crew?*

Q T : They tried. They didn't have the support. The crew was happy. We paid a good wage.

J H : *Wouldn't the union have gotten them more?*

Q T : Well, they wouldn't have their jobs—union people would have their jobs. I'm coming from an amateur point of view. The system never helped me whatsoever. Never protected me. Never gave me a leg up. And now that I'm here, they're going to come to me and say, "You got to play ball our way"? If I'm going to make a movie for $4 million, it is not to give the company a break—it's because I think it's a $4 million movie. I've got to be able to make a small movie. This is an art form. It's not a textile plant.

J H : *You're not a member of the Writers Guild?*

Q T : Writers Guild *or* Directors Guild.

J H : *What about the Screen Actors Guild?*

Q T : I am a member. You have to join SAG, or you won't be able to work. SAG is the one union I tried for years to join and could never get in.

J H : *How would you describe your politics, Quentin?*

Q T : [*Silence*] I guess I'm a liberal. Definitely not a conservative—I'm definitely not a Republican. Most people, when they're on one side or the other, don't paint with a small brush, they paint with a f---in' roller and wipe everybody into pansy liberals or dictator fascists.

J H : *The last Sundance Film Festival featured a number of movies with tough guys, profanity, violence, criminal capers gone awry. How do you feel about these faux Tarantino films?*

QT: Personally, I love it. I adore it. I get the biggest kick out of it. If I've made it a little easier for artists to go that way, work in violence—great, I've accomplished something.

JH: *Does it bother you that Bob Dole singled out two movies you wrote,* True Romance *and* Natural Born Killers, *as "nightmares of depravity"?*
QT: That's political campaigning. He's getting all this air time because he attacks the media. He hasn't even seen the movies. I got a zillion phone calls. They wanted me to be on *Nightline* with Dole. I didn't play that game. Win the presidency on your own, buddy. It's like George Carlin's thing: They've just come out with an order to ban toy guns, and we're going to keep the f---in' real ones [*laughs*].

JH: *Europeans often make the point that Americans are more puritanical about sex than violence.*
QT: I want to buy $1,000 worth of tickets for *Showgirls*. I want *Showgirls* to make more money this year than any other movie. If NC-17 was a viable option, it would just blow the lid off some filmmakers, because that's where they live, that's where they breathe, that's where their natural instincts take them. I mean, it's so ridiculous: NC-17 means commercial death. Based on what? The performance of a movie taken from the diaries of Anaïs Nin [*Henry & June*]? That was the final word? Why don't I buy that? Why do I not think that this has been put to the test?

JH: *Does any film violence strike you as gratuitous or distasteful?*
QT: I don't respond on a moral level. It's bad art—no different than if I saw a really good musical with really s---ty sequences.

JH: *Do you think movies have any effect on behavior?*
QT: If I hadn't loved movies so much and wanted to be an actor, I might have been a criminal. I was very romanced with that way of life. When I was a teen-ager, I totally believed: I'm not going to get some 9-to-5 job that I don't like just so I can drive a Honda. I'll take what I want. I did time in the county jail at three different times—all for bulls---—but, like, I'd rather go to jail than pay the money.

JH: *You mean parking tickets?*
QT: Yeah, like tremendous warrants. I always had illegal cars.

J H : *So, as far as you're concerned, there's no correlation between enjoying violence onscreen and enjoying it in life.*

Q T : I don't enjoy it in life at all. I never liked fighting. I don't fight by Marquess of Queensberry rules. When I fight, I fight like I'm trying to kill you, because I am assuming you're trying to kill me. One of the reasons I don't have a gun is, if I had a gun and a 12-year-old kid broke into this house, I would kill him. You have no right to come into my house. I have to assume the worst. There would be no holding you for the cops, no shooting to wound. I would empty the gun until you were dead. I feel that way about my art as well. I know that at the end of the day, no one will ever mess with the movie to the point that I'm unhappy with it.

J H : *Has that ever happened?*

Q T : Totally never happened. I don't even fear it. I would burn the negative. Twenty million dollars — *voom!* — it's gone.

Tarantino and Juliette

MIM UDOVITCH/1996

QUENTIN TARANTINO HAS A cold, and since it's his, it's one motherfucking badass cold; he is unshaven, wearing jeans and a T-shirt, and, even in a weakened state, capable of projecting an upbeat egotism so enormous that it almost amounts to generosity, a sort of open house of the self. Juliette Lewis is tired, slender, and chic in a tailored black jacket with a nipped-in waist, a synthetic blue shirt, and an air of cosmic smoldering. Together, at the Hamburger Hamlet, they have, as they point out, a funky vibe. Tarantino is expansive, reflexive, and hyper, in his work and in his person, while Lewis is internal, instinctive, and serenely sensual. The two bonded on the set of *From Dusk Till Dawn* (opening next month), which was written by Tarantino and directed by Robert Rodriguez, and in which they costar—in a stunning reversal of the old caricature, Tarantino is a director who *really wants to act.*

However different their routes, Lewis and Tarantino are both living at the heart of Mondo Hollywood: They are successful on their own terms within the framework of the Industry; the work of each is inimitable in its individuality; and in a way that has less to do with their work than with the weird psychic demands America places upon celebrity, both have been known to get on people's nerves. (Especially Tarantino, whose image has gone from demigod to despot in near record time; recently, critics have begun attacking him for movies—*The Usual Suspects, Things to Do in Den-*

From *Details*, February 1996, pp. 112, 114–117. Reprinted by permission of *Details* and the author.

ver When You're Dead—with which he had absolutely nothing to do. "It's natural, it's gonna happen," says Tarantino of the wave of backlash headed his way. "If you don't read it, it can't hurt you. And if people think I'm an egotistical loudmouth asshole, then yes, they're wrong.")

Nevertheless, in an age of grumpy celebrity, both love their jobs. "I mean, every independent filmmaker you talk to will just rag on and on about how fucked everything is," says Tarantino. "And it's like: Well, if it's so fucked, why are you doing it? If life is so tough for you, stop making movies!" "Acting for me is a release sometimes," says Lewis. "I almost get giddy and light, and it's just amazing because I'm stepping out and creating this whole other, nonexistent world in front of a little camera. And other times," she adds, pragmatically, "it's just work."

MIM UDOVITCH: *All right. Are you ready?*
JULIETTE LEWIS: Oh God, we're playing truth or dare.

MU: *Why are movies so bad?*
JL: I think it's the big war between the money people and artists. And that money people have this idea that it's either independent-artsy or it's commercial-bad. But movies can be both.

MU: *So why do they cling to the idea that they can't?*
QUENTIN TARANTINO: Well, I don't think they do anymore. The rules that they've been playing by don't quite work anymore and everyone's kind of like realizing it right now. It's because basically that whole Touchstone formula that was existing in the '80s, that couldn't miss, is missing now. It doesn't work.
JL: Yeah! Like *Home Alone* was a huge hit and no one predicted that. No one can predict *Congo*.
QT: Yeah, the formulas of the last ten years don't work anymore. The movies that are like sequels to the real big ones work because the audience has an investment in that franchise. But either the movies that used to be making $100 million are barely making $20 million or they're not even making that. I think right now is the most exciting time in Hollywood since 1971. Because Hollywood is never more exciting than when you don't know.

M U : *It's like alternative rock, which is an alternative to what, really?*

Q T : Exactly. I did that Kennedy show on MTV, *Alternative Nation,* all week long when *Pulp Fiction* opened and I said that: "Alternative to what?" It's the biggest-selling shit out there.

M U : *You have to let Juliette talk more.*

Q T : She was the one doing most of the talking!

M U : *Okay, let's plug* From Dusk Till Dawn. *What do you play?*

J L : I play a preacher's daughter, Harvey Keitel's daughter. He takes the kids on a vacation, in their little camper, and he's questioning his faith because his wife died, so he's a little bit mad at God, and then through this, we meet up with these two little thugs—and that's Quentin and George Clooney—and they kidnap our little family. Of course the two thugs get in a fight and then it's vampire hell.

Q T : One of the cool things about the vampires in the movie is they're just a bunch of carnivorous banshee beasts, they're like rats, they're these horrible things. There's none of that soul-searching or the angst of living forever and having to suck other people's blood, all that revisionist vampire stuff. They're just a bunch of monsters, and you should kill as many of them as you possibly can, because they're trying to kill you.

J L : And then my character turns into a real badass and it's cool. She has to turn into a warrior to kill these monsters.

M U : *So basically she gets in touch with the inner badass. An underrated aspect of the character.*

J L : Yeah! Well, you don't get it challenged much in life.

M U : *Well, you seem to be in touch with your inner badass. What's George Clooney like? He's a fox-and-a-half, in my view.*

J L : I guess. He's cool, and a lot of people, if they're cool they're foxy. I remember finding Scorsese sexy from being around him.

M U : *You know, from a distance that doesn't come through for me, but I'm willing to take your word for it. Do you get crushes on directors?*

J L : Not directors. I get these five-minute crushes on like room-service guys, valets, grips, actors—but not truly, just for five minutes.

MU: *The room-service waiter thing I can totally get with.*

JL: Actually what's a little more of a challenge is the bellhop, because he's a little more of the silent type. I don't act on it, because I can't really, I'm so guarded. And guys don't really come on to me.

MU: *Is that a fact?*

JL: Yeah! Or if they do, I don't really know. I just became aware of it last year when I was in New York.

MU: *You were in New York? Well, there's your problem. New York is not a good city for the single girl. But you escaped to a fun set on* From Dusk Till Dawn.

QT: The big thing in Barstow, California, where we were on location, was a gigantic factory-outlet mall.

JL: Oh yeah. DKNY. They had all that.

MU: *Did you score any major things?*

QT: I didn't. I have to say that since designers started sending me free stuff to wear, it's kind of taken the fun out of shopping for clothes. One of the big things about going to that factory outlet was that like me, Juliette, George Clooney, and Cheech Marin would go to this thing. Now you have to understand something about Juliette. . . .

JL: Oh, here's the big observation! I like this one.

QT: Juliette is a true chameleon. If she was walking around the Redwood Forest she would all of a sudden look like a lizard on a tree. And so we go walking around this outlet mall and we all realize our demographic like that. I walk into kind of like a hip place, and the counter girl will be: "Oh my God, it's Quentin Tarantino!" And when we walk into a K-mart kind of thing, all of these ladies, the fat ladies in the stretch pants are like: "George Clooney! Dr. Ross!" But Juliette is rarely approached, and not because she's not famous.

JL: Because I was wearing red shorts and a red-and-white tube top and sandals . . .

QT: And she looked like a native. People didn't even remotely turn their heads. If they recognized her, they thought they went to school with her.

JL: Yeah, but if I wore something like this, then . . .

QT: Then you'd stand out. You are a fucking badass. And I'm just here, from being sick all day, wearing a T-shirt.

JL: But Quentin has cool outfits.

QT: But you look *bad*. Bad*ass*. But anyway...

JL: The waitress has to come, Quentin, because we have to get our hamburgers.

MU: *And I have talking points.*

QT: Okay, well, hold on, hold on, I'm not finished with my story yet. So all the young wannabe hip people, they knew who I was, the white-trash people knew who George was...

JL: Oh boy.

QT: ...and Juliette just *looked* like trash...

JL: Yeah, yeah, yeah.

QT: ...*but,* we all looked like Bobby Sherman compared to Cheech Marin. Cheech is the most famous fucking guy on the planet fucking Earth. I mean it's like he walks through there, people would stomp us to death to get to Cheech. We go into the Dairy Queen and Cheech is in business, man. There's like a line. Truck drivers...

JL: Yeah, and little kids because of *The Lion King.*

QT: Yeah, yeah, exactly! And it's like: "*Heeey,* Cheech, smoke a bowl! Cheech! Mr. Marin, can I get your autograph? Cheech, where's Chong?" He's the most famous guy in America!

MU: *What do you think are people's fantasies about Hollywood? What is the Hollywood myth?*

QT: I don't know. To me that's the problem with marketing research and executives—it's everyone assuming that they know what the public's thinking. I know what *I'm* thinking.

JL: The public would have to be asked.

QT: I know what I'm thinking. When I do a movie, I know what I want to see and I'm going to bet there are other people out there like me. I don't know if there's much of a myth of Hollywood anymore. But what I find interesting is something like the E! channel. The whole idea is to demystify celebrities and make the people that watch the E! channel think they're friends with the celebrities, because you're just constantly seeing a barrage the entire time you're watching.

MU: *But don't you think that's the same as the old-time stars doing homey things—like when Joan Crawford would be with her kids reading* The Night

Before Christmas *over the radio the night before Christmas? It's like this highly mediated reality.*

J L : I do. I think with the media...

Q T : No, can I interrupt you, just for two seconds? I think it's the exact opposite. Because it's like you're taking all the celebrities on the planet and you're trying to make them like they're your neighbors. Where in the old days they wanted the stars to be gods. They didn't *identify* with Joan Crawford or Clark Gable, they *worshiped* them. Where that totally exists now is Hong Kong, the Hong Kong film industry. The stars in Hong Kong are like movie stars in the '30s and the '40s, man. I mean, they are *gods*. In a weird way, just like the old movie stars, they're almost not real people, they exist on the screen.

J L : I do think E! is the '90s version of sensationalizing movie stars. The *normalcy* is sensationalized, like: "Look, she eats French fries with her hands!" And like in articles: "And she crosses her legs and looks up to the ceiling and sighs and rests her head on her fucking hand." You just draw such attention to such normal behavior that it does sensationalize it. All people have their own little mannerisms, so I don't see why movie-star mannerisms are more interesting.

Q T : It's funny, because the thing that I find really bizarre when I read interviews with myself is I start getting ridiculously self-conscious about just being me. Twenty articles talk about how fast I talk and that I talk with my hands and all of a sudden I'm like: "Oh, maybe I shouldn't talk so fast. Maybe I should comb my hair. Maybe I shouldn't talk with my hands so much." I'm a geek. I'm a freak.

M U : *Don't go changing.*

Q T : But no one can deal with that kind of self-consciousness, and all of a sudden you're afraid to be who you are. Normally I go into photo shoots and I'm so defensive, like I go in there like I'm gonna get into a fight with the guy or the girl who's doing the thing. I'm like: "No, no, no, I'm not gonna lay in a bucket of blood and I'm not going to put my face against a brick and you're not going to shoot me with a razor blade in my mouth or pins in my face. You're going to shoot me like I'm Sharon Stone. I want to be handsome in this photo, all right?"

J L : (*crosses her legs and looks up to the ceiling and sighs and rests her head on her fucking hand*) Even I've been guilty of this. You can't understand how someone can do an intense part and not have some kind of neuroses. That's the only thing that sucks sometimes, is you can be talking to someone and you're just being normal, but they think at any time your head's gonna spin, like in *The Exorcist*.

Q T: Everyone makes all these jokes or observations about how I'm mentoring John Travolta as far as his career choices in other movies. Well, he's mentoring *me* in photo shoots.

M U: *Okay. The next question is, Joe Eszterhas: Why?*

J L: Who's Joe Eszterhas?

Q T: He's a screenwriter. He's actually bad-mouthed me quite a few times. I don't know about quite a few times, but . . .

J L: I'll go break his shins for you.

Q T: . . . he did this profile on TV and I never saw it, but apparently he spent ten minutes of the twenty talking about how he writes *real* screenplays and he's a *real* screenwriter, and I'm just . . . jerking off.

M U: *But he wrote* Jade *and* Basic Instinct *and* Showgirls. *Those aren't jerking off?*

J L: Oh my God! And he said that about *you*? You can't even respond to something like that!

Q T: To tell you the truth, I thought *Showgirls* was fucking great. I'm thinking about writing an article in *Film Comment* in complete and utter defense of *Showgirls*.

M U: *What did you like about it?*

Q T: I'll tell you exactly what I liked about it. Joe Eszterhas's script was the least of it. I think Sharon Stone made him a star, she's really enjoyable in *Basic Instinct*. But the thing that's great about *Showgirls*, and I mean great with a capital great, is that only one other time in the last twenty years has a major studio made a full-on, gigantic, big-budget exploitation movie.

M U: *And that was?*

Q T: *Mandingo*, which is one of my favorite movies. *Showgirls* is the *Mandingo* of the '90s.

J L: Quentin has these thoughts.

QT: And the thing is, what's so great about it is that no one else but Paul Verhoeven would have the balls to shoot that the way it should be shot. He knew he was making an exploitation movie. Roger Corman started this whole subgenre in exploitation films on video—*Stripped to Kill* is the first one—and they're always about like a bunch of topless dancers and there's usually some killer wiping them out, the best one being a film called *Naked Obsession* with William Katt. And *Showgirls* is a $40 million version of that. The thing that was also great is the sex in *Showgirls* was dirty. There was nothing pretty. The only scene that didn't work for me at all was where Elizabeth Berkley and Kyle MacLachlan have sex in this pool. But the scene where she lap-dances on him and dry-humps him, that was a good scene, man!

JL: I just think all that shit's boring.

QT: But in *Showgirls*, just as the sex started to get boring in the last fifteen minutes, they played the violence into it. And Elizabeth Berkley turns into Pam Grier and fucks up this bad guy and she does a great job. And you leave the movie on a high note.

JL: How does she kill him?

QT: She doesn't kill him, she just beats the shit out of him.

JL: With her hands?

QT: Well, she's tall, she's like a redwood, and she's got these big boots and he's raped her best friend. I mean horribly. So she takes out a switch-blade...

JL: Cool, knives are good.

QT: Unfortunately, she doesn't carve him up with the knife...

JL: Oooooh, why doesn't she use the knife?

QT: ...but the guy's really big and she beats him to death, damn near!

JL: Did he get the knife away from her?

QT: No. She gets him down so he won't say anything and then she proceeds to do these like intense roundhouse kicks with these big boots on.

JL: Kick boxing. Knew it.

QT: And she fucks him up, man! It's really cool.

JL: Wow. You know what I'd like to know? I'd like to know all the rumors on me.

MU: *I don't think I've heard any. I think you satisfied the need for rumors by coincidentally living with Brad Pitt, another famous person, at the height of your fame. That just filled the hole.*

J L :   And the rumors after that, about being with other famous people? I've never been with any other famous people. Just because I'm in the same age bracket as Johnny Depp and Leo DiCaprio doesn't mean we all screw together.

M U :   *And you do tend to hear gay rumors about almost everybody.*
J L :   Yes, the gay rumor goes wild. For everyone. Like with Leo, he was like: "Is Brad gay?" And I said, "Leo, *you're* gay, don't you know? Haven't you heard?"
Q T :   I always thought it was really cool when Jami Bernard interviewed me for her book on me, she goes: "How do you feel about (1) the rumors that you're gay, and (2) the fact that the gay community has embraced your movies and claimed you as one of their own?"
J L :   Whoa! Quentin has a gay rumor too!
Q T :   And I go: "Really? That's cool, man. I totally dig it."
J L :   Because they're the underdogs or whatever. I have kind of the under-dog connection too.
Q T :   You kind of look like Underdog.

M U :   *And I've heard you're starting a band. Are you thinking of leaving acting?*
J L :   The band, yes, but leaving acting, no. I thought of that last year. You get real jaded, I guess, temporarily.

M U :   *What had you all jaded?*
J L :   Love. Love. Enormous, enormous love, going awry.

M U :   *What do you mean?*
J L :   From sixteen to twenty, I was with one person and truly, truly in love, and then all these elements in his life and mine were changing, and those are enormous years as it is....

M U :   *In the wake of breaking up with Brad Pitt, you were reevaluating your life?*
J L :   Yes, because it wasn't cut-and-dry, it wasn't totally breaking up, so I lost myself there for a second. I felt bad about myself, and the thing about doing movies when you're going through personal stuff is you've got to feel good enough or have some amount of pride to even say: Okay, I can be in front of a camera, I can be fifty feet high. It's a distant thing now, but

a couple of years ago it was a huge change, and I had to remember that I had once lived alone, and had my own pride and my own ideas. There was much more to it than the relationship, it was also where I was in my life. But it's old now, and I actually care about Brad and I think he and Gwyneth are cool. And I think he's found a good girl.

M U :   *Okay. The last question is, what are you looking forward to?*
J L :   Just the future. The future at large.
Q T :   I'd like to be in a situation where I can direct a movie, then act in a movie, direct a movie, then act in a movie. Because one of the big problems with directing is it takes so fucking long. It was great to give my heart and soul to something and then when shooting was over, it was done. And I liked being another person, and thinking another person's thoughts.
J L :   And he's really menacing and threatening and perverted, it's really gross.
Q T :   Other than that, I guess I'm too self-obsessed to think of anything that isn't personal. I used to have directors where I was counting the days until their movie came out, but I don't think that way anymore. I'm looking forward to sleeping late.
J L :   I'm looking forward to seeing who becomes the love of my life.

M U :   *I'm looking forward to seeing that too. I mean, not who becomes the love of your life, although, of course, I'd like to know that as well.*
Q T :   All of America is looking forward to that.

Out of the Past: Quentin Tarantino — On Ambition, Exploitation, and Playing Psycho

DON GIBALEVICH/1996

QUENTIN TARANTINO LOVES MOVIES. That's why he makes the damn things. And while this isn't exactly a groundbreaking revelation, it's impossible to talk to the man without spending a lot of time on the subject. Today, as Tarantino relaxes after an afternoon photo shoot, hunched over a plate of excellent fish tacos in the lounge of an airplane hangar turned photo studio, he can't help but wax eloquent on the subject of classic kung-fu movies. When someone mentions *Master of the Flying Guillotine,* his face lights up with the sort of excitement most of us reserve for reunions with long-lost childhood friends.

"That's one of my favorite movies of all time," he enthuses. "Jimmy Wang Yu. Have you ever seen the first one of that? That's a sequel...*Master of the Flying Guillotine* was a *sequel.* The first movie shows how he became the incredible one-armed boxer. It's called *The One-Armed Boxer* in Hong Kong and the UK, but in America it was released as *The Chinese Professionals.*" If this guy was your roommate, you could throw away your shelf of movie guides — he's got them all hardwired into his brain.

Strangely enough, this walking encyclopedia of film can't remember the first movie he saw as a child — but he does recall his mother taking him to a double bill of *Deliverance* and *The Wild Bunch* when he was nine. Movies became his life. Even today, Tarantino sees the years before video as a golden age of moviegoing, no matter how schlocky the movies might have been.

From *Axcess,* Vol. 4, No. 1, February–March 1996, pp. 58–64. Reprinted by permission of Axcess Ventures, Inc.

"There were certain movies that I just adored," he recalls. "One of my favorite movies of all time is *Rolling Thunder,* particularly when I was younger. Whenever I'd read it was playing at the Palace Theater in Long Beach on a triple feature with *The Howling* and something else, I'd take the bus to Long Beach and see it. If it was playing at the Arcade in downtown L.A., I'd take the bus over there and go see it. I'd follow *Assault on Precinct 13* wherever the hell it was playing. It was always great seeing it. It was neat."

Tarantino—probably the only guy alive who can say that something's neat and get away with it—explains that his youthful enthusiasm for exploitation films was, in part, a product of geography. "I lived in the urban area of the South Bay. In the city of Carson, a big black, Hispanic, and Samoan area, there was a theater called the Carson Twin Cinema. They showed all the exploitation films as they opened, and they also showed all the mainstream Hollywood fare on its way out of town. They'd get the new kung-fu movies, or the blaxploitation movies, or the good ol' boy movies, on their opening weekend—the one week that they were playing—or *A Star Is Born* on its last trip before it went into oblivion. There was this one double feature that they whipped out at least twice a year, and that was *Five Fingers of Death* and *Enter the Dragon.* And they knew, when they showed *Five Fingers of Death* and *Enter the Dragon,* that it was just going to be fuckin' pandemonium. People would always go see it. Black guys, the Crips, yelling at the screen, all the Samoans there, people getting into kung-fu fights and shit . . . it was a blast. It was so much fun. Video has taken that away, a little bit . . . the communal aspect, the ritualistic aspect of it."

In fact, Tarantino's first job was at a movie theatre—of the adult variety. "I never really cared for porno movies," he asserts. "I only worked there for about a year as an usher at age sixteen. I lied about my age . . . but not because I wanted to see the movies. I just needed to get a job, and I got one. I'm semi-familiar with the porno film world from that period, which in some ways was the last bastion of interesting porno films. They didn't seem that interesting at the time, but now, in retrospect, they're very interesting compared to the crap that they make now, the made-to-video stuff. Just the fact that they were all shot on 35 millimeter film goes a long way. It's really weird, because the production quality of porno films got better and better until they switched over to making them straight on video, and then they were horrible. But I remember in the '80s, working in a video store with all the different porno films, I'd take one home and look at it and go, 'God, this is almost the production level of a TV show. Maybe a little better.' There still was a quality of anything can happen, in some of the '70s movies, which is kinda gone now, almost completely. Just the fact that they were actually going out to play in theaters gave them more of an urgency than they have just throwing them in a video store. The same thing happened to exploitation films. I love exploitation films, and I would go see exploitation films all the time. But the thing is, it's hard for me to get any enthusiasm to even watch them on video—and I would go and see just the crappiest movies at the theaters growing up, and even in my twenties. But the exploitation film industry isn't dead. It's just on video. There's no drive-ins. Taking the theatrical experience out of it, something has been lost in the making of it. It shouldn't be that way. It doesn't really make any sense that it would be that way, but there is an urgency gone from the filmmaking, just knowing that ultimately they're going to be seen on television, on Showtime and on video. That has taken some of the specialness out of them. Not that those films back then were *that* special. But there was an urgency about them. And the ones that broke through really did break through, qualitywise."

Not content to wallow in nostalgia, Tarantino is taking active steps to preserve this legacy. "I'm starting a small distribution company through Miramax that'll release four films a year, and it's called Rolling Thunder Pictures. We don't make movies, we just release them. The first film is going to be a great Hong Kong movie called *Chunking Express*. The second one is going to be this old exploitation movie from the '70s called *Switchblade Sisters*. It's a trippy movie, done by Jack Hill, the guy who directed *Coffy* and *Foxy Brown*." Quentin may be the only guy in the room who knows what he's talking about, but he's also the guy who's making certain we all have the chance to enjoy these films in their proper setting.

Tarantino's latest undertaking finds him starring with *ER*'s George Clooney in *From Dusk Till Dawn*, a gleefully gruesome vampire action flick directed by Robert Rodriguez from a screenplay by Tarantino. (Despite the ongoing controversy over Tarantino's acting skills, he continues to act— criticism flows off him like water off a duck's back.) As might be expected, this horror movie is deeply informed by his love of genre films—and his disappointment at recent horror fare. "When studios make horror films, they just don't commit to actually making a horror film. I don't know what the fuck it is that they're making. They don't really have much faith in the horror film audience. They're trying to make horror films that will get the people who never go see horror films, so they water them down."

Tarantino stresses that this is *not* the case with *From Dusk Till Dawn*. "This is a full-on drive-in picture. We totally made a horror film for the *Fangoria* crowd, which hasn't had a horror film made for them in a long time, but we got to do it on a big scale. We went full out to give them a cut your head off, slice your throat, bang your head against the wall repeatedly horror film."

From Dusk Till Dawn is a project that's been kicking around for quite some time. "This was the first piece I was ever hired to write," Tarantino reveals. "For fifteen hundred dollars." The original treatment was sketched out by Robert Kurtzman of the special effects outfit KMB, leaving Tarantino plenty of room to develop the tale of the dangerous Gecko brothers (George Clooney and Tarantino) and their desperate rush for the Mexican border. Taking a preacher (Harvey Keitel) and his family hostage, the Geckos seek refuge in an all-night strip bar called The Titty Twister—only to discover that its inhabitants are ancient Aztec vampires who plan to make an early breakfast of them all. Tarantino guarantees that the ensuing battle for survival will keep audiences riveted to their seats, overwhelmed by a healthy overabundance of blood.

"Because I wanted the vampires to be able to bleed freely and flow through rivers of blood, I made their blood green—so there's no mistake who's getting killed here. Demons from hell are getting killed. Not human beings. I mean, human beings are getting killed, but they're getting killed by demons from hell! But when our heroes fight back at the demons, then you see who's being killed. And you can kill as many vampires as you want. They don't exist!" Having forestalled this potential ratings problem, Tarantino was free to focus on his character, Richie Gecko, and leave the driving to director Robert Rodriguez.

"I'm like this psycho fucker," he announces with obvious relish. "Quentin was never on that set, it was always Richie Gecko. Everything I experienced, I experienced through his perspective, not through Quentin's perspective. I can't talk objectively about him, because I *am* him. Richie has all his reasons for why he does what he does. But he's definitely not controllable. There's a really cool sequence when George Clooney is telling

Harvey Keitel, if you don't try to escape and indulge us just for tonight and just do what you're told, we'll let you go in the morning. And then Harvey looks at me and goes, 'You won't let him touch my daughter?' And then George kinda looks down at the floor and then looks back up and goes, 'I can handle Richie.' But we've just seen that he *can't* handle Richie. He wants to be able to take care of me, for me, but he can't. He says 'I give you my word'—but the last time he gave his word to a hostage, I killed and raped her!"

While the Gecko boys sound like members of a seriously dysfunctional family, Tarantino rushes to their defense when someone suggests that they don't get along. "They actually love each other," he maintains. "We love each other immensely, that's obvious in the movie, but George's character Seth—who's been in jail for eight years—sees that I'm not controllable. I'm doing things that I shouldn't be doing. I'm doing things how it's not done. And he's like, 'What the hell's going on? He's killing people indiscriminately, he's raping women—what the fuck is up with this?' But because we're all going to this hole-in-the-wall place in Mexico, it's okay... 'I'll just take care of him, and once we get to Mexico it'll all be fine. He'll never be in this situation again, he'll never ever have to have a gun again. If I just get him to Mexico, I can take care of him and he'll be fine.' So Seth is working under that situation. Richie thinks *he's* the one who's taking care of business. And at one point in the movie you actually see things from his perspective."

That this is a madman's paranoid perspective is putting it mildly. But in his own way, Richie is taking care of Seth as much as Seth is taking care of him. "If *From Dusk Till Dawn* is inspired by anything, it's inspired by Jim Thompson's book of *The Getaway*," Tarantino explains. "Instead of two lovers, it's two brothers in love. In fact, even where they're going to is the place that the characters in *The Getaway* are going, this mythical place called El Rey. When there's nowhere else to go, you go to El Rey. And that's where the Gecko brothers are going to." Like many Thompson fans, Tarantino rues the fact that this sequence of *The Getaway* never made it to the screen in either version of the movie. "It was the greatest thing in the book."

Needless to say, Tarantino isn't one to leave the good stuff out of any of his own projects, whether he's writing, directing or producing. It's an impressive rise to prominence by a self-professed "video geek." The story of his life has been told and told again. Rabid fans of *Reservoir Dogs* and *Pulp Fiction* already know that he served time as a video store clerk before becoming the hottest ticket in Hollywood. Tarantino doesn't see the point in making a big deal out of this, however. "I always wanted to make films, so it was just a matter of getting the gumption to get my life started...as opposed to just staying at the comfortable hovel that I was in."

But what was it about Quentin Tarantino that made him the guy who broke out, rather than the clerk who's still reshelving Humphrey Bogart movies at the local Blockbuster?

"I never looked at it as breaking out of the video store," he explains. "I didn't go to college. To me the video store was like my tenure at college. I don't mean because I learned anything there...but I don't know how much people learn at college. It's more the life experience. When your four years are up, you have to actually officially start your life, but you end up hanging on to that free zone. Video Archives was my free zone. And eventually my own ambition got me out of there. But the ties that bind are strong. You get comfortable in those places. And that's the killer. The next thing you know you're thirty years old and still work at a video store.

"That's the situation that most people our age are in. People of our generation have got caught in this kind of weird minimum wage cycle. You're working at the Footlocker selling shoes at the mall. You know all the people at the Footlocker. You know all the people in the surrounding stores, and it's a lot of fun—you date the girls that work there, you pick up on the customers, and you all go out to have beer afterwards. You go to the movies together, and it's all real great. If you're even halfway diligent, you start becoming assistant manager in about four or five months. It's not that hard. If you just start doing your job, they move you up. First your're assistant assistant manager, then you're assistant manager, and then you're the manager, and everything is going fine—but then something happens and you're fuckin' fired and you're out in the street. It might not even be your fault. Now you gotta go and get a new job. You could try to get a job at Northrup or Hughes Aircraft—a real job where you can actually start building a life, if that's what you want to do—but those jobs are hard to get! But you can get a job at the Nike shoe store tomorrow. They'll hire you in a day. Boom—you get hired and you meet a whole new crew of people. You hang out with them all fuckin' day, and you pick up on the girls, and everything's just fucking great and fun and you're having a good time and you go to the movies with them and hang out with them and you smoke pot with them and you do whatever the hell it is you do with them. And then you're the manager, and they move you to another store across town and you work there, and you know those people, and then, boom — you're fired! So now what do you do? You've spent six years working at these places, doing jobs that kids get to pay for their gas."

Tarantino pauses, as if contemplating how his life would have gone if he'd stayed on this track. "That's the circle that a lot of people in our age group fit in, just going around and around and around. I started realizing this by seeing it in my friends, about four years into the experience. So I never got into the circle."

It's a sure bet that Tarantino would have never been invited to the Beijing Film Festival if he hadn't worked up the "gumption" to hop off the minimum wage merry-go-round. "It was a very big adventure," he recalls of his week in mainland China. "It was pretty terrific. *Pulp Fiction* had never played theatrically, but the video piracy in Asia is just remarkable, so all the young kids had seen, or owned, video copies of the movie. The film students at the Beijing Film Academy totally knew who I was. And all the rock musicians there and all the young kids totally knew who I was." It just goes to show that a little ambition can carry you a long way. For Quentin Tarantino, it's probably taken him farther than he'd ever imagined. But has Hollywood glitz and international fame gone to his head?

Maybe, maybe not.

While he *does* leave the interview in a limo, he still owns the same old Geo he's been driving for years.

My Evening with Q

LANCE LAWSON/1997

Part I

Following the final credits of *The Glove*, Quentin Tarantino and friend Lance Lawson loitered in the theater a while to talk of many things—"of shoes and ships and sealing wax, of cabbages and kings; and why the sea is boiling hot, and whether pigs have wings." Oh, and they also talked about movies.

E@H offers up a portion of that dialogue for your delectation.

LANCE LAWSON: *Five years from now, how do you imagine your home entertainment system?*
QUENTIN TARANTINO: Well, I don't anticipate a lot of changes because I'm pretty much a low-tech guy. I keep going back to my prints, man.

LL: *I know you've been a laser aficionado since the early days. What do you think of the DVD and its future?*
QT: Well, you can't say lasers can't become obsolete when albums became obsolete in no time at all. I mean, the switchover from vinyl to CD was so quick, I didn't realize it was even happening until it had already happened. It seems like one day you'd go to Licorice Pizza, and there was nothing but records, and then the next day there was nothing but CDs,

From *Entertainment@Home*. Part I: Vol. 1, No. 3, May 1997, pp. 40–42, 44. Part II: Vol. 1, No. 4, June 1997, pp. 53–56. Reprinted by permission of *Entertainment@Home*.

with LPs in this small little section. And then the records were gone altogether.

As far as the special features that DVD offers, I know what language *I'm* going to watch movies in, and I don't need to be offered pan-and-scan when I'm going to be watching letterboxed anyway. As far as being able to offer different-rated editions, well, I don't like that just as a filmmaker. If I make my R-rated movie, then that's the movie I want out there. Now if I sell it to television and cut it, then that's my decision as a filmmaker: I've consciously sold it to television and agreed to cut it. But, to have hotter or milder versions of it floating around—I want people seeing the movie I made.

LL: *As of now, Universal and Disney have made no commitment to putting out software for DVD. Do you think that will change?*

QT: I'm sure it will if the hardware's out there demanding movies. But, you know—and this sounds so silly—I like the size of laserdiscs and their packaging. I don't want them to be smaller. It's like albums vs. CDs: I just like the size and feel of them. The size is just cool... it's kinda dynamic looking, it opens up displaying decent-size pictures... it's just cool looking!

LL: *Laserdiscs seem to be losing something of an exclusive feature in that the letterboxing of videocassettes is becoming more and more common. Do you think this is due to growing acceptance on the part of consumers?*

QT: I think it's a situation where customers are more aware now of letter-boxing in a way that they weren't. But, at the same time, I can't imagine that the studios would be doing it unless they felt there was a market for them.

You know, *Pulp Fiction* was one of the first big movie video releases to be released simultaneously in pan-and-scan and letterboxed versions. There was discussion whether we wanted to release only a letterboxed edition, and we decided there was no reason to make Buena Vista Home Video's life a living hell. And in a weird way, I like my pan-and-scan version. Most filmmakers don't master their pan-and-scans. Usually, it's their cinematographer working with the video engineer, and when they're done, they show it to the director. And you usually do that right after you've made the movie.

Now, *Reservoir Dogs* was no problem to pan-and-scan because we shot it in Super-35, so there were just minor adjustments made. But with *Pulp,* there was no way I could keep the movie I made in pan-and-scan. Rather than artificially cut back and forth between two characters that should have been in the same frame, we would just slowly pan between Sam and John, sorta like Scorsese's slow hallway pan in *Taxi Driver*. It has to be a different emotional response when the yuppie guys in the apartment open the door and see Jules standing there, as opposed to opening the door and seeing Jules and Vincent standing there. But otherwise, I'm very happy with it.

L L :   *Is the changeover to Side 2 on* Reservoir Dogs *officially recognized as the worst changeover in the history of lasers?*
Q T :   [Laughing] Yes, I think that is official now. You know, we did every-thing regarding the mastering of that laser except that break to Side 2, and it's the worst I've ever seen. Although at this point, it is almost sooo bad that it has a certain notoriety. I come to look forward to it.

L L :   *What long-term effect do you see DSS having on both local cable fran-chises, as well as the home video market?*
Q T :   I'm a bad person to ask that question because I'm not sure what the consequences are. I just got DirecTV, so there's not really a need for cable. And if DSS could offer movies to homes like Spectravision does in hotels, that would go a long way toward kicking the shit out of video. Because the hotels seem to have that weird window of having films that have left the theaters but haven't yet come out on video, there's the added attraction of being able to tape high-quality copies off the air.

L L :   *This DSS ad brought to you by Jack Valenti and the MPAA.*
Q T :   [Laughing] No, you're all right as long as it's for home use, and you're not selling them.

L L :   *Speaking of cable, when is cable going to get a crack at* Reservoir Dogs *and* Pulp Fiction, *or are they destined to be* The Rocky Horror Picture Show *of the 1990s?*
Q T :   No, actually, *Pulp Fiction* has played on Starz! channel, and was part of a Miramax/Disney package deal. Our cable sale was just fantastic! And they pretty much made the most out of the fact that they were the ones that had *Pulp Fiction*. And *Dogs*, I think, plays on the Independent Film Channel.

LL: *Really? I've never seen* Dogs *on IFC, and I don't know anyone who has* Starz!.

QT: Neither do I [laughing]. I'm glad *Dogs* didn't get passed around HBO, Showtime, and Cinemax. Most people have seen it either at the theater or on video. And I'm glad *Pulp* hasn't been all over HBO. It's actually kinda unique . . . we released *Pulp* and the film played for a year. So, that normal video window of six months after the theatrical release—forget that, we're still in the theaters! At that point, the video guys were making their plans, when I said, "Hey, we've kinda gotta cult thing going here, and the quickest way to kill a cult is to make it easily accessible." I thought we should hold off a whole year before releasing it on video. The video people said to strike while the iron's hot, but it goes back to something I observed at Video Archives. The video customers *know* when a video should be available, and they're going to be coming into video stores in droves looking for *Pulp Fiction*.

LL: *You say you have a love/hate relationship with video. It seems like you're making quite a case for the "love" side.*

QT: Well, you make these films for the theater experience, and outside of that you're left with this rather unglamorous presentation of your films. You don't even want to have to think about the fact that people are having conversations and doing the crossword puzzle while your movie's playing. [Laughs] But I do like the fact that when a movie stops playing in the theater, that's not its last day in court. I've really noticed that with the video release of *From Dusk Till Dawn*. People are always yelling out their car windows, "Hey, it's Richie . . . Richie Gecko!" [Quentin's psychotic character] There was this obvious big burst of recognition directly after the video release. I've made a case for the benefits that access to video gives, but the availability devalues films at the same time. That's why I've really gotten into collecting film prints. Just having a 16mm or 35mm film print means you can't take it for granted. It's more important because it's not so disposable. In an ironic way, by making art available we make it more disposable. Another really weird side effect [of video] is I find myself getting really excited over regular television. We're so used to watching prerecorded material and having that control over it—to stop it, to pause it, and so on—that, when we watch broadcast television, it seems like live television in contrast, because it's going, and it *ain't* stopping for you.

LL: *And people nowadays certainly take for granted the time-shifting capabilities of VCRs, as if there was never a time when that capability didn't exist.*

QT: Oh, exactly! We'll go out Sunday night and we'll tape *The X-Files*, whereas, back in the '60s, it was, "Hey, *The Man From U.N.C.L.E.* is coming on, we'll be right here." It was now or forget about it.

LL: *On an early* Politically Incorrect *episode on* Comedy Central, *you made a rather stirring—and some would say stunning—defense of 1970s television: "We had* The Brady Bunch, *we had* The Partridge Family, *we had* Kung Fu, *etc." What do you think of network television in the 1990s?*

QT: It's kind of funny. I didn't watch much television in the 1980s. I would get hooked on a show and watch that one show for a while, for a season or two, and then burn out, but I didn't really watch regular television. I pretty much used my TV as a monitor: I watched videos on it, and I taped films on it. And this went on all the way up until I began editing *Pulp Fiction*. And then a really funny thing happened. Shooting the film is just so hysterical, it's like running off with the circus. In contrast, editing is like a 9-to-5 job. I would go home at the end ᴏɪ a day and just veg and lay on the couch and watch television. That was really the first time I had that experience, you know—the way most Americans use their television. So, before this, I had never seen *Home Improvement,* and I had no idea who *Grace Under Fire* was, so I just started watching all these shows and getting caught up in them. But, I still can't get in the habit of watching a particular show, except for *The X-Files*. There are shows I wish I watched more, because I feel like I'm not supporting them and that'll bug me, you know what I mean? I've watched *Millennium* and that seems cool, although I missed the first one, and that's all anyone ever talks about. Plus, I tend to watch some things that are in syndication. I never watched *The Fresh Prince of Bel-Air* when it was on network television, but channel 5 here in L.A. has a solid hour of it starting at 6 p.m. And then, at 7:30, there's *Seinfeld* every night. But the only show other than *The X-Files* which I never miss, and I've followed it since its days on Comedy Central, is *Politically Incorrect*. It's got to be killing Dave and Jay because it's remote zap time come midnight: it's automatic. Back to back with *Nightline*, it's deadly.

LL: *I remember a couple of years ago, right before you directed your episode of* ER, *you told me that* ER *was the American equivalent of* The Decalogue *[the*

legendary 10-part series of moral tales done for Polish TV by Krzysztof Kies-
lowski]. Personally, in addition to The X-Files, *I always thought that it would be*
cool if you directed episodes of Homicide *and* NYPD Blue. *I think* Homicide, *in*
particular, just keeps getting better and better.

QT: That is a good show. I saw the episode directed by Whit Stillman,
starring Rosanna Arquette. And I like that girl, Michelle Forbes, who has
joined the show. I think she's really cool. But, you know, my problem with
those shows, and maybe I don't watch them enough to get used to it, but I
get kind of tired of their jumpcuts and handheld camera swooning. It's
kind of a false style in a weird sort of way—it's not organic. I don't mean
that it cheapens the material, but I wouldn't want to have to shoot it that
way simply because they shoot every episode that way. I would want to
have fluid camera movements and shoot it in 70mm. Enough of this
shooting it on 16mm, scratching it up, and calling it a "style."

LL: *If you directed an episode, you don't think they would give you that lati-*
tude? Oscar-winning documentarian Barbara Kopple directed a Homicide *a few*
weeks back, and that seemed to stretch the boundaries a bit.

QT: Well, I don't mean to sound too strong on this. When you adopt a
style like that for your show, you're kind of asking to be made fun of a
little bit. Regarding Kopple, I would imagine a documentarian's style is
exactly what they're going for any old way. I mean, the thing is, it was
very interesting directing the *ER* episode. I liked the *ER* style: I like that
Steadycam whipping around, shots that go on for 4, 5, 6 minutes without a
cut. But it was funny, at one point when I was doing the episode, word
came down that John Wells, one of the executive producers, had a problem and wanted me to go back and shoot more coverage on a scene we
had just done. Now, nobody's *ever* told me to go back and shoot more
[coverage]. I said, "I want John to talk to me about it," because I'm just
used to getting the benefit of the doubt on stuff like this. And then one of
the producers said, "Well, who would tell you on your own movie?" And
then I realized she was right... this is *their* show... this isn't my show.
I'm coming in and I'm directing the episode, and then I'm leaving. In TV,
the producer is The Man, the *auteur*. It was a writer-producer oriented
show: all the writers were producers and John Wells was The Man, and it
was great.

LL: *Television programs have begun displaying a ratings guide at the beginning of each broadcast. What do you think of that?*
QT: I don't have a problem with that. And it's kind of cool, because it's the producers deciding what the rating should be. It's the producers judging the material, and nothing's being restricted, nothing's being censored. So it's not an outside body labeling you. I would love to be able to go, "I think my movie's an R," or "I think my movie's a PG."

LL: *You don't think, in the long run, particularly with new mature dramas, that the ratings might end up a red flag scaring off advertisers?* NYPD Blue *took a financial bath that first season because advertisers didn't want any part of it.*
QT: If advertising is affected by it, I think it's just silliness. If the advertisers were smart, they would take advantage of that adult audience watching *NYPD Blue* and market accordingly. They should be advertising cars and beer and razor blades, and not Cap'n Crunch, so the rating shouldn't matter. Either the audience is there or it isn't: just advertise to your audience, whoever they are.

LL: *HBO has had great success with original productions and Showtime has followed suit. A few films like* Red Rock West, The Last Seduction, Freeway, *and* Paradise Lost *have actually gotten subsequent theatrical releases. What do you think of this production source and could you see yourself doing a made-for-cable?*
QT: Some of those HBO, Showtime, and TNT movies are really cool — even some of the USA Network movies are cool. My favorite television movies are not coming from the networks, but from these guys. I think they're making really great stuff. Right now, I'd pretty much want to stick to theatrical releases, but it would be cool to do like a mini-series or something. I haven't talked to anybody about it, but in the back of my mind I've thought it would be cool if I could do the Len Deighton trilogy, *Game, Set,* and *Match.* It's a trilogy of spy stories, and if you could do all three stories as a mini-series, that would be really cool. I thought of the idea of doing a television show where I had a commitment for a year, where I had at least a year, and I could have the whole season with it. And basically for that year — it takes about a year to do a movie anyway — for a year, that would be the only thing I did: I would write and direct every episode of the show, and it would be something that had a continuing kind of arc. So

that's the kind of television thing I would like to do. In Europe, that's what they do all the time. That's what Lars Von Trier (*The Kingdom, Medea, Breaking the Waves*) does, that's what Fassbinder (*Berlin Alexanderplatz*) did, Kieslowski (*Blue, White, Red, The Decalogue*) did: they move back and forth between film and television all the time.

LL: *You've stated that you're not that computer literate. Do you have any idea how many Tarantino websites there actually are?*
QT: Well, I've heard there's a whole bunch, and there's a whole lot of stuff out there. But I've yet to be at a friend's somewhere where they're all set up and can say, "Okay, Quentin, go ahead, take off! Check this out for the next two hours." I'm always hearing tons and tons of rumors about stuff that's supposed to exist on the Internet, I've just never really explored it. But, I kind of like the fact that it's out there, that it's all going on. I get a major kick out of that.

LL: *Panasonic and Philips are marketing telephones now for around $400 that will allow you to email without a computer: a blinking light notifies you that you have email waiting, so it seems like computers are creeping into more aspects of our lives. Are we getting closer to HAL 9000?*
QT: Just leave me a message on my answering machine! You know, a client in Japan I did a commercial for gave me this headset that's like a virtual reality mask, and it's attached to a VCR. And I thought, this will be really cool, it will be like watching a movie at the Cinerama Dome, only it will be attached to my head and right in front of my eyes. Instead, it's like a Viewmaster attached to your head! The only thing special about it is that it's stuck to your face! Wherever you turn your head, the picture follows. I put on *Pulp Fiction,* and Tim (Roth) and Amanda (Plummer) are going with me wherever I turn, and I thought to myself, I could probably live my entire life without this contraption. So some technology is just silly.

LL: *Speaking of elements which have an effect on home entertainment, both Ennis Cosby and Lawrence Austin, the owner of The Silent Movie Theater in Hollywood, were gunned down in one week. Knowing you were a patron of The Silent Movie Theater, do you think these kind of notoriously violent events tend to keep people at home rather than going out for their entertainment?*

Q T : You know, unless you live in a *really* bad neighborhood to begin with, I don't know. I think when people hear about these kinds of events, they go, "Oh my God, oh my God, this world we live in!" But a week later, when someone suggests going to see *Liar Liar,* they're like, "Sure! Good idea, I'll see ya at the theater." And for the people it *does* affect, I really think you shouldn't let it. You really can't be scared of the world.

L L : *On a lighter note, Steven Spielberg's* Director's Chair *CD-ROM is out now. What was it like working on that project and what do you think of CD-ROMS in general? Our friend (filmmaker and fellow Archivist) Roger Avary is convinced they will be obsolete in a couple of years.*

Q T : Well, I don't know if they're going to be obsolete or anything, but it was cool doing it with Steven. What it was was a thing [originally] called *MovieMaker,* which they described as "film school in a box." And, like, Mira (Sorvino) said, "Oh, I'd like to see that," but you can't see it, you have to make it. As a player, you're going to get a bunch of rushes, and you put the movie together. We shot it as a comedy, and we shot it as a serious movie, and the viewer/moviemaker cuts it together any way he wants at these different levels. As an actor, it was kind of a blast. We did it as as straight dramatic thing, and we did it as a wild, *Airplane*-style comedy... completely taking the piss out of it, being wild and raw in it. And so, it was kind of funny... see, I did it just before *From Dusk Till Dawn,* and I was kind of intense at the time because I was really in the head of Richie Gecko. But, then Steven asked me to star in this thing, and he was going to direct it, so we did it, and as we were doing it, I thought, "This is really wild. I don't know anyone who's had this kind of exact opportunity, where you do a scene full-on, straight and dramatic, and then you turn around and do the next take like a Zucker brothers comedy. And I thought, "Wow, that's really kind of neat acting gymnastics!" And Steven Spielberg is the best director of actors I've ever worked with: he's just wonderful. It was so cool to work with him on that.

L L : *What's the story of the sequel to* From Dusk Till Dawn?

Q T : Well, there's going to be *FDTD* 2 and *FDTD* 3, but neither will be a sequel in the traditional sense. One will be a prequel, and one will be a follow-up taking place a couple of weeks after the original. Robert [director

Rodriguez] came up with one idea, and I came up with another. Robert came up with a story, which his cousin wrote, and it's called *Dusk Till Dawn: The Hangman's Daughter*. It's a western, and it basically tells the origins of the character, Santanico Pandemonium, and how she ended up at the Titty Twister Cantina. So it's a prequel of about 100 years. On the other one, Scott Spiegel, Boaz Yakin, and I came up with the idea for a story, which Scott wrote, about a group kind of like Texas Reservoir Dogs, where these Texas bank robbers are getting ready to rob this bank in Mexico when a detour is made to the Titty Twister. So they end up robbing vampires, and it's really lewd and crude and a total balls-out action film.

Part II

LL: *Sales of home video and audio products, which account for about a third of the consumer electronics industry's annual revenues, actually declined in 1996 for the first time in five years. What do you make of that, if anything? Do you see it as a trend, and do you think DVD will have an effect?*

QT: I don't have any idea whether DVD is going to catch on or not. And I don't know whether declining sales are part of any particular trend. I think that, for some people these days, there's a definite fear factor. They're afraid that the equipment they buy today will be obsolete tomorrow. And also, I think there's a certain saturation of the market, and that has to do with the interest level. Probably by now, anyone who really wants a laserdisc player has one.

LL: *You talked a little in Part One about your master plan to delay the video release of* Pulp Fiction *in order to increase the cult value of it, but we never really talked about whether you felt this strategy paid off.*

QT: Oh yeah, it paid off big time! As I said before, the video customers know when a video should be available—they've been trained. And, basically, what a lot of people don't realize is that you're not selling videos to consumers. Your primary customers are the video stores. After a year of having been bothered about a movie not [being] available, there's very high awareness on the part of the video store. It's like at Video Archives [in Manhattan Beach, California] when we were asked a million times for *Big Wednesday* before it was released. Well, when it finally is released, you end up buying four copies rather than one. So, that's what we [did] with *Pulp*, and it ended up the bestselling priced-for-rental video in history, leapfrogging *Terminator 2, Dances with Wolves,* and *Ghost,* I think. And I'm positive my strategy of holding it up a year, which the Weinsteins [Miramax owners Harvey and Bob] and Buena Vista Home Video backed me on, was a major key to it ending up number one.

L L : *You came to Video Archives with such extensive film knowledge, I'm glad you were able to pick up a few things.*

Q T :   Oh yeah, another theory I devised at Video Archives was when *Lethal Weapon* came out. It made something like $70 million at the box office. I was working at Archives when it came out on video, and any customer who had any interest at all in action films eventually saw *Lethal Weapon.* Two or three years later, they came out with *Lethal Weapon 2.* That movie ended up making something like $150 million at the box office — a big leap! And the reason for it was, thanks to video, the audience for it had just doubled.

The same thing happened with *Reservoir Dogs. Dogs* opened in America on the art-house circuit and did about $3 million, which was actually good. Some people expected it to break out, but it did better than any other five independent films put together, because everyone was fighting for screen space at the time. Nothing opened wide, and only *The Crying Game* was able to blast off. But *Dogs* got so much publicity from the festival circuit that we sold over 100,000 video units, which was unheard of at that point for a non-A title. Three years later, when we did *Pulp Fiction,* I knew we had a much bigger potential audience. A huge audience had been exposed to *Dogs* in one format or another, and that was now an audience waiting for the release of *Pulp Fiction.*

L L : *You talked a little in Part One about the availability of films on video making the art form more disposable. You had something you wanted to add?*

Q T :   Yeah, I remember when I got my first VCR and my mom told me I could buy any video I wanted. I went in the store and picked out *The Great Escape,* and it was so cool...I had my *Great Escape!* But we take that for granted now. Once anything becomes accessible, we begin to take it for granted. I know I've got a stack of *Zatoichi* movies over there, and another stack of something over there, and it just kind of takes the specialness out of the whole thing. When I used to be into exploitation films in the '70s, I went to the movies and saw them every week. Now I've got them on video and laser, and I don't even watch half of them!

That's why I've really gotten into collecting prints. It's like a big breath of fresh air. Plus, with prints you not only have a film, but a responsibility. There may come a time when that's the only existing print of that movie in the world—you never know. So you have to take care of it; you *owe* it to film.

LL: *We made mention in the last issue that you once compared* ER *to Kieslowski's* The Decalogue, *which would be putting it on quite a pedestal. Do you still follow* ER *and would you still find that comparison favorable?*
QT: (laughing) I do feel like its first season was like that, but I really haven't been following the show. I've just gotten off the viewing schedule, and I've been meaning to catch up. I've been wanting to call them up and get some videotapes, 'cause now I'm scared to turn it on. I was so closely involved with it, but now two years of soap opera has happened, and I'm way behind. I've seen little bits and pieces, and that makes me want to kick myself for not watching more.

LL: *There was talk a while back of you directing a Nike commercial to air during the Super Bowl. What became of that?*
QT: That was just a rumor. I don't know where that got started. I'm offered commercials and music videos all the time. I just don't have any desire to do it. I might do a music video if it was a minute and a half, but three minutes is just too long! (laughs) You usually use up all your good ideas in the first minute and a half, and then just repeat them. But, basically, it comes down to the fact that if I'm not working, I just don't want to work.

LL: *The average cost of a studio pic is now $35 million, plus $15 to $20 million for prints and advertising. This has driven the cost of a first-run movie ticket to $8. Do you think this has a measurable effect on home entertainment?*
QT: I don't know how you can measure the effect on home entertainment, but I believe it has an effect on people going to the movies. When I was at the Cannes Film Festival, I had the great fortune to be sitting at a table with Robert Shaye of New Line and Harvey and Bob [Weinstein]. I started talking about the price of admission, and Robert defended it. [He said] it's expensive, but if you compare them to anything else that's grown in the last 10 years, movie tickets are still affordable and still cheaper than

going to a nice restaurant for dinner. And it's cheaper than going to a nightclub and buying drinks, and it's cheaper than going to a Broadway play, and cheaper than this and that. . . .

Now, he is correct about that. But it's my belief that the citizens of America, at the end of the day, feel that a movie ticket should cost five bucks. [Of course] when you *really* want to see a movie, let's face it, they could ask for 10 or 11 dollars, and you'd pay it. Am I right?

LL: *Yeah, I don't think many of the folks waiting at the Chinese Theater to see* Star Wars *would have dropped out of line because it was $11 instead of eight.*
QT: Exactly! But I think these higher prices have gone a long way toward killing the *habit* of moviegoing. I mean, before, when movies basically cost $5 to get into, people would go to the movies as a matter of course. For instance, Monday was "movie night." Or, "It's the weekend, let's go to the movies, all right?" But now it takes the same consideration that you'd use when thinking about going to a restaurant. It has become more of a special event. So, consequently, the audience is younger 'cause it's the kids who would be going out on dates anyway. And, because they're young, many of them have never known a time when movies cost five bucks! But for the majority of us old fogies, we still kinda think that ticket prices shouldn't be above that. And the minute you have to start thinking about the money, then the art form has become a little too expensive.

LL: *We've made brief mention of your upcoming film,* Jackie Brown. *What can you tell us about it?*
QT: It's an adaptation of one of my favorite Elmore Leonard novels, *Rum Punch,* and, as far as casting goes, it *looks* like it's going to be Pam Grier, Sam Jackson, Bridget Fonda, and Robert Forster. I'm moving the setting from Florida to the South Bay [southern California], and we're hoping to begin filming in July. I'm not sure of a release date, 'cause it'll be the first time I'm not having to get a film to a festival! *Reservoir Dogs* was rushed to get it to Cannes. This we aren't rushing to get anywhere. We might have a goal once we get it into production, but right now we can take our time. But I like to make a film from start to finish in six months . . . do it like a low-budget film. [Editor's note: Since Lawson's interview, the production schedule of *Jackie Brown* has been accelerated in anticipation of a Christmas '97 release. In a nod to both the film's star Pam Grier and Tarantino's girl-

friend Mira Sorvino, the name of the film's production company is Mighty Mighty Afro-dite. Tarantino has also added Robert De Niro to the cast as Samuel L. Jackson's ex-con partner in crime.]

LL: *Speaking of your decision to cast Robert Forster as Max, I remember laughing out loud when you announced your intention to use John Travolta in* Pulp Fiction. *John recently signed to do* Primary Colors *for $20 million. Can we expect Forster to be pulling down eight figures per picture five years from now?*
QT: (laughs) Robert's really cool . . . he's going to be great.

LL: *Concerning Mr. Travolta, your resuscitation of his career was amazingly prescient. It is generally understood that you had to talk him into doing* Get Shorty. *And my favorite review of* Michael *began with the statement, "John Travolta should never accept another film assignment without first consulting Quentin Tarantino." How often do you speak to Travolta these days, and do you get a percentage of his future earnings?*
Q: (laughs) John and I keep in touch on a regular basis. We get together and have dinner. He hadn't seen *From Dusk Till Dawn*, so he came over, and we watched it. John is cool . . . he's just the sweetest guy. And, yeah, I did talk him into doing *Get Shorty*.

LL: *Many people who were skeptical of your acting career were turned around by your chilling turn as Richie Gecko in* From Dusk Till Dawn. *You seem to have all cylinders working with writing, directing, and acting. If you were forced to choose just one craft in the future, which would you choose and why?*
QT: Well, luckily I don't have to choose because I love all three. But the thing about directing . . . if I was just an actor or a writer, I wouldn't have the control that you do as a director. And, as far as being a writer, someone once said to me, "No other director would have the faith in Quentin's words that he does," and I think that's true.

LL: *Just ask Oliver Stone [*Natural Born Killers*].*
QT: Yeah, right.

LL: *You showed me the documentary* Full Tilt Boogie, *which I thought was outstanding.*
QT: Yeah, I think it's great! I put up the money for it, but it was directed by Sarah Kelly, who's just terrific. Roger [Avary, writer/director of *Killing*

Zoe] called me right before I began shooting *Pulp Fiction.* Sarah had been a production assistant on *Zoe,* and Roger highly recommended her, so she ended up being a P.A. on *Pulp.* Anyway, she's extremely talented... and she did this documentary about the making of *From Dusk Till Dawn.* But this ain't your typical "making of/behind the scenes" crap. It's not an HBO "first look"; it's an amazing documentary about how a movie is made. Anyway, it opened the South by Southwest Film Festival in Austin, and Miramax signed a distribution deal for it on the spot.

LL: *It's that time... desert-island selection. You're going aboard the spaceship trailing Hale-Bopp, and you can only take 10 lasers/videos along. What are they?*
QT: Oh God, 10 of my lasers... I'd probably choose 10 prints if I could. Yeah, I wouldn't take videos or lasers.... As far as which prints... I hate this kind of question because I usually end up blurting out something and then read it later and go, "Oh God, no!" I don't know... I'd take *The Ipcress File, Zatoichi and the Black Cape, Abbott and Costello Go to Mars*... I don't know.

LL: *All right, I didn't mean for you to hurt yourself. Thanks for inviting us over.*
QT: Oh, sure, it's been really cool! Now, what movie should we watch?

Quentin Tarantino: Press Conference on *Jackie Brown*

TRANSCRIBED BY

PETER KEOUGH/1997

QUENTIN TARANTINO ANSWERED QUESTIONS about *Jackie Brown* at a Miramax Films press conference at Los Angeles's Wilshire Regency Hotel in early December 1997, several weeks before the film's Christmas Day opening in New York and LA.

Q: *After* Pulp Fiction, *weren't there a lot of expectations for your next feature?*
A: It all boils down to the work you want to do, the work that speaks to you. I didn't want to follow up *Pulp Fiction* with another epic. I wanted to do something smaller, something more character-oriented. If *Pulp Fiction* was an opera, *Jackie Brown* is more of a chamber piece. However, if I had come up with an original story in epic scope I liked, I would not *not* have done it because of the movie I'd done before. Maybe if I've done five movies that were of a similar nature, maybe I'd change the sixth. I'd probably get a bit more self-conscious. But not after just two movies.

Q: *Will some fans be disappointed that it's not an original? That you're recycling?*
A: It's an adaptation of Elmore Leonard's novel, *Rum Punch;* that's not a recycling. Every Kubrick movie is an adaptation of a novel; he only does adaptations. I also think there are a lot of fans who have been waiting to watch me tackle Leonard's work because of our like minds and sensibilities. Also, original writers need to do an adaptation, or something along those lines, every once in a while so a certain sameness doesn't creep into the work. As an actor, as a director, as a writer, you try to be as different as

you possibly can, show as many faces as you possibly can, but at the end of the day it's all still coming from the same well. This piece is me, and, in its own way, *Jackie Brown* became more personal in some areas simply because of the once-removed quality to it.

Q : *What was the first Pam Grier movie you saw?*
A : *Coffy* was the first. I saw it at the Carson Twin Cinema; I'll never forget it. A double feature with *The Mack*. My two favorite blaxploitation films! I also saw *Foxy Brown* and Pam's women-in-prison movie, *The Big Bird Cage*, and *Black Mama, White Mama*. I've just been a big fan for a long time. She is a truly great icon, and she holds a very special place in cinema history. When the blaxploitation phenomenon was going on in the '70s, you had Jim Brown, probably their single biggest star, and they would always say about Brown that he's sort of the black Clint Eastwood. Fred Williamson had the mantle of the black Burt Reynolds; Jim Kelly was the black Bruce Lee. But Pam Grier wasn't the black version of anybody, because there had never been a heroine who specialized in doing action movies, a full-on woman who didn't try to act like a man. Not until women in Hong Kong movies started doing kung fu did that kind of role come up again.

Since, Pam has really worked and stretched herself as an actress. She's done a lot of stage, and her performance in the film, *Fort Apache, The Bronx*, is just fantastic. That's truly great character work. I've always wanted to direct her. Finally I found a piece of material that just presented itself as perfect. Somebody said to me, "Well, did you read her?" I answered that you don't write a Charles Bronson movie and have Bronson read for it.

Q : *From the minute you read* Rum Punch *did you picture Pam Grier as the heroine, Jackie Brown?*
A : Not from the minute I read the book. After I finished the book, I started thinking, okay, what am I going to do with this? And then I natu-rally start thinking of casting choices. Pretty much after I thought of Pam, that was it. Everyone else was blown away.

Q : *Samuel L. Jackson had already played a killer in* Pulp Fiction. *Did you think of casting him in a different way in* Jackie Brown?
A : There's really not a part for him other than Ordell Robbie. To me, Sam is just the perfect Ordell. He jumped off the page as Ordell.

Q: *Do you feel you've matured as a director with* Jackie Brown?

A: I think from *Reservoir Dogs* on, I showed a maturity as a filmmaker. I don't think there's ever been a lot of whiz-kidness, hey mom, watch me direct, aspect to my work. I feel I was always pretty pure to it. The razzle-dazzle came in the script form, the structure. But even that wasn't show-offy, it was organic to the piece. But the tone of *Jackie Brown* has a maturity. There's a maturity to the characters, to the...*pain* that the characters feel, to their desperation. There's some pain to the characters of *Pulp Fiction*, but not to the very realistic level that's here. *Reservoir Dogs* is different because it's so immediate, so compact, that live hour in that warehouse. By virtue of the immediateness it can't be very reflective.

Jackie Brown? This is a movie built on resonance.

It's really funny. People come to me after a screening and say, hey, I really like your movie. It's not like I don't believe them, but I kind of think, wait two days to tell me that. This movie is built to hang in there. *Jackie Brown* is built for you to like it even more two days from now, and that's new ground for me. I'm used to making ass-kickers. And this is a different work. It's not an ass-kicker. Well, it's an ass-kicker when you watch it with a black audience. When you watch it in the Magic Johnson Theater. But for other audiences—and we're trying to get all audiences in there—it's much more of a resonant work. It's different when you change gears as an artist.

Q: *How does the music fit into the filmmaking of* Jackie Brown?

A: The thing I'm coming from is listening to music to be the guide to a movie. That's the beat or the rhythm the movie's to play at. I fancied *Pulp Fiction* as a modern-day spaghetti western. The surf music just fit in there perfectly. In the case of *Jackie Brown*, old-school Soul is the rhythm and feel this movie takes place to. Not high energy stuff, but Bill Withers, the Delfonics song you hear. That's how we're supposed to take it in. Once I decided that, it became the easy process of diving into my record collection and finding the right pieces.

Q: *Could you comment on the frequency of the "n" word in* Jackie Brown?

A: I've been quoted before as saying that when you're talking about the "n" word, you're talking about probably the most volatile word in the English language. I actually find the use of the "n" word....Gosh, it's a word I can't even say out loud. It has that much power! Should any word have that much power? My answer is no. Any word that has that much power should be de-powered. If I could snap my fingers and it would be done, I'd do it.

Q : *And in your work?*
A : That's not my job. I don't have any political agenda in my work. I am a writer and I'm writing characters. I promise you that the use of the word "nigger" is true to Ordell. That's the truth as far as he is concerned, the way he talks. To not have him say that would be a lie. And if you notice, Jackie doesn't use "nigger" a lot. She uses it very specifically, at specific moments, because she's a different human being than Ordell. It's different human beings: they're not blacks, they're not whites, they're different human beings.

Q : *What about the "T" word—Tarantinoesque?*
A : People keep asking me, "So how do you feel about all these scripts being referred to as 'Tarantinoesque?' " And I get development people telling me, "Oh, every fourth script I read has your influence on them." And sometimes I see a movie that I think possibly could be influenced by my stuff. I'm afraid I'm just getting a big head. But at the same time, I remember that people have said that same stuff about my work—that I ripped off my Mexican standoffs from John Woo, and that I took this from that movie and that from this movie. And so much of it is just not the way it is. So those poor guys and girls are taking a bad rap because they work in a genre I'm working in, because I'm popular in that genre and have a distinctive voice. It's kind of unfair. Just as if someone does a neo-noir they're told, no, that's John Dahl's territory.

Q : *Do you want to direct the next James Bond?*
A : Yes, as a matter of fact, but not necessarily the kind of Bonds that they're doing now. That's not an insult to the kind that they're doing, but I'd be really interested in *Casino Royale* set in the '60s, like in the novels.

Q : *Are you, these days, primarily a director, a writer, or a producer?*
A : I don't think of myself as a producer, though I've helped a few people out, get a few movies off the ground. During the year I was writing this

film, I was a writer. That's what I did for a living. During the shooting, I was the director. During the time I was doing *From Dusk Till Dawn,* I was an actor. I'm going to Broadway to do a show, *Wait Until Dark.* At the end of January 1998, we start rehearsal—I'll be an actor.

Q : *Are you annoyed at people who say that your acting is only a sideline?*
A : Like you say, they think I'm screwing around when I'm acting, and I shouldn't be screwing around. I should be doing my work. Well, those people don't know me and they don't know how serious I am. But that's okay, it's not a battle that's going to be won in a day. It's going to be won over a long career. I'm just as serious about acting as I am about directing. As I am about writing. I'm as proud of my work acting in *From Dusk Till Dawn* as I am proud of my writing and directing work in *Pulp Fiction.* I didn't put myself in *Jackie Brown* because there wasn't a part right for me. That's how serious I am.

Q : *Why do you want to act in* Wait Until Dark?
A : Harry Roat is a great character, the first character I've been offered that made me salivate to jump into it. I'll be doing it with Marisa Tomei, who does about a play a year. It's not like a movie actress doing a little theater turn. She's a really wonderful actress who, if I put it down, then she can pick it up. We can just go where we go. It's just going to be very exciting. It'll be great because, if I didn't act in *Jackie Brown,* you better believe I wanted to, that I was having a poison-ivy acting reaction! I was itching for it the entire time! When I was directing Robert De Niro, you better believe I wanted to mix it up with him. I wished I was doing scenes with him, putting it down, having him make me better, possibly me making him better. You better believe I wanted to do it. But I had to sit on it and give it all to my direction. Because there wasn't really a right character for me in this movie. I was very clear on that. But that acting muscle was aching—that muscle was yelling—so I've got to go right off *Jackie Brown* into that play, and I just can't wait.

Q : *How do you deal with celebrity?*
A : Well, I'm used to it now, and it was never a bad thing. But it takes a little bit of time to get used to it. The only time it's really a problem is when you're on a romantic date with your girlfriend, or something along those

lines, and you'd rather be left alone. Basically though, people are coming up to me all the time with an amazing amount of positivity. I try to talk to them. I actually have contact with the people who like my stuff. The only problem is — I mean it's really nice to hear — but when people say, you're work is great — as far as conversations go — it's kind of a conversation killer. Where do you go after that? I look forward to hanging out in a bar and having a nice conversation, but not about my movies. One of the biggest problems with becoming famous is that people stop talking to you and start asking questions.

Q: *And there's pressure to read people's scripts.*
A: I can't read scripts. I just can't read them! Young filmmakers who put a tape of their student film in my hand — I'm really honest. I say, oh, I'd like to take a look at this. I don't know when. It might slip through, and I might not see it. I might not watch it for a long time. But thank you for the tape and if it presents itself, I'll watch it. Oh, I get a lot of them!

INDEX

Made in the USA
Lexington, KY
21 January 2011